Ace the IT Interview

Ace the IT Interview

The Best Interviewing Strategies for IT Professionals

Second Edition

Paula Moreira

New York Chicago San Francisco Lisbon
London Madrid Mexico City Milan New Delhi
San Juan Seoul Singapore Sydney Toronto

The McGraw-Hill Companies

Cataloging-in-Publication Data is on file with the Library of Congress

McGraw-Hill books are available at special quantity discounts to use as premiums and sales promotions, or for use in corporate training programs. For more information, please write to the Director of Special Sales, Professional Publishing, McGraw-Hill, Two Penn Plaza, New York, NY 10121-2298. Or contact your local bookstore.

Ace the IT Interview: The Best Interviewing Strategies for IT Professionals, Second Edition

1234567890 QPD QPD 01987

ISBN 978-0-07-149578-3
MHID 0-07-149578-9

Sponsoring Editor
Megg Morin

Editorial Supervisor
Janet Walden

Acquisitions Coordinator
Carly Stapleton

Technical Editor
Mike McCoy

Copy Editor
Claire Splan

Proofreader
Susie Elkind

Indexer
Claire Splan

Production Supervisor
James Kussow

Composition
Alden Prepress Services Pvt. Ltd.

Art Director, Cover
Jeff Weeks

Cover Designer
James C. Korn

For Pano

About the Author

Paula Moreira is currently the global IT training manager at a large financial services organization. She and her team support an IT staff of about 2,000. Paula began her career as a techie and has spent the last 15 years working in IT education and career development.

About the Technical Editor

Mike McCoy is chief technology officer at InnovaSystems in San Diego, where he manages a team of over 120 software engineers and architects. He is recent graduate of the Masters in Executive Leadership program at the University of San Diego.

Contents at a Glance

Contents

Acknowledgments

This book is made possible through the help of many dedicated IT professionals who give back to the profession by assisting with projects such as these. I thank them for their contributions. And to my dear and trustworthy friends who, when called upon at the last minute, never cease to amaze me with their generosity of time and caring.

First of all, a very special thank-you to all who made the first edition possible: Abbi Perets, Dean Hardy, Don Berard and the team at StarDot (www.stardot.ca), Mike Landau and the team at SetFocus (www.setfocus.com), Ed Tittel and his team, Ryan Storgaard, and Ephreum Ruphael. In addition, I would like to thank Mike McCoy, Dattu Inampudi, and Soma Tekumalla for their work on this new edition.

To the great staff at McGraw-Hill/Osborne—Megg, Carly, and everyone else—thank you for making this project so easy and supporting me through the whole thing.

Last but not least, I am grateful for the support and encouragement of all my family and friends near and far. And to the man who gets to live with me through these book projects—Pano, ILU always.

–*Paula Moreira*
August 2007

README.DOC

I don't know about you but I'm not one for reading introductions. I'm glad the title caught your attention because within these few paragraphs could be the key of how to get your next job.

Now that I have you here, let's talk a little about the IT job market. Quite frankly, it couldn't be better thanks to the dot com bust. That event single-handedly managed to discourage the next generation of college students from seeking a job in IT. So if you lived through those times and were looking for the silver lining—there you have it.

Some may think that with the shortage of IT folks organizations will hire any warm body off the street. Some will, but others won't. They will hold out for the right candidate and you need to differentiate yourself. You need to be prepared! There is absolutely no reason to make job hunting more stressful by walking into an interview cold, without any background information about the job or the position. And what about preparing yourself for the types of questions the interviewer is most likely to ask based on the position you're applying for? You didn't walk into the Prometric Testing Center for your last certification test without using a variety of study aids. Why would you subject yourself to an interview without preparing first?

For IT professionals, preparation comes in several layers: the softer questions regarding personality and work ethic, and then the technical side specific to the job at hand. That's how I've organized this book. The first four parts handle the stuff that you're probably least familiar with—how to dress, make a great first impress, and how to stand out. The last part is the Interview Encyclopedia, packed with hundreds of questions that are likely to come up on your next technical interview. By no means memorize these questions (or get caught with cheat sheets during your interview), but at least review and practice how you would answer them based on your strengths and experience.

You'll be doing yourself a favor and helping yourself stand out in the crowd.

–Paula Moreira
August 2007

Part I

What You Need to Know About Getting Hired

In This Part

Chapter 1

What Really Happens in the Interview Process

Welcome to *Ace the IT Interview!*—a guide to how to get the job you want in IT. This entire book has one mission: to turn you into a *Valuable IT Professional* or V(IT)P! V(IT)Ps are IT professionals who managers know will get the job done right. They are problem solvers. They are team players looking to contribute to something bigger than themselves. They are employees who stick around for the long run. Are all IT professionals V(IT)Ps? No! But by reading this book you're one step closer.

In this chapter, I'll help you understand what IT hiring managers are looking for from V(IT)Ps and how they go about selecting the right V(IT)P for the job. This chapter covers

- Hiring from the IT manager's perspective
- Debunking some of the myths associated with interviewing
- Handling different interview styles and situations
- Preparing for different interview styles

Hiring from the IT Manager's Perspective

You certainly picked the right industry to be in if you like being in the thick of things. Today's IT organization is more than the helpdesk. IT professionals are truly seen as business partners with the rest of the organization in achieving business goals. Today's typical IT organization now has the staffing and other proper resources to get the job done. This is great news. Or so you think. It also brings more accountability. For today's CIO or IT manager, that means staffing their departments with reliable, responsive, hard working, and customer-oriented people who know how to do the job and get it done on time and under budget. Finding these folks is often a challenge even if there are plenty of people available on the market. Why would this be so with a very pro-employer job market? Because there's a big difference between being able to do the job and *demonstrating* that you can do it through a job interview.

Why Not Just Use Assessment Exams?

You might be thinking that interviewing is just about checking out whether you have the right technical skills. Wrong! Think of interviewing like dating—it's an opportunity for two people (you and the hiring manager) to determine whether there's a long-term fit. That means aligning working styles, expectations about the job, ideas of teamwork and leadership, and how to measure results. If it were just about the technical skills, assessment tests would do the trick.

There's a lot more to this process than whether you can write the code or give the right answer over the phone. It's about *two* people checking each other out—not just the interviewer assessing the interviewee.

Consider this book like a matchmaking service. I'll get you through the first date and if things go well, then I'll help you decide whether you want to go on a second date or move on to something more serious and long term—employment with a company that's right for you.

The Hidden Needs of IT Managers

You know you want a job. But do you really want just *any* job? Chapter 11 will help you determine whether the jobs you are offered are the right fit for you. But for now, let's turn to what the hiring IT manager wants from the V(IT)P, even if the job ad never mentioned it.

When you think of the needs of hiring managers, you probably tend to think of just their immediate need to get a warm body to fill a seat. Isn't that what the job ad and the HR recruiter said? Not true. Though filling an immediate opening is at the top of the IT manager's mind, there's a lot more happening under the surface. Your technical capabilities will definitely contribute to getting the job, but there are many competent techies out there who have sent out hundreds of résumés without a single job offer in hand. So what's the secret?

First of all, the secret is really in what's never expressed verbally by either the recruiter or the hiring manager.

STAND OUT!
Employers hire solutions, not people.

All hiring managers (IT or not) have four basic questions that must be answered before they hone in on the perfect candidate. These needs drive the way they make their hiring decisions. By preparing to address these needs, though, you can make an impression and stand out among the other hundreds of candidates. The basic questions are

- Can you do the job?
- Will you stick around?
- Will you fit in?
- What will you cost?

Can You Do the Job?

This is the easiest part to prepare for. After all, you have the job description. You know you have experience in the required technologies: SQL Server, .NET, XML, and Service-Oriented Architecture (SOA). But what about using these technologies to build a business-to-business solution that connects a hospital's procurement system to its suppliers? Do you have experience there?

Determining whether you can do the job means understanding the technology, the company, the industry, and the position. This means doing some research. In Chapter 3 I'll introduce you to some great researching techniques so you can be prepared. As you begin your search for the right organization, start thinking about the experience you have, both basic technical experience and the specific projects where you applied that technical experience.

Hiring managers want to know whether you'll be able to apply your technical skills to their particular challenge. You can tailor how you present your experience so that it's easy for the hiring manager to see you solving their challenge, meeting their requirements, and fitting in with their existing team.

I'll talk more about individual job competencies in Part V later in this book.

Will You Stick Around?

According to a study by the Saratoga Institute, the average cost of hiring a new employee is approximately $8,500. This doesn't include the amount of time managers spend away from their regular responsibilities recruiting and interviewing. Add to this relocating, training, and breaking in a new employee and we're talking about a very expensive proposition. Each day that a new employee spends on the job represents an investment for the organization. No employer wants to see his investment evaporate after only a few months. So another characteristic of a V(IT)P is that you convey an impression of stability and commitment. This may be tough if you've spent the last couple of years job-hopping. Chapter 7 covers some strategies for how to handle these situations.

Will You Fit In?

Great, you scored a 99 percent on your assessment exam. You've proven you know what you're talking about when it comes to Windows Vista and .NET. But all of your answers have been provided as one-word responses. As the hiring manager tries to draw out a little more information from you, you stare back at him, as if questions like why you got into programming are none of his business. Not good. Though you've passed the technical competency part of the interview, you have just failed the social competency part.

You've got to keep in mind that you're going to be part of a team. You're not going to get the job unless that team thinks they are going to be able to work with you. Remember, they already work there. You're the outsider. Some of the things they look for are similar personalities, work ethics, dedication, desire to be on the technology leading edge, same processes, and so on. If you have 20 years experience as a project manager and you're interviewing for a company with a relatively new (and young) development team, you're probably not going to fit in. They may not be ready for the processes and structure. There's nothing wrong with this. It's better to learn it right up front than after you've quit your old job and moved your family across country.

What Will You Cost?

Your cost goes beyond your salary. It includes the amount of training you will require, the amount of time it will take you to learn the industry and the business processes, and also the project at hand. It also includes benefits, relocation, and other perks. IT salaries have actually stabilized over the years. Hiring managers are being much more discriminatory about the benefits they provide.

If you want to stand out in the IT hiring manager's mind, focus on presenting the value you bring to the organization. Emphasize that you bring a quick ramp-up to the job because you've worked for a competitor or worked on a similar project using the same technology.

Debunking the Myths of the Interview Process

The interview process is nerve-wracking for everyone, no matter how many interviews you've been on throughout your career. This isn't what you do for a living—writing code and catching hackers is. There's no such thing as a professional interviewee, though if you've been in the open job market for a while, it might seem as if you're coming close.

To help ease those apprehensions, let's take a look at some of the most common myths surrounding interviewing.

Myth: The Interviewer Holds All the Power

Let's first address the issue of how you perceive the interview by answering a question. If a recruiter calls you out of the blue to tell you about a terrific position he is seeking candidates for, does that mean you have to pursue the opportunity? Of course not! You have a choice. And it's the same thing with interviewing. Remember, it's like a date.

Maybe it's because they may be out of a job, unhappy about their current job situation, or just low on self-esteem, but a lot of people hand over all their power of choice to the interviewer. They assume that the interviewer holds all the cards, a deck that he has craftily stacked against them in order to probe them, wear them down, and expose their every flaw.

Yikes, where's the fun in that? If this is the interview, can you just imagine what working for this person would be like? Why would you want to do that?

Many job-seekers think of an interview as a one-sided activity. The interviewer has all the power to direct the conversation and the outcome of the interview. This couldn't be further from the truth! Just like dating, you get a say in evaluating whether you want to work for this company. You do so by interviewing the interviewer. I've dedicated all of Chapter 9 to the questions that you should use to turn the tables and interview the company. If they don't answer your questions to your satisfaction, you can turn down any job offer presented to you. Imagine that—you may actually want to walk away from a job offer.

The key to keeping this perspective is in how you think of yourself. It's the difference between being a "job-seeker" and a V(IT)P. Defining yourself as a job-seeker prevents you from taking advantage of opportunities. It carries a stigma of an unemployed job candidate who's so desperate to get a job they'll take the first one that comes along. If you are too eager, easy to please, and represent yourself as a "perfect" (not The Perfect) candidate, employers will think there's something wrong with you. They may take advantage of low self-esteem to get a great new employee dirt cheap!

Remember, a V(IT)P is a Valuable IT Professional. A V(IT)P knows the following things are true of himself or herself, the prospective employer, and the job market:

- Employers hire people who can solve their problems. They hire solutions, not headcounts.
- The employer wants to hire you, and he will help you win the interview.
- V(IT)Ps see themselves as problem solvers who can help an employer achieve their goals.
- V(IT)Ps know that not every open position will offer the opportunity to best use their skills. They will walk away from any situation where they cannot be perceived as a problem solver.
- The interview is a two-sided conversation to see whether there is a fit between the available position and the V(IT)P.
- The right position with the right company is out there. It is simply a matter of finding it.

Let's take a closer look at the differences between a job-seeker and a V(IT)P. Unlike the V(IT)P, the job-seeker:

- Comes across as desperate.
- Uses phrases like "I want…," "I need…," and "I'm looking for…"
- Has an "employee" mentality
- Lets the interviewer ask all the questions
- Describes the interview as "I am being interviewed by XYZ."

By contrast, the V(IT)P:

- Is confident, poised, and self-assured
- Comes across as a problem solver, a troubleshooter, a consultant
- Is considered a contributor
- Is prepared with his own questions
- Is well-informed about the company
- Listens for problems the employer is trying to solve and responds with examples of how he can contribute based on past experience
- Describes the interview as "I am speaking to XYZ about how I might be able to help them reach their goals"
- Actively participates in the interview process

Contrary to popular belief, interviewers rarely set out to interrogate applicants. Their objective is simply to get to know the candidate well enough to make a good match with the position to be filled. Few interviewers are warped enough to enjoy watching you squirm. If there's any squirming to be done, it will most likely be the interviewer, since he knows full well you will judge the entire organization by the professionalism that he shows you.

With that said, there are interviews designed to assess how you will perform under pressure. These are called "stress interviews." Rarely do you have a stress interview on the first interview. I'll talk a bit more about stress interviews later in this chapter.

Myth: Employers Are Experts at Interviewing

Having been a hiring manager for many years, I can personally debunk this myth. Most IT interviewers have a full-time job doing something else, such as CIO, IT director, data center manager, engineer, or helpdesk manager. Most have not been trained as interviewers—in fact, they've had relatively little experience interviewing people. Interviewers often feel awkward and uncomfortable in the role of interviewer. At best they see it as an interruption of their "real" work. To make matters worse, they don't spend much time preparing for the task. Most likely, they scan your résumé for a few minutes while you're waiting in the lobby.

Most IT managers' interviewing experience is acquired after years of some hits and many more misses. They extend job offers with their fingers crossed behind their backs while quietly whispering a prayer to the hiring gods. Unfortunately, they use everything from instinct to bizarre criteria to make their hiring decisions, instead of asking qualifying questions that will help them identify whether the candidate before them will be able to do the job. Very rarely do interviewers remember how well the employee did in the interview, much less which questions they asked. Most of them build their interview question base by asking themselves, "What did I wish I had known before I had hired that last employee?"—as that employee is walking off the job.

The way to get the upper hand is to learn how to drive an interview. In order to drive the interview you must first research the position and the company. First, you should clearly understand your current job—the technology involved and processes, such as project management, change control, and quality assurance. Compare your current job description to the proposed job description. Make a list of questions that will help explain the responsibilities a bit more. Refer to Chapter 9 for a list of questions that you should ask any interviewer. The beauty of taking over an interview goes further than just transforming a dull meeting into a productive one. It immediately positions you in the eyes of the interviewer as a problem solver. (And they appreciate not having to come up with all the questions.)

Myth: Employers Know What They Are Looking For

This myth actually works in your favor. Managers who have a clear idea of the skills, requirements, and personal characteristics of their ideal candidates are definitely in the minority. They may have a vague, general notion of what they're looking for. They may also have a job description that aids them in defining the job responsibilities. But few managers take the time to think through what type of individual it takes to actually do the job. On top of that, interviewers may not know what questions to ask to assess whether the candidate is qualified for the position. This is particularly true if they have never personally hired anyone for this type of position or are replacing a long-term employee. Some good examples would be developers of new technologies and the creation of a new internal team when the function was once performed by an outside vendor, such as helpdesk or development.

Although you can't control these situations, you must be prepared to handle them. If you think you've walked into an interview where they aren't quite sure what they need, here are some questions you can ask:

- Is this a recently created position?
- Who performed these duties in the past?
- What were their strengths?
- What was missing from how they performed the job?
- What policies and procedures are in place to support this team/position?

You have the opportunity to define or redefine the ideal candidate by presenting how *in your experience* you see the needs of the organization being met. And here I literally mean *in your experience*—using examples of problem solving and accomplishment to redefine the expectations of professionalism for this position. By setting the bar to at least meet your value to this organization, you will be one step closer to being the perfect candidate.

What typically happens when an employer doesn't have a clear idea of who they are looking for is that they end up weighing candidates against one another. That's the least ideal situation for you.

Myth: A Technical Interview Is All About Your Technical Skills

Yes, the interviewer will ask you about your technical skills. Will he ask detailed questions about objects, methods, and file names? Maybe, but most likely not. Beyond entry-level positions, the likelihood that all your interviewers' technical knowledge will actually match yours is very small. What he is more interested in is how you applied your technical skills to solve a business problem, in the hope that you might be able to help solve his. Understanding what types of questions he might ask is extremely important. Part V focuses on these questions as they may apply to the job you are interviewing for.

You need to build up your general interviewing skills more than you probably need to enhance your technical skills.

Different Styles for Different Managers

It would be great if all hiring managers made decisions the same way, or would it? Imagine if all managers were model decision-makers, with their spreadsheets, scoring cards, and assessment exams—an intimidating prospect for most job-seekers. Let's take a look at some different styles of interviewers you may encounter on your way to the perfect IT job. Throughout your interviewing process you will run up against these different styles of decision-makers. Sometimes their styles will work in your favor, other times not. You must be prepared for what to expect and not take a negative reaction personally.

Model Decision-Makers

These are your textbook hiring managers. They are methodical and objective in how they evaluate, typically using a predefined list of hiring criteria. They also use group opinions and as many sources of information as possible, including interviews, credentials, and references. What's positive about this type of decision-maker? Once they've made their decision, they act swiftly. They are in the minority.

Quantitative Decision-Makers

You'd better be a good test taker, because that's what these folks look at. They'll want to know what scores you received on your MCSE or other certification exams. These decision-makers will ask you to take assessment exams and will want to see your past certification exam scores. Be prepared with this information as well as letters of recommendation and reference lists.

Gut Decision-Makers

These guys are at the opposite end of the spectrum from the quantitative decision-makers, preferring to rely exclusively on their intuition. They believe their gut tells them more than any assessment exam, because they've got 15 years in the business and have seen it all. Or maybe not.

Just-Get-Me-a-Warm-Body Decision-Makers

You are very likely to run into lots of these folks in your interview travails. Often recruiters fall into this category because they need to fill a position so quickly that they throw all traditional hiring methods out the window and take the first warm body who responded to the ad. You might think this is a job-seeker's dream situation, but you should really think twice about accepting any position too quickly.

Interview Styles to Be Prepared For

There are many ways to conduct an interview. As an IT professional, you're going to run into basically four different interviewing situations: the traditional, the behavioral, the performance, and the stress interview.

Traditional Interview

This is the interview that most of us are familiar with. It's a process that's fairly structured. Even most inexperienced hiring managers have this one down. It goes something like this:

- The interviewer begins with small talk to put you at ease and to establish rapport.
- The interviewer either starts describing the position and the organization or begins to review your résumé.
- The interviewer then moves into a discussion of your capabilities, asking you to describe your skills and personal qualities.

- The interviewer closes with a chance for you to ask questions and thanks you for coming in.
- As you shake hands and prepare to part, the interviewer may provide some information about the next steps in the process.

This is a tough interview to control because the interviewer is asking most of the questions. Here are some tips on how to gain control early:

- As the interviewer is describing the position and the company, ask questions.
- Be ready with "asset statements" (see Chapter 4).
- Find some common interest that you can use to build rapport and lighten up the conversation.

Behavioral Interview

Most experienced IT managers will use the behavioral interview approach because it tells a lot more about the candidate. What makes it different is how questions are phrased. It is more scenario-based and by far more specific to the job that you're interviewing for. Part V has many examples of behavioral questions for each of the positions that I've profiled.

Here's a comparison of a behavioral question versus a traditional question. A behavioral question might go like this:

"What would you do in this situation?" You are working alone when the following calls come in:

- The CEO can't access his e-mail.
- Your good friend can't print.
- A crabby user can't log in to the network.
- The Internet router goes down.

"Prioritize the calls and describe why you would service them in that order."

Here's the same question asked as a traditional question:

"How would you prioritize support issues?"

Performance Interview

Typically, performance interviews involve taking an assessment exam as a preemployment screening device. I cover assessments extensively in Chapter 8. Basically, assessment exams are a great way to demonstrate that you have the skill set for the job and to earn you the interview.

Stress Interview

Stress interviews include brain teasers and situations that are meant to make you nervous. They are designed to see how you would handle stress. You see these types of interviews in more structured interview situations with large recruiters and large organizations. Typically, the higher your salary, the higher the likelihood that you'll run into the stress interview. Urban legend says that Microsoft and Google like to interview in this way.

Checklist

Before you go on, make sure you:

- ☐ Understand the difference between a job-seeker and a Valuable IT Professional (V(IT)P)
- ☐ Understand that a job interview is an opportunity for you to assess whether you want to work for that company
- ☐ Realize that a technical interview is more than just a review of your technical knowledge

Part II

What to Do Before the Interview

In This Part

Chapter 2

Acing the IT Résumé

Your résumé represents the first impression that you will make on any prospective employer. Consider it your calling card or letter of introduction. Single-handedly, it will be the reason why a prospective employer will invite you in for an interview. Hiring managers may be reviewing hundreds of résumés for a single opening. Consequently, it's critical that yours:

- Matches up to what the employer is looking for in the ideal candidate
- Paints you as a "safe" hire—one who can do the job and who will fit in with the team
- Enables the hiring manager to see you successfully handling the required tasks and responsibilities

You may think your current résumé does all the above, but are you really getting the number of call-backs you were expecting, or are you wondering why you're not? This chapter will take you through the key elements of an outstanding résumé. For additional tips and tricks, be sure to check out *Ace the IT Résumé!: Résumés and Cover Letters to Get You Hired*, published by McGraw-Hill/Osborne (2007).

The Ace Résumé Test

Take the Ace Résumé Test to evaluate whether your résumé might need a face-lift:

- ☐ You still list MS-DOS as a technology on your résumé.
- ☐ You've sent out 100 résumés and haven't received a single call-back.
- ☐ Your résumé is four pages long.
- ☐ Your résumé still includes your high school GPA.
- ☐ You have no experience but you are trying to get a $60K+ job.
- ☐ You are a career changer and realize that getting an IT job is not as easy as all those advertisements say.
- ☐ You have been at the same job for so long that you have no résumé.
- ☐ Your résumé begins with the line "I want to get a job in IT..."

- ☐ You have been to all the career sites on the Web and they haven't helped you improve your résumé at all.
- ☐ You want to get your dream job and make the big bucks.

If you answered yes to any one of these questions, read on. You need help!

STAND OUT!
Your résumé is the hiring manager's first impression of you. You want to come across as a strong, competent, confident candidate. Taking the time to ensure that your résumé portrays the right image will be the first step you make in getting the IT job you're dreaming of.

You Must Believe!

What differentiates a successful résumé from one that receives little response is the *attitude* with which it is developed. It's the frame of mind of the candidate that makes all the difference. At the core of getting noticed is a firm belief in yourself and your abilities. The same confidence that you will need to successfully maneuver the interview needs to come across on paper. Notice, I said *confidence*, not cockiness. Confidence plays the most important role in getting noticed. If you are currently unemployed, it could be difficult for you to move from the woe-is-me attitude to the confident attitude, but this is crucial. If you have a hard time mustering confidence, try to recall your accomplishments or past victories. Recall the praise of your past employer or the problems you solved that eluded lesser individuals. You *must* genuinely believe two things (and you'll want to repeat these aloud until you are comfortable):

- The right opportunity with the right company and the right team is out there for me.
- I have skills that employers need and that will add value to their company.

When you truly believe that you have something to offer, the juices will start to flow and the magic will happen. As you sink into the groove of your accomplishments, more and more accomplishments and recognition will come to you. You start to see how what you have to contribute is valuable. There will be a change in the words you use, the examples you provide, and the impression you create in the recruiter's or potential employer's mind.

STAND OUT!
The sole purpose of your résumé is to get you invited for an interview. It's not your life story no matter how much you think you've accomplished.

As an IT professional, it may take you a few tries to find this groove, especially since IT professionals don't tend to be great marketers, which is where the problem lies. While marketers like to embellish and sell the features and benefits of a product (including themselves), most IT professionals stick to facts and analytical data. Techies tend to stay with what works and doesn't work about their products. They leave the features and benefits to the marketers. Consider this chapter a quick lesson in how to market the most important product of your career—you!

> ***STAND OUT!***
> Hiring managers are human. Their hiring choices are a reflection of themselves. They are looking for candidates who will demonstrate their ability to hire high-quality team players who will not only get the job done but will proactively contribute to the success of the overall department.

Reading the Hiring Manager's Mind

Managing risk is a key management task. Employers are at risk every time they make a new hire. You are sitting in front of someone who has been burned before by other former employees. They hope that you will be able to do the job technically, learn the unique policies and procedures of their company, and work effectively with the existing team. Your job is to minimize the risk factor associated with hiring you by providing a résumé and demonstrating an interviewing technique that inspire confidence in you. Here are some of the ways you can do that.

Reducing the Time to Productivity

When you start a new job, you will have a lot of downtime. You'll probably end up doing laps around the building just to find the bathrooms. Then consider getting to the point of being able to figure things out for yourself, like checking your code into Visual Studio Team Edition without wiping out everyone else's, the proper etiquette for escalating helpdesk calls, and how to differentiate between calls from the president's admin and calls from the mailroom clerk. While you view this ramp-up time as an inconvenience, your employer sees it as nonbillable hours down the drain. Every moment you take to learn your way around the company and its technology is money lost for the company. Clearly, IT managers favor candidates who bring with them industry experience and advanced system and software skills. The more experience you demonstrate, the higher your résumé will rate. And it gets better. If you demonstrate experience within the same industry, your résumé will rate even higher.

> ***STAND OUT!***
> Companies pay for doers and problem solvers. Did you increase productivity or efficiency? Did you save the company money? Did you reengineer a business process? Did you identify a problem that had been overlooked? Did you suggest new cost-saving programs for the company? Provide examples of money saved, efficiencies improved, and staff retained (if you're a manager) that demonstrate the direct progress or accomplishments of your work.

What do you do if you don't have experience? Then you must rely on transferable skills that may be industry independent. Many times, IT professionals include only their technical skills on their résumés. Just as important are the "soft" skills that you've learned throughout your career. When presenting transferable skills, you should be specific about how they can apply to IT. You want to help the hiring manager see how your skills would apply within their organization. Make him realize the loss he will suffer if you go to work for another company.

Some examples of transferable skills are

- The ability to learn technical information quickly
- A proven history of improving operations and increasing profitability
- The ability to handle challenges, with proven history of increased productivity
- Strong communication skills
- Experience working as a team member as well as independently
- A history of being a self-motivated, hardworking team player
- The ability to prioritize and work proactively
- Experience as a troubleshooter and problem solver
- A proven ability to work in a fast-paced, challenging environment
- Willingness to do whatever it takes to get the job done

STAND OUT!
The number one way to demonstrate that you have growth and promotion potential is by continuously improving your skills through training and certification. If your résumé doesn't demonstrate the new things you've learned since earning your degree or certification, go back and add those things.

Training Means Growth and Promotional Opportunities

Remember the part above about IT managers fearing that you won't stick around long enough for them to recoup their investment in training you? You can show you are a good fit for the company by providing clues into your training history and your learning approach. It is evidence that you're willing to invest in your own self-improvement, and that you're open to change and to working with new technology. Today's hot software will be tomorrow's legacy application. Remember, IT departments are change agents within their organizations. If you're not flexible, you're in the wrong field.

Your résumé should include a list of all the certifications you have achieved. You can also include additional coursework that goes beyond the call of your normal day-to-day job. The more advanced training you include on your résumé, the higher the hiring manager's comfort level in selecting you as his ideal candidate. Continuous learning demonstrates to the employer that you will continue to improve your skills and develop yourself to become a more knowledgeable and productive employee. Plus, you will probably end up sticking around for more than a year.

STAND OUT!
Most HR recruiters are not technical! They don't know the detailed differences between a CCNA and a CCIE, so you have to make it easy for them to match you up to the key qualifications they are looking for based on the job posting.

Getting Past the HR Recruiter to the Hiring Manager

As I've already talked about in Chapter 1, the IT hiring manager is like a king in his castle. He is surrounded by gatekeepers and screeners—recruiters, HR managers, and even he himself will be sorting through stacks of résumés. Your job is to make it to the top of the stack that gets invited to an interview. The trick? You can show you are a good fit for the company by providing clues into your training history and your learning approach.

Reading Between the Lines

The job ad will tell you a lot about what the hiring manager is looking for from candidates. Depending on where the ad is posted, you will be able to get the details you need to target your résumé. When you read a job ad, you should look for the following information about the position:

- Job title
- Industry
- Job skills and responsibilities
- Years of experience required
- Software/hardware experience required
- Education required

This information should tell you exactly what needs tailoring on your résumé. Here's a quick summary:

Job Title Today it's all about keywords! Rather than using the traditional "Objective" statement, simply list your keywords at the very top.

Industry If you have experience in this industry, make sure you call it out in your summary of qualifications as well as experience in similar industries.

Job Skills and Responsibilities Determine where there is a direct match. If the ad calls for particular tasks that you may have rolled up into more general descriptors, break these tasks out again. If the position calls out for additional skills that you may possess but left off your résumé, add them back in. The goal is to have as many matches as possible with what is included in the job posting.

Jargon Look for acronyms and include these in parentheses in your résumé.

Service-Oriented Architecture (SOA)

Business Process Management (BPM)

Enterprise Services Bus (ESB)

Asynchronous JavaScript and XML (AJAX)

Representational State Transfer (REST)

Web Service Definition Language (WSDL)

Effectiveness After adjusting your résumé, ensure that it still reads as powerfully as before the edits.

STAND OUT!
IT managers are busy people. On average they spend less than 90 seconds scanning a résumé. Lay out the most relevant information in the first third of your résumé.

The Anatomy of a Technical Résumé

Your experience and education will not make your job hunt easier if you don't nail the essential elements of your résumé. There's more to it than just words on the paper (and more than just a list of software packages). How you lay out your skills and past experience and how these look when you print it out can make a big difference. Formatting and layout may come easier to a graphic artist than a techie, but anyone can do it using these templates.

The Sections of Your Résumé

The following are the standard sections of a résumé:

- Header
- Keywords
- Summary of Qualifications
- Education
- Certifications
- Technical skills
- Experience

Here's what to include in each.

Header

This is the easiest part of your résumé, but there are a few things you'll want to watch out for. What to include:

- Name
- Current address
- Home phone and cell phone
- E-mail address

What *not* to include:

- Funky e-mail addresses (such as beerguzzler@hotmail.com). You should also be aware that some companies may have filters that prevent employees from sending to or receiving e-mail from free e-mail accounts.
- Current employer's daytime phone number (use your cell phone number instead).

STAND OUT!

What's the most important part of your résumé to any recruiter or hiring manager? The summary of qualifications section! They don't want to have to read through two pages to find out what technologies you know. Make sure that you make it easy to pick out your experience, technical skills, and why you're perfect for the IT job.

Summary of Qualifications

This is the most important section of your résumé! Pay attention. This is how you will hook and reel in your hiring manager. Skip the objective statement—go right to the summary of qualifications statement. That's right, everyone already knows you're looking "to obtain a challenging position that utilizes your experience and knowledge for the overall benefit of the company." What's important is *how* you can do this. So the summary section should be focused on the specifics that will lead to this contribution.

Here are samples that help illustrate a great summary statement. As you can see, you can either bullet this information or write it out as a paragraph. As long as you're concise and use effective language it won't make a difference.

> **Infrastructure Specialist** with experience in design, implementation, and support for WAN/LANs, wireless networks, DNS, DHCP, and Active Directory. Additional experience includes disaster recovery, capacity planning, and business continuity. Excellent problem solving skills and interpersonal skills.

Or

- Results-oriented professional with 17 years experience in IT, customer service, and finance.
- Ability to create a shared vision and translate strategy into a workable traction plan that includes any needed governance.

- Excellent communication skills, interfacing well with management, coworkers, and clients.
- Comfortable working in a fast-paced environment, building and leading cross-departmental integration teams, and working with cutting-edge technologies.

Technical Skills

The most important part of your résumé after your summary section is your skills section. It should include a concise list of skills and technologies that you have experience with. If you don't make it easy to pick out your qualifications, you run the risk of immediate disqualification. So make it easy. Here is an example:

TECHNICAL SKILLS

Operating Systems Windows 98/NT/2K/XP/Vista, Windows Server NT/2000/2003, Macintosh OS to OS X v.10.3.5, SQL server installation

Databases Microsoft SQL Server 2005, Microsoft Access, FileMaker Pro, Crystal Reports

Networking WAN/LAN protocols, server administration and configuration, TCP/IP, FTP, DNS, SMTP configurations, HTTPS setup, firewall configuration, VPN, NT/AD domain registration, network appliances

E-mail Outlook, Exchange Server configuration, Microsoft Live Communication Server

Peripherals BlackBerries, Smart Phones, Pocket PCs, Storage Area Network (SAN), VMWare, Network Backup Servers

Hardware Dell and HP servers, desktops, and notebooks

Education

Depending on how long it's been since you graduated, the education section may appear near the beginning or end of your résumé. If you recently graduated, it's a good idea to list it near the top of your résumé. This will easily explain your lack of extensive work experience. Degrees should be listed with the most recent first. Include the name of the educational institution, the degree, and the date granted. If you graduated with honors, include that as a second line. If you are still working toward your degree, list the date as "Anticipated." If you will not be graduating, list the college name, the dates attended, and then a categorization of the courses that you took—for example, "Java Programming, Web Fundamentals, Adobe Photoshop, and Communications."

It's also important to demonstrate that you continue to keep your skills current. You can do that in the education section by including a list of courses you've taken. These can be combined with your certifications. Take a look at the next section's set of examples to see how it's done.

Certifications

Certifications should be listed under their own category. Again, depending on how recently you earned these, you may want to use the dates of receipt as a justification for the lack of on-the-job experience. Abbreviations for certifications are fine and actually preferred. There's nothing worse than filling up a short résumé with extra words! Make sure you're using the right acronyms. Also, there's no need for periods within the acronym.

These days, certification is not just available from Microsoft, Novell, and Cisco. Companies like Brainbench.com offer many valuable certifications that prove you can do the job. Though they don't necessarily have the same weight as an MCSE, they will help you stand out nonetheless. If you've earned these, list them. For example:

Certifications

CompTIA A+ Certification

Microsoft MCSE

Brainbench Technical Help Desk

Brainbench Computer End-User Support Specialist

As mentioned in the previous section, you should also list additional courses that you've completed even if you don't end up getting an entire certification. Here's how to do it:

Certifications

CompTIA A+ Certification

Microsoft MCSE

Brainbench Technical Help Desk

Brainbench Computer End-User Support Specialist

Additional Courses and Training

Cisco CCNA: Interconnection Cisco Network Devices

Exchange Server 5.5: Server Administration

SQL Server 2005

Migrating to Vista

STAND OUT!

Listing experience goes further than the job title and employer. It means demonstrating how you used your skills. Employers and recruiters want to see the types of projects you worked on. Don't just regurgitate your skills section. Give them the details!

Experience

Here's where most techies get confused about what to include and how to present it. If you have a lot of on-the-job experience (five years plus), your life is a bit simpler. The skills you've accumulated over these years will easily fill up one page. Your problem will be scaling down how much to present. The rule of thumb is simply to go back ten years. Anything more than that will be outdated. If you feel that you have valuable skills acquired over more than ten years (such as management skills), consider including them in your summary section—for example, "15 years experience in IT management."

Recent graduates and recently certified techies may want to consider the skills-based résumé that focuses more on skills competencies than on work experience. It may also benefit those who have acquired many technical skills in a short period of time, or for those whose skills are more impressive than their job titles.

Experience is experience. It doesn't matter whether it is paid or not. If you have volunteer or internship experience that is relevant to the job you are applying for, list this in the same format you would use for work experience. Give yourself a title and support it with a list of your accomplishments.

STAND OUT!
Your résumé is a marketing brochure of you. Start each statement with an active verb that indicates your actual role. For a list of active verbs, check out www.acetheitjob.com/.

In presenting the details of your experience, you want to make sure that you keep it focused on how you applied the skills that you listed in the previous sections. This means describing the types of projects you worked on and how you made a difference. In an upcoming section, I'll show you a foolproof way to do this.

The Technicalities

Technology has certainly complicated the issue of what format your résumé should be in. But before you complain too much, think back to the days of the typewritten résumé and just be grateful for how easy word processors make it to reformat your résumé today.

These days you need both a PDF résumé and a text-only résumé.

STAND OUT!
The French word résumé means summary—so keep it brief. This means one page, or at the most two pages.

The following are steps to create an e-mail–friendly résumé in ASCII format:

1. In your word processor document, set one-inch margins.
2. Open your existing résumé or create a new one.

3. Select all of the text, and then select a font that is fixed-width 12 point, such as Courier 12. This will give you 65 characters per line, which will accommodate most e-mail programs.
4. Save your résumé as a text-only file with line breaks. If you have been instructed to use hard carriage returns at the end of paragraphs instead of at the end of lines, save as text-only without the line breaks.
5. Open this new file in Notepad or any other text editor that you have on your system.
6. If your traditional résumé is longer than one page and contains your contact information or page numbers on every page, remove that information. On the computer screen, your résumé will read as one continuous page.
7. Review the appearance of your résumé in the text editor. This is exactly how most recipients will see it.
8. Replace all characters that are not supported by your text editor. For example, bullets may appear as question marks or other characters (*, >) in Notepad. You can replace the bullets by using asterisks or hyphens. You can create a horizontal line for effect by using a series of hyphens or other characters.
9. If there are long lines of text in your editor, use Notepad's Word Wrap feature under the Edit menu. This feature inserts hard returns, allowing you to format the résumé to meet your specified margins.
10. Copy and paste the text of the résumé into the body of an e-mail when you are satisfied with the way it looks.
11. Create a short cover letter using the same steps described above. Insert the cover letter above the résumé within the e-mail message.
12. Send a copy of this e-mail to yourself and to a friend who is using a different e-mail program before sending this text résumé to the recruiter or employer.
13. If you are attaching a résumé to an e-mail, be sure that it has been virus scanned with the latest virus definition files in place. Sending an infected document to an HR recruiter will end your hopes of proceeding further in the interview process.

STAND OUT!

E-mailed résumés are preferred by hiring managers because they provide the greatest flexibility in distributing and archiving. The preferred method is for the résumé to be sent as an attachment.

The Final Test

What is the key that makes your résumé a true winner? Hidden in the next few pages you'll find the answer. It's a simple technique called the "So what?" test. Herein lies the magic that will have employers picking your résumé above all others.

The "So what?" test, when properly applied, is what makes your résumé a true winner. Too many people litter their résumés with boring job descriptions and endless lists of software, hardware, operating systems, and so on. Potential employers are busy people. They don't have time to sift through endless terminology and long-winded language. They want to know what you can do for them. First, identify your accomplishments and special recognitions. Then for each of the answers that you provide, ask yourself, "So what?" That will help you come up with the difference your accomplishment made and *why it mattered*.

STAND OUT!

If you don't follow any other advice I offer in this book, follow this. The key to standing out is to ensure your résumé passes the "So what?" test. Read on.

Here are some helpful questions to get you started:

- Were you asked to take on more responsibility?
- Were you asked to lead or participate in a special project?
- Did you create or assume new responsibilities?
- Did you receive a bonus for exceeding your goals or objectives?
- Did you do anything for the first time at your company?
- Were you promoted?
- Were you praised or acknowledged by customers, coworkers, or vendors you worked with?
- Did you receive perfect scores on certification exams or college examinations?
- Were you a member of an honor society in college?
- What project accomplishments did you successfully deliver that had high visibility with management?
- Have you received company recognition awards?
- Were you a contractor who was hired on as an employee (indicates you added so much value at your last position that they had to hire you)?

STAND OUT!

Don't ever insert "References on request." You will provide your list of references later, when requested, on a separate sheet with their contact information.

Summing It All Up

The hardest part of résumé writing is making a commitment to start. Once you start to get your skills down on paper, you have something to work with. For additional résumé templates and worksheets to help you get started, visit www.acetheitjob.com/. You won't get it all right the first time, so make sure you keep refining how you present yourself. If you're not getting the response you expected, make sure you run your résumé by impartial parties for their input. Remember, your résumé is the first step to getting you the interview. It is well worth the investment in time.

Figures 2-1 through 2-4 on the following pages include some samples of IT résumés.

Ted Franks 212-555-0989 (cell)
1001 Park Avenue, New York, NY 10023 tedfranks@gmail.com

Professional Summary

- 7 years of experience as a **Business Analyst** and **Client Relationship Manager** in the **financial industry.**
- Good understanding of basic principles of **financial markets and instruments,Basel risk management,portfolio risk,trading** and **settlements** concepts.
- Excellent **client relationship management**, communication and presentation skills.
- Worked on multiple projects in a **fast paced environment**. Good team player.
- Pursuing a certificate in **Financial Risk Management**

Technical Skills

Business Analysis

- Rational Unified Process (RUP)
- Unified Modeling Language (UML)
- Software Development Life Cycle (SDLC)
- Object Oriented Analysis and Design Concepts (OOAD)
- Business Process Re-engineering (BPR)
- Test Lifecycle
- Multi-tier Web Applications
- Data Warehousing
- Business Intelligence (BI)
- Data Modeling (ORDBMS)
- Service Oriented Architecture (SOA)
- Prototyping
- Agile and eXtreme programming methodologies

Business Documentation

- Documented Business Requirement
- Use Case Specification
- Functional and Non-functional Specification
- System Requirement Specification
- UML diagrams (Use Case, Class and Sequence)
- Traceability Matrix
- Project Estimate
- Change-Version Control
- Training and User Manuals
- Master Test Plan Review (Integration, System and Acceptance)

Methodologies	RUP, SDLC, OOAD, UML, Data Modeling , SOA, Agile, eXtreme
Modeling Tools	Rational Rose, MS Visio
Project Management	MS Project, Rational RequisitePro
Testing Tools	Mercury and Rational-Quality Center (Test Director), QuickTest Professional, LoadRunner, VrGen, Rational ClearQuest, Manual Testing
Databases	Oracle, Sybase, SQL Server, Informix
Reporting Tools	Crystal Reports, Rational SoDA
Source Code Control	CVS, PVCS, Rational ClearCase
Operating Systems	Windows, UNIX (Solaris), Linux
GUI	Visual Basic

Career Experience

Business Analyst Reuters, NY Jan. 06–Present

Major Project: Time series analytics implementation. Time Series Analytics provides the ability to extract desired time series across financial instruments for any period, frequency, and tenor and provide analytical metrics. Created as a Microsoft Windows application interoperating with Reuters networks and historical market databases hosted in different global locations. Developed according to Reuter's standards for usability, performance, and reliability.

Responsibilities:

- Helped the technical team with the busine ss proposal documentation and presentation.

FIGURE 2-1 Sample business systems analyst résumé

Ted Franks•212-555-0989 (cell)•tedfranks@gmail.com

Page 2 of 2

- Met with client groups to determine user requirements and goals.
- Analyzed business requirements and segregated them into high-level use cases and class diagrams.
- Developed documentation (Requirements Document, Functional Specification, and Testing Plans).
- Conducted weekly meetings to facilitate discussion between the different users to resolve issues.
- Set up definitions and process for test phases including product test, integration test, and system test.
- Maintained requirements traceability matrix throughout the project.
- Performed system testing to ensure that the compiled software components of the applications adhered to project standards, performance criteria, and functional specifications.

Environment: RUP, Rational Requisite Pro, Rational ClearCase, Rational ClearQuest, MS Visio, UML, SQL, C++, CORBA, and object databases.

Business Analyst HSBC, NJ Nov. 04—Dec. 05

Major Project: Consumer lending Website. Designed and developed consumer lending Website for HFC (HSBC Finance Corporation), a member of the HSBC Group. Website allows customers to apply online for personal, real-estate, and auto loans and get instant response.

Responsibilities:

- Worked with business requirements document and user centered design (UCD) to create UML use case, class, and sequence diagrams for developers.
- Assisted with data conversion activities and all levels of testing.
- Participated in the logical and physical design sessions and developed design documents
- Designed new process flows for the existing system as well as for the enhanced system.
- Conducted and led statusreport meetings with the business and the IT team on a weekly basis.
- Conducted technical review sessions and facilitated other project meetings as required.
- Worked with project management to schedule, manage scope, and analyze change requests.
- Documented test cases during requirements gathering, analysis, and design phases.
- Responsible for addressing, diagnosing, and resolving issues that arise on a day-to-day basis for the team. Also responsible for documenting the causes, analysis, and final resolution to the issues/errors.

Environment: Rational RequisitePro, MS Project 2002, MS Visio, Test Director, Java, Windows NT/2000.

Education

New York University, NY – Pursuing a **Certificate in Financial Risk Management**
Coursework in securities and investment management, measurement and management of financial risk, as well as the nature and operation of markets in futures, options, swaps, and other derivative instruments. Anticipated completion: June 2007.

Rutgers University, NJ — Masters in **International Relations**

Seton Hall University, NJ – BA in **Management Information Systems**

FIGURE 2-1 Sample business systems analyst résumé (*continued*)

Joseph Mathews jmathews@yahoo.com
675 Highlands Avenue · Kansas City, Kansas 56445 (876)555-1212

PROFILE

- Extensive experience with LAN installation, network reconfiguration, connectivity, network security, and Internet and software/hardware configuration
- Track record for implementing, optimizing, and maintaining high-performance and high-availability network systems
- Proven ability to lead and motivate teams in order to maximize levels of productivity
- Excellent communicator, with experience working at client sites to facilitate project implementations, support, and training
- Exposed to diverse internal and external technical environments, recognized for ability to manage multiple tasks simultaneously
- Creative, analytical thinker with demonstrated ability to troubleshoot problems, determine strategies to resolve issues, and consistently implement effective solutions
- Microsoft Certified Desktop Support Technician (MCDST)

TECHNICAL SKILLS

Hardware: IBM, Dell, Gateway, Toshiba, Notebooks, Compaq Printers HP, Epson, Okidata, Toshiba Peripherals Tape Backups, Memory, Modems, Motherboards, Network Cards, PCMCIA, I/O devices, Networks Hubs, Routers, Cabling, 10/l00Base-T

Platforms: Windows 95, 98, NT, 2000, XP, Macintosh, Citrix, Terminal Server, RedHat Linux

Software: Microsoft Office (Access, Excel, FrontPage, Outlook, Outlook Express, PowerPoint, Project, Publisher, Visio, Word), Netscape, Adobe Illustrator, Lotus Notes

Databases: SQL Server, Lotus Notes, MS Access

Tools: Remedy Call Tracking Application, Asset Insight (Inventory Management), DameWare Utilities

PROFESSIONAL EXPERIENCE

Help Desk Support Team Leader

GE Capital ITS, Kansas City, Kansas 4/2004–Present

- Managed 18 agents supporting 20,000 employees. Responsible for ensuring that the team provided 1st level support for Nortel Networks' employees worldwide. Created a graduated perk system for rewarding help desk staff for outstanding performance as monitored by spot checks and silent monitoring, creating plans to help poor performing agents achieve their objectives, and if needed recommending them for termination.
- Prepared, analyzed, and acted upon the team's daily performance in relation to customers SLA's (Service Level Agreement). Improved average calls per hour 22% to the highest in the organization.
- Conducted coaching/training for the team to achieve team goals and organized team-building events and methods of motivating the team.
- Managed escalation issues in PC and customer service environment.
- Prepared reports and presentations for upper management.
- Decreased talk time through effective use of call handling techniques.
- Created a project tracking system to ensure all projects started were successfully completed.

FIGURE 2-2 Sample helpdesk analyst résumé

Joseph Mathews jmathews@yahoo.com

Help Desk Analyst

GE Capital ITS, Kansas City, Kansas 8/2000–4/2004

- Provided 1st level PC support for Nortel employees worldwide, maintaining 80% 1st level resolution. Coordinated with 2nd and 3rd level support groups to ensure that the appropriate support group was informed of the issue, and then monitored it to ensure the issue was resolved to the customer's satisfaction.
- Skilled in diagnosing and repairing server/workstation network connectivity issues (Win9x, WinNT, Win2000, OS/2).
- Supported Office 2000, Palm Pilots, Netscape, IE, RAS, Cable modems, DSL modems, VPDN, Exchange and Notes environment.
- Worked as afield technician troubleshooting PC, Laptop, and hardware issues
- Used Remedy support tool.

Senior Desktop Support Technician

ABC Computer Group, Kansas City, Kansas 9/1995–2/2000

- Supervised four junior technicians.
- Created a database for tracking repairs and replacements.
- Developed new processes for handling incoming stock for tracking.
- Setup and directed trade shows.
- Trained customer employees in several PC-related topics.
- Tracked stock and maintained records of inventory.
- Handled escalations and irate customers.

EDUCATION

DeVRY Institute of Technology, Kansas City, Kansas 6/1999
B.S. in Computer Science

FIGURE 2-2 Sample helpdesk analyst résumé (*continued*)

Jason Brass jasonbrass@gmail.com

24 Elm Street • Farsville, NC 88767 • 889-555-9878

Desktop Support • Help Desk • IT Support • CHDP • CompTIA A+

SUMMARY

- Certified Help Desk Professional and A+ certified senior member of the desktop support team providing support for 2,000 users across a five-building campus. Experienced in maintaining 24/7 presence in a mission-critical production environment.
- Interact positively with a diverse range of end users and groups. Communicate well with customers via the phone and email. Provide hands-on support as needed.
- Successful resolution of hardware/software issues. Meet or exceed established SLAs by positively establishing customer expectations and communicating processes and procedures.
- Motivated self-starter and team builder with an aptitude for learning new skills quickly.

TECHNICAL PROFILE

Operating Systems:	Windows 98/2000/XP, Windows 2000 Server, RedHat Linux
Networking:	Active Directory, TCP/IP, DNS, DHCP, TELNET, SSH, TFTP, FTP, firewalls, Sonic VPN, Cisco VPN, Citrix Secure Access Gateway, RSA Administration
Databases:	MS SQL Server, Microsoft Access, ACT CRM
Applications:	Lotus Notes, MS Outlook, MS Office 2003, SAP, Siebel, Dreamweaver, Macromedia Studio, Adobe Acrobat Professional and Reader
Support Tools:	Heat, Remedy, GoToAssist, Network Streaming Remote Support, Intuit Track-IT, Ghost, Norton Anti-Virus, Magic, DameWare Remote Control, Trend Office Scan, Symantec AV Corporate Edition, CA ARCServeIT, Veritas Backup, Symantec Enterprise Products
Hardware:	Dell desktops, laptops, and servers; IBM desktops and laptops; HP desktops and notebooks; Sony Vaio laptops; network cabling; NetGear routers and hubs; Cisco routers; Sonic firewall; HP routers and hubs; 3Com routers and hubs; Linksys routers and hubs; 802.11g wireless routers; HP, Toshiba, and Lexmark printers.

SKILLS

Desktop Support

- Install, configure, and troubleshoot desktop equipment for new users and deployed desktop applications as needed.
- Assign user accounts on both LAN and Web servers and granted permissions to shared resources.
- Create and edit documentation for installation and training manuals for employees.
- Install and configure antivirus software on user desktops.
- Analyze frequent problems and consult with network manager, VP of Information Systems, and Software Developers to design and offer training sessions in order to address end-user problems.
- Collect frequently asked questions and write formal answers to ensure accuracy of responses and consistency with other Help Desk personnel.
- Monitor available network and desktop disk space to ensure sufficient space for regular and backup operations.

FIGURE 2-3 Sample LAN administrator résumé

Jason Brass jasonbrass@gmail.com 2

- Maintain server and desktop event logs and respond to critical system events and failures.
- Perform nightly network backup and data recovery functions.

Help Desk

- Provide telephone and remote technical support.
- Provide first level support for end-users using Citrix Presentation Server–based applications.
- Assign and troubleshoot Citrix Metaframe application permissions and sessions for end users.
- RSA Secure ID Administration.
- Create and maintain Vantive user accounts.
- Maintain SAP R3, Enterprise Portal, and Business Warehouse accounts.
- Evaluate various application errors for user and escalating problems based on the experienced errors. Perform root/cause analysis.
- Document support issues and resolutions in Help Desk Software. Follow up with end users on resolution satisfaction.

EMPLOYMENT HISTORY

Help Desk Analyst 2006 to Present
Simms Inc., Atlanta, GA

Senior Computer Technician 2002 to 2006
Kyocera Wireless Corporation, San Diego, CA

Help Desk Technician 2001 to 2002
PDSHeart, Conyers, GA / West Palm Beach, FL

CERTIFICATIONS

Certified Help Desk Professional, STI Knowledge 2005
CompTIA A+, New Horizons, Atlanta, GA 2004

FIGURE 2-3 Sample LAN administrator résumé (*continued*)

Thomas Banks (410)555-5678
2343 High Road • Catonsville, MD 23433 thomasbanks@gmail.com

Technical Direction ▪ Infrastructure Planning ▪ IT Director ▪ Team Management ▪ Budgeting ▪ Strategic Planning ▪ Vendor Selection ▪ Project Management ▪ Business Analysis ▪ IT Security/Strategy ▪ Network Management ▪ Process Improvement

Seasoned technical specialist and leader with more than 20 years of combined experience impacting corporate performance through skillful alignment of technical resources with enterprise objectives. Experience in orchestrating the design, development, and deployment of IT strategies within diverse business platforms. Proven leadership in identifying and eliminating operational discrepancies with the upgrade of existing systems and implementation of customized solutions. Experienced in developing talented teams focused on exceeding objectives.

PROFESSIONAL EXPERIENCE

Information TechnologyDirector

EASY PRINTS INC. *Raleigh, North Carolina* *2003–Present*
Provider of commercial printing services with annual revenues of $100M.

- Led IT strategy including solutions development, budgeting, network design, help desk, and computing functions. IT department comprised of 11 team members servicing 5 multi-state locations. Managed $2.1M budget and assisted in monthly P&L reviews. Supported 350+ user environment.
- Improved overall IT project management success by establishing an IT Steering Committee and IT Policies/Standard Operating Procedures. These efforts were estimated to have saved the department $210K annually.
- Saved $96K in telecommunications costs annually by renegotiating existing contracts and further reduced non-labor expenditures by 40% in 2 years through IT vendor standardization.
- Consolidated technical platforms including migration of 42-server Windows NT environment to 18-server MS Windows 2003 environment, and CheckPoint Firewall to Cisco PIXs Firewall environment.
- Enhanced technical operations within a 120,000 square-foot warehouse facility by implementing wireless network environment. Improved warehouse management operations by implementing a new barcode scanner system.
- Reduced data entry and manual processes with the implementation of interfaces in .NET environment that connected two main corporate systems.

Information TechnologyDirector/ Service Bureau IT Manager

KIMBERLY CLARK *Greensboro, North Carolina* *1999–2003*
Garment label printing company servicing markets in Hong Kong, China, and Mexico. Annual revenues totaled over $60M.

- Successfully consolidated three IT departments with into a single unit that reported directly to the Executive Vice President. Promoted to serve as primary leader of the organization's global IT department with locations in the US, Hong Kong, and Mexico.

Figure 2-4 Sample IT manager résumé in a skills-based format

Thomas Banks 2 thomasbanks@gmail.com

Managed networking, pre-press support, global development, help desk, business community relations, workflow design, and business process improvements. Served as member of the Board of Directors for the Mexico facility.

- Facilitated annual revenue growth from $24M to $60M by eliminating a 24-hour delay in the transfer of production specifications to overseas locations, and standardized workflow order management to a single process for all product types by initiating the implementation of an in-house ERP system.
- Produced over $800K in new revenue within the first year of introducing a graphic/variable data management application for a new business unit that facilitated rapid turn around of order delivery.
- Generated more than $153K savings annually through expert re-alignment and cross training of technical staff.
- Enabled consolidation of financial data from local/overseas locations with the introduction of ACCPAC Professional Series 6.5 accounting package (GL, AP, AR, and multi-currency).

Senior Systems Analyst

PIXAR GARMENTS *Cleveland, Ohio* *1996–1999*

Apparel identification company with locations in Asia, Latin America, Europe, and North America. Annual revenues totaled over $350M.

- Recruited to direct the implementation of a new MRPII system within the organization's Ohio and Hong Kong locations. Identified and collected user requirements, defined business process for system configuration, and programmed modifications.
- Enhanced performance of MRPII system through modification, introducing ordering, quoting for printing products, and consolidation of shipments.
- Eliminated lost paperwork with the design and development of a Job Tracking System.
- Achieved successful completion of this complex project (with a history of failures), implementing system within both locations in 11 months.

Additional Experience

IT Manager, Development Services, Outsourced Solutions Inc., Baltimore, MD 1994–1996
Development Manager, Biomed, Inc., Cleveland, OH 1992–1994
Network Operations Manager, American Red Cross, Cincinnati, OH 1990–1992

EDUCATION/PROFESSIONAL DEVELOPMENT

Master of Business Administration in Operations Management
Wake Forest University, Raleigh, NC

Bachelor of Science in Information Processing Systems
University of Cleveland, Cleveland, OH

Figure 2-4 Sample IT manager résumé in a skills-based format (*continued*)

Checklist

Your résumé is your calling card. The goal: to get you an interview. Use the checklist below to ensure that you haven't forgotten anything.

- ☐ Did you create a powerful summary section that provides a concise summary of your experience, skills, and benefits that you bring any organization?
- ☐ Did you ensure that the most important information regarding your skills and accomplishments appears in the top third of your résumé?
- ☐ If you lack significant hands-on experience, did you create a skills-based résumé that highlights your knowledge and skills rather than the jobs you've held?
- ☐ Did you ensure that your résumé contains the keywords found in the job listing?
- ☐ Do your accomplishments and experience pass the "So what?" test?
- ☐ Did you spell-check and grammar-check your résumé?
- ☐ Did you have a friend or mentor check your résumé for content and typos? Not all typos are detected by a spell-check or grammar-check.

Chapter 3

Getting the Interview

You've perfected your résumé, uncovered your skills, and discovered how talented you really are. Now that you know it, you can't bear another moment in your present position. You've got to get out there and snag the job you really deserve, the one that'll pay the big bucks and be your ticket to easy street. In fact, you'll just quit your old job right now, and concentrate full time on finding a new gig. With your stellar skills, it'll take, what, a week, maybe two?

Easy, tiger.

One step at a time. First, concentrate on getting the interview. I'll walk you through the process. There's no need to quit your job this early in the game—in fact, having a job puts you in a stronger negotiating position.

If you're out of work, you may be able to spend more time on your job search, but remember: this book teaches you to work smarter, not harder.

In this chapter, we'll focus on the shortest distance between job ad and interview. Here's a look at what's in store:

- Networking: the best way to find a job
- How to dissect a want ad
- Getting past gatekeepers
- Cold call scripts
- Becoming a people magnet

STAND OUT!

It's hard to believe, but the best way to find a job is actually through word of mouth. Seventy percent of the time, landing the job you want will happen because of "who you know," according to author Robert S. Gardella in _The Harvard Business School Guide to Finding Your Next Job_. Get to know lots of people. Now!

The Other Kind of Networking

It's difficult to believe it when you're scanning through the thousands of job postings online or in your local paper, but most jobs are never advertised or publicly announced. Companies much prefer to fill vacant spots via personal recommendations, word of mouth, or networking. It's a hidden job market just waiting to be tapped.

Even though everyone knows about the benefits of networking, most job-seekers don't bother to take advantage of their contacts. Those who do make halfhearted attempts at networking don't do so with a clear goal in mind, and they rarely follow up properly.

Many job-seekers mistakenly believe that their contacts can't possibly help them get a job. Granted, your technophobic aunt may not seem to be a likely prospect, but her best friend might be the owner of a highly successful technical recruiting firm. You won't know unless you ask.

STAND OUT!

Get to know your dentist, doctor, chiropractor, local coffee shop owner—these people know lots of people. Let them know that you're looking for a new opportunity and ask them for recommendations on any customers or clients who may be able to help you in your search.

Define Your Networking Goal

To network effectively, you have to spend some time preparing. Sit down and figure out exactly what it is you want. Is there a specific job you'd like to have? Write down the details: junior developer at a large financial company, QA engineer at Microsoft—spell out whatever it is you want to be doing. Then identify what you hope to gain from your personal connections: information about that position, the inside scoop on the company's corporate culture, or the name of the hiring manager.

Your Personal Network

When you know what you want, tell everyone in your personal network—your friends and family. These are people who genuinely care about you and want to see you succeed. Give them the opportunity to help you. When they ask how you are, say:

> "Great! I'm trying to get [information about/a job at/whatever it is you want]. Do you know anyone I can talk to who might be able to help?"

Don't feel you're taking advantage of these people. In fact, you may well be in a position to help them, too. Whatever they reply to your questions, thank them, and follow up by asking, "And how are you?" As long as you genuinely care about the answer, you're still a good person.

STAND OUT!
Joining a professional user group is one of the best ways to increase your technical abilities but also to network. User groups offer a social setting where you meet other technical professionals from other companies in your area. They are often aware of career opportunities within their organizations and will seek to recommend people they know and trust that will get the job done. Join a user group today!

Your Professional Network

Beyond your personal network, you must also reach out to your professional network. How can you create such a network? Quite easily, actually. Join a professional user's group, attend trade shows in your industry, take a class or a seminar, or talk to coworkers.

If you can't find a job fair or trade show, you're not looking hard enough. Go to your favorite search engine and type in **trade show [*your desired position or industry*] [*your city*]** and see where the search takes you. Or go to www.psijobfair.com/ for an extensive listing of IT job fairs.

Never go anywhere without copies of your résumé and business cards. If you don't have business cards, have some printed. For under $100, you can have four-color cards printed with your name, a title, and your contact information. You'll present a more professional air.

Don't be afraid to ask for help from people who are successful in your field. Most people are flattered to be asked for assistance and advice with your job search. It makes them feel important.

Manage Your Network

To get the most from your network, you need to be organized. Keep track of your contacts using a PDA or a spreadsheet. Track your personal and professional contacts, and be sure to jot down a few notes each time you talk. If someone makes a suggestion, say, "Thanks, that's a great idea. I'll try it, and I'll call you next week to tell you how it went." If you use a PDA or smart phone, you can immediately schedule follow-up reminders. Other tips for managing your network:

- *Set goals.* Talk to five new contacts each week, for example, or ask ten contacts for referrals on Tuesday.
- *Always ask for business cards.* A paper file is a great backup system.
- *Care about your contacts.* Make sure you occasionally call people just to say hello and ask how they are. Send paper thank-you notes to people who have taken the time to speak with you. Send a small gift to someone who really went out of his or her way to help you.

Make Your Network Work for You

When you do get a meeting with someone who has been referred to you as a possible contact, be prepared. Questions you can ask:

- How is my résumé? Would you hire me? What would you change?
- Is my cover letter effective? Do you have any suggestions to improve it?
- Do you have any advice or ideas for me?
- Who else should I be talking to?
- Are there any groups I should join?
- What would you do if you were me? Who would you ask for advice?

Be a People Magnet

Want the secret to being a people magnet? Learn to listen more than you talk. Hear what people are saying, watch for opportunities, and always take notes. People love to talk about themselves, so give them the opportunity. Ask a question, then stand back, zip your lip, and let people share their knowledge with you.

The Best Time to Network

Most people don't think about networking until they're out of work. But the best time to network is before you need a job. Successful networking takes time. You have to cultivate contacts and gradually get the information and the results you desire. It doesn't happen overnight.

In addition, if you're down to the wire—the phone bill is due, you're on your fourth week of ramen noodles, or your car is about to die—you're going to be tense. More likely than not, you'll communicate that tension to your contacts. And desperation is a big turn-off. So do yourself a favor and start networking today, even if you have a job.

What Does That Ad Really Want?

When you first begin perusing want ads, you'll probably figure out the shorthand very quickly. You don't have to be a genius to understand "5+ yrs exp. C#," for example. A finer art is reading between the lines in a job ad. This skill is one you should hone. Even the skimpiest want ads can prove to be quite revealing when you know how to read them correctly.

If an ad sounds too good to be true, it probably is. For example, ads that promise incredibly high salaries, tons of vacation time, terrific benefits, and large bonuses every year sound pretty attractive—until you realize that no company name is given. If you decide to answer such an ad, don't be pressured into making any commitments over the phone. Ask lots of questions, and pay attention not only to the answers you receive, but how those answers are given. Does the person on the other end of the phone hesitate a lot? If so, your antennae should go up. Luckily, there aren't too many of these ads in the computer job section.

Ads that don't disclose a company name or location should also make you wary. If an ad specifies no phone calls and gives only a post office box to which résumés can be sent, think twice about applying. Such ads can be legitimate, but ask yourself why the company doesn't want to be identified.

One particularly deceptive kind of ad takes this form:

> **Exciting Careers in Technology**
>
> The IT industry will continue to grow in the future as more people and businesses become technologically advanced and the demand for IT skills increases! Thousands of jobs are expected to open up for those people with the right training. You too can have an exciting and rewarding career in IT as a developer, web designer, programmer, or manager. For more information, contact Tim at 555-1221. START YOUR NEW CAREER TODAY!

Notice that the ad does not mention any one specific opening. Rather, it talks in general terms about the "industry" and your "rewarding career" opportunities. But the big tip-off here is the word "training." That means the ad was most likely placed by a local trade or technical school looking for students.

On the other hand, there are plenty of ads placed by genuine companies and recruiters. Recruiter ads indicate an additional level of "security" for the company—it's just one more hurdle for you to jump through on your way to the employer. (Don't worry, I'll show you how to do that.) Of course, it's important to remember that most recruiters for staff IT positions get paid when they place people with companies. Their goal is to get you placed and collect their fee. They may not necessarily be looking out for the best opportunity for you. Ads placed directly by companies who clearly identify themselves offer you the best opportunity to tailor yourself to specific positions. So your first step, when considering a classified job listing, is to evaluate the source of the ad, and how reliable that source is.

Making the Call

If an ad appears to be in order, don't just e-mail or fax in your résumé, pick up the phone and call. You can increase your chances of getting noticed by adding a voice to the résumé. Granted, if an ad specifically indicates that no phone calls will be accepted, then use the communication medium requested—fax, e-mail, or snail mail. But if there is a phone number listed, put your fingers to work.

> ***STAND OUT!***
> IT organizations are always recruiting, particularly for helpdesk employees and developers. Even if an organization does not appear to have a current ad on a job board or a newspaper, checking in with them for opportunities is a good idea. An unsolicited résumé and application landed me my first position with Novell as a technical instructor.

Uncovering Hiring Needs

More often than not, the job of your dreams will not have a posting on Monster or CareerBuilder. Does that mean they're not looking? Of course not. Companies are always looking for IT professionals, whether they know it or not. So how do you find out what opportunities are available? You should be familiar with the first way: check out the career opportunities section of their Website.

Recruiters and Employment Agencies

The subject of recruiters is a touchy one for IT professionals. Just check out the major IT message boards and you will find lots of horror stories that would persuade you to hang up on the next recruiter that calls you. Yes, there are a lot of shady IT recruiters out there, but there are some very large reputable IT recruiters as well. When in doubt, stick with the big guns in your region. Ask your friends and colleagues if they know of reputable recruiters.

If you are contacted by a recruiter, be prepared to ask for some information, such as his name, company name, and telephone number. Ask about the specific position; location, start date, and industry of the employer/client are good places to start. If the recruiter can't answer those, there isn't a job.

If there is a job, ask some tech-specific questions to get a sense of what the employer is looking for. Many recruiters aren't tech-savvy, so ask him to read you the job requirements. If you find a recruiter that you feel comfortable with, build the relationship. Recruiters see many job opportunities before they're posted and can talk you up to a prospective employer. Be professional and honest about whether you think you can do the job, and you'll make an ally out of someone who can put you on the top of a recruitment list.

Outsourcing Firms and Temp Agencies

You'll probably have more luck when you contact outsourcing firms and temp agencies. The very nature of the service they provide demands that they maintain contact with a large database of individuals. A direct approach will work best:

> "Hi, my name is Karen Smith, and I'm a software developer. Do you have any clients who are looking for a C++ developer with six years of experience?"

Let them respond; they'll probably ask more questions about your specific skill sets. You should be prepared to list your "technical specifications" quickly.

ON THE RECORD

Why Work with Recruiters?

Recruiters sometimes get a bad rap—but they can also be very valuable allies in the search for your ideal job. I asked a senior recruiter for StarDot PRG Inc., a technical placement firm in Calgary, for some insight as to how recruiters can help candidates with their job search:

"If you are a mid-level professional, teaming with an IT recruitment company can provide yet another source of opportunities. There are many jobs that are not publicly advertised for by employers. Employers rely on companies like ours for sourcing all their IT personnel."

"We work very effectively with consultants in helping them find their next contract. The benefits of working with a recruiter include opening you to a new job market. For example, if you are a contractor you are busy running your own business. If you pick four or five recruitment companies to help find your next assignments, that frees you up from having to actively find work. That way you always have feelers out in the industry and you can concentrate on doing work."

"It's important to establish a good relationship with the recruiters you pick. You can call them up to find out what's going on in the industry, the latest popular projects that employers are looking for. They will definitely open up more opportunities to you than just doing a general search."

Recruiters like StarDot find their best candidates through word of mouth. The second best source of candidates is through the posting on their Website. If you have a colleague who has a good relationship with a recruiter, you may want to ask them to make some introductions. After all, personal networking has the highest rate of success when it comes to finding the ideal job.

ON THE RECORD

How to Get Noticed by Recruiters

Hooking up with the right IT recruiter is a great way of finding a position that matches your skills and career objectives. IT placement companies, such as Kelly IT Resources, the IT division of leading placement company Kelly Services, offer you the opportunity of temporary contracts, contract-to-hire, and full-time employment. Medium to large organizations turn to placement companies to recruit for hard-to-fill positions on their IT staffs. One may have just the right position waiting for you.

Certainly, posting your résumé on Kelly's Website is one way to get noticed by the company. Andrew Trestrail, vice-president of Kelly IT Resources, offers some additional insight on how to really get noticed by their recruitment team.

"In this job market, you have to be proactive about your job search," says Andrew. This means going beyond plastering the job boards with your résumé. It means networking with others in similar professions to find out what opportunities they may be aware of. One way of building these relationships, according to Andrew, is to "join special interest groups and user groups in your area—hot spots for recruiters looking for competent individuals to fill their open spots." If you don't have a local user group, there are plenty on the Internet that you can join. Believe it or not, recruiters look there as well.

Continues on next page

"We attend user group conferences because we know that we'll find dedicated professionals who are interested in growing their careers. These are the types of individuals we want to hire," says Andrew. "Referrals from our existing employees and contractors are another great source of placements." That's because a referral generally comes from a trusted employee, with work habits and performance history Kelly knows about. "Referrals come with an automatic reference from the person who referred the candidate. When someone refers a candidate it says a lot about their confidence in that person's skills."

If you are currently looking for a new job opportunity, it's also important to get the word out through friends and family. Ask them whether they can put you in contact with any of their acquaintances who may be able to help you. As Andrew put it, "It's like the shampoo commercial—you tell two friends, and they tell two friends, and they tell two friends, and before you know it you've got a lot of people helping you with your job search."

What to Say

If you've been shaking in fear ever since reading that bit earlier about preparing a pitch that's 15 to 30 seconds, relax. I'm not going to leave you to come up with a speech all on your own. I'll help you create one that will get results. Here's your motivation: cold calling is one of the fastest and most effective ways to put yourself directly in line for your dream job.

You have skills to sell. Employers need your talent. They're actively looking for it. And as much as you don't want to pick up the phone and call them, they don't want to have to go looking for you. If you make the call, you save them the trouble. You're doing them a favor when you call to find out if your skills and experience mesh with their needs and requirements. It's a simple, direct way to get information about prospective employers and give information about what you have to offer.

The key to a cold call script is brevity. Introduce yourself, emphasize your qualifications, showcase your special talents, and ask about open positions. Then stop talking. Like this:

> "Hi, this is Karen Smith, and I'm calling to ask about open software development positions. I have six years of experience, and for the past two years, I've worked as a team leader overseeing four major releases of a financial software package each year. What's your process for hiring senior developers?"

Now, unless public speaking is your forte, you've got to give yourself some reminders within the script. So go through it again and add cues:

> (SMILE) "Hi, this is Karen Smith, and I'm calling to ask about open software development positions. (BREATHE) I have six years of experience, and for the past two years, I've worked as a team leader overseeing four major releases of a financial software package each year. (BREATHE, SMILE) What's your process for hiring senior developers?"

You should print a copy of your script double-spaced, in a very large font. Then you can refer to it confidently, and you won't lose your place.

When you call a company you've researched, and you're hoping to land a specific position, always take the time to personalize your call. Bear in mind that the listener is always interested in what you can do for him. Did the company just release a new product that you use and love? Do you have a suggestion for the next release and the know-how to implement the changes? Then, by all means, add it to your pitch:

> "Hi, this is Karen Smith, and I'm calling about the developer position advertised in the *L.A. Times*. I have to tell you that I use your StellarSoft package daily, and it's the best developer tool that I've used. But I noticed that you still don't have a patch to correct the security flaws in your mail client. Are you planning to address that in the next update?"

STAND OUT!

Have your résumé handy so that you can quickly read off your qualifications and technical skill set.

Let the person respond to your question, then steer the conversation back to the purpose of your call:

> "I'd love to be part of the team that works on that project. For the last two years, I've been the senior developer on a major software security project, and I think my expertise would serve StellarSoft well. Could you tell me a little bit more about the position that was advertised?"

By this point, you've made your expertise clear, and you have a personal connection to rely on when you send in your résumé. In fact, you can write a personalized cover letter, address your résumé to the person you spoke with, and mark the envelope (or the subject of your e-mail) "Confidential: Personal."

Phone Tips

Of course, when you make the call, you must be organized. Here's a checklist to use every time:

- ☐ Clear your desk of unnecessary papers.
- ☐ Keep your script and any notes about the company you're calling in clear view.
- ☐ Have a copy of your résumé, a calendar, a notepad, and pens.
- ☐ Be ready to follow up on any URLs given to you. If you have a computer with a broadband connection, you'll be able to refer immediately to any Websites you discuss. If your connection is dial-up, just mark down URLs to check later—you don't want to waste time.

Start a file on each position. Fill in basic information before you call: company name and web address, for example. Then record who you speak with first—the interviewer's name, position, direct contact number, and the interview date/time. Where is the position based geographically? Why is it vacant?

If you make follow-up calls, record all the information for those calls as well. Mark down the name of the hiring manager and when a decision will be made.

Always write down any new information you get, as well as your general impressions. Don't trust your memory. After a few calls, everything will begin to run together. Be especially sure to write down the name of the person you speak with—and check the spelling on the spot!

One other important note: sometimes cold calls will feel like social calls. Don't fall into this trap. Always keep the conversation professional. The saga of the latest office politics is not appropriate material, no matter what.

The goal of your phone call is to get an interview appointment. When you get it, thank the person for his or her time, and hang up. If you stay on longer, you could sell yourself out of a job.

Put It in Writing

If an ad offers you no choice but to make your first contact in writing, whether it's via e-mail or snail mail, you'll want to craft your cover letter with care. Imagine that you're a busy assistant in a crowded office. The company needs to find a C# developer with three to five years of hands-on experience.

For just one moment, get inside this assistant's head. He doesn't know C# from HTML. It's all techno speak to him. But he's the person who determines the 20 résumés—from the pile of 427 that poured into the office four minutes after the job was posted on Dice.com—that the hiring manager will see.

He's the person, in other words, who you have to impress.

The trick here is to make it impossible for him to overlook your résumé. You do that by tailoring your résumé to the job ad.

In this example, the first line of your résumé qualifications section would read "Experienced C# developer, 4 years of hands-on experience." Look at the major points of the job ad, and make sure you hit them in your résumé and cover letter. Figure 3-1 provides a sample cover letter for a candidate responding to a job ad for a web developer.

Dear Sir/Madam,

While my attached résumé will provide you with a general outline of my work history, my problem-solving abilities, and some achievements, I have taken the time to list your current specific requirements and my applicable skills in those areas.

Your requirement:	**My experience:**
Computer Science degree	**B.S. in Computer Science**, San Diego State University.
Web programmer with three years of experience, preferably in the insurance or financial industry	**Five years** experience as a web developer and applications programmer for a Fortune 500 insurance company.
Experience with multi-tier development using ASP, COM+, SQL Server, Visual Basic, JavaScript, and DHTML	Led the development of the **extranet solution** used by all State Farm independent insurance agents nationwide. The project was developed in **ASP, COM+, SQL Server, and VB.**
Experience with content management, change control, and collaboration software	Key member of the IS development team to deploy a **formalized project management system** which included change control and **content management systems.**
Excellent documentation and communication skills	Excellent **written and oral** communication skills. Frequently deliver **technical presentations** to **management.**

I look forward to meeting with you to further review how my experience will contribute to your organization. I will be following up later this week.

Kind regards,
Lucille Woods

FIGURE 3-1 Sample cover letter

Use the Language of the Job Ad in the Interview Request

The job ad is your greatest clue to what the hiring manager wants to hear. Spend a few minutes analyzing the ad, and you'll be able to craft a cover letter that will serve its purpose: to get your résumé read and to get you invited in for an interview.

Look for the job title and responsibilities. What industry is the company in? How much experience do you need? What software and hardware experience must you have? Is an advanced degree necessary?

Obviously, you want to make sure you meet the company's criteria. But that's not enough. You need to be absolutely certain that the company knows you meet their criteria.

Yes, it's a pain to tweak your résumé every time you send it out. That's exactly why you should: most other candidates won't bother. They'll send out the same cookie-cutter form time and again, and wonder why the phone doesn't ring. You, on the other hand, will be left in the enviable position of choosing between several lucrative offers.

Steps to Success

1. Print out the original job listing.
2. Highlight the job title. Rephrase your career objective so that it includes the job title as your desired position.
3. Highlight the industry. If you have experience in this industry, make sure that you call it out in the description of your past positions.
4. Highlight the particular job skills and responsibilities. Review your own résumé to see whether there is a direct match. If the employer mentions particular tasks that you may have rolled up into more general descriptors, break these tasks out again in your résumé.
5. Note when employers want additional experience that you may already possess but have not specifically listed on your résumé. Add it back in. Job search engines are keyed from the original job description. The more exact matches the better.
6. Look for any acronyms listed in the job description. Incorporate these acronyms in parentheses in your résumé.
7. Reread your résumé to ensure that it has not lost some of its power as a result of the edits.

Keeping the Job Search Alive

Remember that hiring managers look for and respect professionals who seek to constantly better themselves. That's the kind of person who will never be satisfied with mediocrity. And that's the kind of person companies love to hire. Demonstrate your commitment to excellence by keeping current in your field. Communicate that commitment by saying, "I've taken several steps to stay on top of the latest developments in the industry." Read on for ideas on specific steps you can take.

Continue Improving Your Skills During Downtime

If you're in between jobs, take advantage of your downtime, and enroll in a course that's related to your field. If you're a developer, consider a class in a new language. If you're hoping to make the switch to management, take a class to help prepare you for the transition. Look for short courses that won't interfere with potential interviews or job offers.

Taking a course has benefits beyond the knowledge you'll gain. You may make new professional contacts. If an interviewer asks why you're not currently working, you can say that you wanted to take a few weeks to immerse yourself in new skills training.

Online Courses

Online courses are easy to work into even the most crowded and unpredictable schedule. Again, courses may be fertile networking ground, and you're learning valuable information at the same time.

Another idea to consider: *teach* a course online. It's a great way to gain instant credibility in your field. It positions you as an immediate expert, and it looks great on a résumé.

Read Trade Publications

You should always read your industry's publications to keep up with new developments. You'll learn about conferences and exciting opportunities, and you'll be able to get a real feel for the trends in your market. And if you love what you do, it will be pleasure reading, not work.

If your industry does have a publication that you enjoy reading, consider writing an article for the magazine. Again, it establishes you as an expert—someone any company would want to hire.

If the idea of writing an article intimidates you, find out if the magazine is looking for interview candidates. Many magazines seek professionals to profile in their pages. You can be that person. The piece will make a terrific addition to your résumé.

Checklist

So are you ready to land an interview? Take a moment to review the following checklist. If you can honestly mark off everything, you're that much closer to landing the interview that can get you the job of your dreams.

- ☐ Do you know how to read a want ad and tailor your skills to it?
- ☐ Have you created and rehearsed cold call scripts that will take you past the various gatekeepers and put you in touch with the decision-maker?
- ☐ Have you perfected the pitch you'll make to the decision-maker?
- ☐ Are you cultivating and maintaining your personal and professional networks?
- ☐ Do you travel everywhere with copies of your résumé and business cards? Do you have to replenish the supply every night?
- ☐ Do you listen when people offer advice? Do you take their advice and follow up with them afterwards?

Chapter 4

Standing Out in the Crowd

In previous chapters, you learned how to create a winning résumé. That résumé did its job: you've been invited to come in for an interview. This chapter will show you how to apply what works on paper to the face-to-face interview scenario.

Too many otherwise intelligent people make the mistake of thinking that by writing a killer résumé, they've done all the preparation necessary for the interview. Not so. With a good résumé, you will land an interview, but without a good interview, you will never get the job. There's still work to be done, and this chapter will walk you through it.

In this chapter, I'll cover:

- The basics of getting noticed
- The crucial step most job-seekers skip
- Gimmicks that don't get results
- Creating powerful asset statements

By the time you finish this chapter, you'll have a better understanding of how to set yourself apart from the pack. In essence, you'll be able to clearly identify—and articulate—why a company should hire you. And your newfound confidence will be an important tool as you set out on job interviews.

Getting Noticed for Good Reasons

It's pretty easy to stand out in the crowd—we all remember the class clown and that weird guy from accounting who speaks only in binary code. That's not the kind of attention you want. Rather, you want potential employers to notice your attention to detail, your perfectionism, your unrelenting commitment to fulfilling departmental and company goals. And yet, you don't want to wave a giant sign and shout, "Look at my accomplishments! See how great I am?"

So how do you get noticed without making it obvious that you're trying to get noticed? And how do you make sure that what people are seeing is the best possible presentation of you?

It all comes down to the way you come across. And it's easier than you think for one simple reason: most people are lazy. By putting in a bit of extra effort, you'll shine brighter than the vast majority of other candidates out there.

Do Your Homework

So, what's the step most people skip? Being prepared. That means research, research, research. It seems straightforward, a no-brainer, even: know something about the company you're targeting. Amazingly, however, most people who apply for any given position know absolutely nothing about the company offering the job. Doing some high quality research will lift you heads above the other candidates. Some of the benefits you'll gain include having the facts to demonstrate a convincing fit between your qualifications and the job's requirements, being able to provide intelligent answers to questions like "What do you know about our company?", and being able to better absorb and evaluate new facts the interviewer throws in during the interview.

But even before you begin researching individual companies, you should invest some time in learning about the industry you're targeting.

Yes, that's right: there are IT jobs in industries beyond the IT industry itself. In fact, most major companies across the vast majority of industries have large IT departments with plenty of room for growth. Whatever you're into—finance, healthcare, retail sales—you can turn IT expertise in that sector into your strength. The trick is to target one specific industry, preferably one that interests you.

> ***STAND OUT!***
> **The more responsibility associated with the job, the more research you must do to stay ahead of your competition.**

Learn as much as you can about that industry. Read everything you find about it—seek out trade publications, attend expos and shows, talk to people in that market. This isn't something you'll accomplish in an hour online—it can take years. But if you will be interviewing with a company in an unfamiliar industry, you can at least make a start by getting up to speed on buzzwords and trends in the industry you're targeting.

It's practically impossible to over-prepare. Very few interviewers will say, "Gee, she knows too much about our industry."

The major questions your research should answer are

- What does this industry actually do, make, or offer to the world?
- Who is their typical customer?
- Who are the major players in this industry, and what are their similarities and differences?
- What are the crucial issues for companies in this industry? Are they in the press? What do they need to have to succeed?

- Is this company expanding or downsizing?
- How many employees does it have?
- How many locations does it have?
- Is it initiating any new products and services?

Check the Occupational Outlook Handbook (online at www.bls.gov/oco/home.htm), a nationally recognized source of career information that describes working conditions, necessary training and education, earnings, and expected job prospects in a wide range of occupations. Also check specific industry associations to see the growth (or decline) of the industry.

Remember, time invested in research pays big dividends. The more information you have, the more power you have at interviews, and the more valuable you are on the job. If you know your stuff cold, you won't just seem more confident—you'll *be* more confident. And confidence breeds success.

STAND OUT!

Demonstrate your interest in the company by showing your knowledge of it and of the skills it wants.

Researching Companies Online

Once you've learned a little something about the industry you're targeting, you can begin to research individual companies. A good place to start is those companies that are industry leaders, but don't overlook the smaller players. There may be opportunities to move up the ladder more quickly than at the corporate giants.

When you evaluate a company, look at how it stacks up against competitors. The questions you'll want to answer for each company are

- What differentiates this company from others in the industry?
- What are its greatest accomplishments?
- What's their corporate culture?
- Who are the company's leaders?
- What are the company's published values?
- Does the company run lean on staffing?
- What is its reputation?
- What kind of management structure does it have?
- What type of employees does it hire?

Most of these questions can be answered online. Check out the company's Website, and be ready to take notes. Look at the words they use to describe themselves and their business. But don't stop at the home page—go deeper into the site. Check out their press section. Most companies have a downloadable media kit. This is the information they want published about themselves. Study it closely.

You can also spend some time reading what's posted on their "about us" pages. Does the company have a mission statement? Use that to get inside their corporate culture.

STAND OUT!
Whenever possible, get biographical information on the managers you will be interviewing with. These days, the quickest way of getting this information is by "googling" the organization or the manager's name, for example, searching "John Smith Acme Software."

Often, companies post bios of some of their principals. Read this information carefully. Is one of them perhaps a graduate of your alma mater? Are you members of any of the same professional organizations? Do you share some of the same values and beliefs? Look for interesting information you can use to get a foot in the door and follow up on eventually in an interview.

STAND OUT!
Most organizations have copies of their annual reports online. These should include listings of the company officers including their CIO!

After you've exhausted the company Website, use your favorite search engine to find any recent press coverage of the company. If you have time, request a copy of their last annual report. Use resources like Fool.com to find out whether the company is climbing or diving. You don't want to go through all this effort to join a company that won't be around much longer.

WHAT EXACTLY IS CORPORATE CULTURE?

The corporate culture of a company is essentially how its employees behave. It's more important than many people think. When you're looking for a job, it's tempting to think you'll fit in anywhere. Don't fall into that trap—ask about corporate culture. Questions to consider:

- Are employees expected to hang out together after hours?
- If everyone else is single, will they understand if you stay home to care for a sick child?
- Will your married coworkers try to fix you up with every delivery guy/girl who comes into the office?

Don't let your desire for a job overshadow your instincts about the people you'll be working with.

> ***STAND OUT!***
> If possible, try to get your hands on the internal newsletter. It will provide you with a better picture of what life is like inside the organization.

What is the company's vision for next year? In the long term? What's the company's overall goal, in other words, and what are the steps they're taking to get there? Even if you'll just be in the IT department, it's important to know how what you're working on fits in with the rest of the organization's goals. You want to believe in what you're doing, because you'll do it better.

Make sure that the general values of the company are in line with your own. If you're on an anti-smoking crusade, working for Big Tobacco will probably be little more than an exercise in frustration.

You'll want to explore the sectors of the company that show the most promise in terms of growth and expansion. Those are the areas least likely to be affected by job cuts if budgets are tight. On the flip side, if one part of the company has lost money three years straight, you may want to think twice before accepting a position that may not be around six months from now.

SPECIAL NOTE ON START-UPS: MANAGING THE RISK

Seasoned IT professionals know that taking a new job with a start-up is a risk. Yet some are willing to accept this uncertainty because a start-up may offer them a position that's high on the corporate food chain, comes with a bigger salary, or has an employee-friendly work environment.

Not all start-ups are bad. The dot-com era definitely tainted the term, but the reality is that there are thousands of new businesses that get started every year that offer employment to IT professionals. Some of these succeed; others don't. Here are some additional things you'll want to know about the company if it's a start-up—just in case.

- How long has the business been around?
- How sound is their business plan?
- How many rounds of funding has it received?
- Who is financing the venture and what's their experience in this market?
- How much money is in the bank?
- How many employees were there at start-up versus today?
- Have there been any layoffs?
- How do their employee benefits stack up?
- Do they pay competitive salaries?
- When does the company plan on breaking even?
- Are you being offered stock options to supplement a below-industry compensation package?

General Web Resources

Again, use the laziness factor to your advantage. Most candidates will check out the company Website and stop there. But you're different. You'll keep your fingers on the keys, and go to other sites designed to give you the dirt on your dream employer.

The Websites you check out will depend on the kind of information you're after. Here are a few of the sites you don't want to miss.

Company Research

The following is a list of Websites that will help you in your search for information about potential employers:

JobOptions.com An employer database containing information on more than 6,000 employers. Searchable by keyword, industry, and location with one-click résumé forwarding to the employer. See www.joboptions.com/.

Hoover's Online Business Reference Directory Industry overviews, specific company profiles. See www.hoovers.com/.

WetFeet.com Industry and company research. See www.wetfeet.com/.

Yahoo! Industry News Industry press releases and current news. See biz.yahoo.com/industry/.

PR Newswire Comprehensive information on market intelligence. See www.prnewswire.com/.

Thomas Register Online Online product and services guide that allows you to search for manufacturers or providers. See www.thomasnet.com/.

About.com Job search and employer search site. See www.about.com/.

Employee Message Boards

The following is a list of helpful employee message boards:

Vault.com Insider information posted anonymously by actual employees. See www.vault.com/.

Yahoo! Groups Message boards by industry and company. See clubs.yahoo.com/.

Career Sites

The following are great career sites:

Monster.com See www.monster.com/.

JobOptions.com See www.joboptions.com/.

HotJobs See hotjobs.yahoo.com/.

CareerBuilder See www.careerbuilder.com/.

> ***STAND OUT!***
> **A simple keyword search at Google.com can turn up the most interesting information on the company and its officers.**

An additional resource is to use a simple keyword search in your favorite Internet search tool. The search engine may turn up not only the company's web page, but also articles about the company. This is an excellent way of assessing the company's track record as well as its PR efforts.

Beyond Online Research

The ease of obtaining information on the Internet means that if the Web is your only research tool, you're no different from anybody else. If you really want to stand out in the crowd, log off for a little while and do some old-fashioned research. Some ideas:

- Contact your university alumni association. Personal contacts offer the fastest ticket to the top. And even if a fellow alum can't get you a job, he can tell you what it's really like to work in the position you covet.
- Contact trade group sites. Most businesses and industries have a trade group on the Internet. Perform a search on the industry and you should be able to find the trade associations for your respective industry. Then make an inquiry through the association to find out things like reputation, controversies, and more information about the officers of the company you are interviewing with.
- Attend expos, conferences, technical briefings, and user group meetings in your field. Many of these events are free. Also, training classes are a good place to meet corporate employees who have been sent to learn about new technologies. If you are signing up for classes, ask the training center which employers they do training for in the area. Bring plenty of business cards with you. Whenever you hand someone a card, they will usually offer theirs. If they don't offer one, go ahead and ask for theirs. The card you collect today might come in handy a month or even a year from now.
- Call the company. If you can't get past the switchboard operator, ask *her* what it's like to work there. Say something like, "Is it great to work for Apple?" She may surprise you and think of someone terrific for you to speak with.
- Here is a creative one. Have one of your older kids call the company and get some research materials for a paper. Most companies are very responsive to requests of this type.
- Realize that you may already know someone who works for this company. Check with your church, synagogue, gym, or friends to see if there is an inside connection you know who can give you information about the company and the corporate culture. Get involved in Toastmasters, your local Chamber of Commerce, Shriners, or other groups or charitable organizations where you may meet employees and prospective employers.

- Hit the library. Did one of the company principals write a book? Read it. Take notes. Have specific questions ready to pose at your interview. You will probably be given an opportunity to ask questions during your interview. Don't be caught off guard. Have some intelligent questions ready when this opportunity presents itself.
- If you find an employee or even just someone who interviewed recently with the company, they can give you an insight into who might be conducting the interview and questions that could be asked.
- If you have questions about a large, public company, call their corporate communications department and pretend you're interested in buying some of their stock. They should answer your inquiries. You can also check company financials through the U.S. Securities and Exchange Commission.

BE PREPARED!

If you get someone from the company on the phone, you want to make every question count. Be sure to have a written list to work from. Try these:

- What do you think is the most important thing for me to know about this position?
- Is there a detailed job description that I could review?
- What can you tell me about the person who previously held this position? Why did he leave?
- If I got this position, to whom would I report? What can you tell me about that person? Is it possible to speak with her?
- Which departments would I interact with?
- How much time would I spend working on my own? In team environments?
- Can you describe your corporate culture?
- When can we schedule an interview?
- What documentation would you like me to bring to the interview? Security clearance, certification verification, detailed references (if not provided earlier)?

Popular Printed References

The following resources can be found at your local library:

- *Business Periodicals Index*
- *Directory of Corporate Affiliations*
- *Directory of Leading Private Companies*
- *Directory of American Firms Operating in Foreign Countries*
- *Dun & Bradstreet Reference Book of Corporate Management*

- *Dun's Top 50,000 Companies*
- *Encyclopedia of Associations*
- *Standard and Poor's Register of Corporations, Directors, and Executives*
- *U.S. Industrial Outlook*

Important Reminders

Once again, remember that most people don't do nearly enough preparation for job interviews. With a little extra effort, you can quickly position yourself as a conscientious candidate—someone hiring managers love. Take the time to research your competition.

> ***STAND OUT!***
> **Job-seekers have access to more information than they ever had before. Research is critical for speaking intelligently during interviews and for differentiating yourself from the competition.**

In tight economies, employers get picky. More people are out of work, so hiring managers can afford to be choosy. They look for exact matches and are less willing to take a chance on someone who doesn't have the specific experience they seek. As a result, you need to be up to speed on the latest technologies.

Has a new version of the programming language you develop in been released in beta or final format? Learn it. Does your uncle need someone to set up his wireless LAN? Volunteer to do it, and make sure you add it to your résumé. Top-notch technical skills that have been put into practice are always in style.

Your cover letter and résumé need to represent the very best about you. Don't hide information or make it difficult to discern. Use clear and concise language. Flaunt your skills! If you're targeting an industry or a company that's doing a lot of business in, say, France, and you speak fluent French, point it out. Don't assume someone else will make the connection.

Be diligent about follow-up. You applied for a position? Call after a day or two to make sure your résumé got there. Are there any issues or concerns you can address right now? Ask if you can schedule an in-person meeting for later this week. You can't get what you don't ask for.

Gimmicks That Don't Get Results

There are always people who concentrate on being flashy and showy, rather than focusing on results. Remember: the first and foremost thought on the hiring manager's mind is, "Will this candidate be team-oriented, self-motivated, and self-disciplined?" People who can't—or won't—answer that question don't get hired. Period.

It's tempting to try to trick a recruiter or hiring manager into reading your résumé or meeting with you. Don't do it. It's one thing to be different; it's another to be remembered for being too quirky. Or being too pushy. Or telling blatant lies. Sell yourself in a professional manner and skip the gimmicks.

No matter how desperate you get, there are some things you should never do, as listed next. These "tricks" can backfire in a big way. IT managers do communicate with each other, and if you pull enough stunts, you can get yourself blackballed from the major companies in your area.

- Never send a gift, balloons, or flowers to a hiring manager to get your foot in the door.
- Never disguise your résumé as a personal letter.
- Never be cute in your cover letter.
- Never talk politics or use sarcastic humor.
- Never fax or e-mail your résumé if an ad indicates you should send it via U.S. mail.
- Never use an inappropriate e-mail address like foxylady@hotmail.com. And never, never use an AOL account. It absolutely screams technophobe.

A Note About Breaking the Rules

Now that you've committed to memory the things you should never do, remember that there's an exception to every rule. But breaking the rules only works if you follow the rules the other 99.9 percent of the time. That said, if you've found the one job that you absolutely know you must have, pull out all the stops. Write a heartfelt cover letter. Let your personality shine through. You won't always get the job, and you might not even get a second glance, but you will definitely stand out in the crowd.

True story: An out-of-work Visual Basic developer saw an ad for a job he desperately wanted—a work-at-home position with a terrific starting salary and full benefits. He was lucky enough to spot the ad moments after it was posted on a job board, and he wasted no time composing and sending the following e-mail:

> *All I'm trying to say is: "Pick me! Pick me!"*
>
> *I know that you've received a gazillion résumés and all of them from people who KNOW that they are the best developer since Charles Babbage.*
>
> *It doesn't happen every day that I see an opening that fits me like a glove (unlike O.J.). Well, this is my story:*
>
> *I'm a software engineer with over five years of hands-on IT experience. I'm up to speed on the latest technologies—I'm fluent in VB.Net, C#, SQL 2005, C++, ASP.Net, JavaScript, VBScript, HTML, ADO.NET, COM, ActiveX, XML, SDL, MSMQ, Access, and Visual Studio Team Center.*
>
> *I have successfully telecommuted and worked in an office environment.*
>
> *I'm easy to get along with, and I'm passionate about IT.*
>
> *I'm looking for a challenging position with a company like Bayside Business Solutions. As a former officer in the Air Force, I have excellent management and interpersonal skills. My in-depth experience as a software developer, software engineer, instructor, and systems administrator will be an asset to your company.*
>
> *Enough about me. Why don't we meet for a cup of coffee—on me—and I'll have an opportunity to present myself in person.*

I look forward to hearing from you.

The e-mail broke just about every rule imaginable, but the "send" button had been hit, and the developer could only sit back and wait.

Meanwhile, his missive was received by the company's secretary, who was so disgusted by it that she forwarded it to the vice-president of development as an example of the trash she had to deal with. The VP, however, loved it. It matched his own quirky sense of humor, and he invited the developer for an interview and eventually hired him.

So there you have it. In this case, breaking the rules worked out—but barely. The developer's plan could easily have blown up in his face and cost him a shot at his dream job.

Increasing Your Confidence

Believing in yourself is an integral part of landing a new job. And it's easy to believe in yourself when you've taken the time to prepare carefully. You know there's an opportunity for you out there—with the right company and the right team. You have skills that an employer desperately needs—and is willing to pay for. I'll show you how to present your accomplishments in the best light for employers to notice them.

A strong image—on paper and in person—will get you in the door. Let's take a look at how to make yourself stand out as the perfect candidate for the job.

Asset Statements

In *Ace the IT Résumé!*, I take you through a three-pronged process of building an effective and attention-getting résumé. Here, I just touch on some of the basics—this book concentrates on acing the interview. I suggest you use the information in *Ace the IT Résumé!* to create the strongest possible résumé.

Just as your résumé should start off with a powerful qualifications section (see Chapter 2 for more details), you should also be prepared with powerful asset statements. Asset statements allow you to hit the key areas of what hiring managers are watching out for—out loud, in your own words.

Your asset statements will highlight specific employer benefits related to your various skill sets. You'll be able to showcase just how your technical skills, management skills, and transferable skills will result in direct gains for potential employers.

STAND OUT!

Find out what role the company wants you to play. Ask, as soon as possible, about the scope of the job and the ideal person's qualifications for it. Then use specifics to describe your matching skills.

Here's how it works:

1. To begin, **identify what the company needs from you.** List, on paper, everything the company hopes to gain by hiring someone for the advertised position.

2. Next, go back through your list and **identify the specific skills you have that the company can use**. Circle or highlight them in your original list.
3. Once you've done that, it's time to focus on benefits. You need to **demonstrate exactly how your skills will help the company**. Most people make the mistake of listing their skills and leaving it at that. You'll take it one step further. Take a look at the two examples below.

Example 1: Features

The company needs:	**I have:**
Strong VB.NET skills	Strong VB.NET skills
Experience with ASP.NET	3 years ASP.NET experience
Web skills	5 years web development experience

Example 2: Benefits

The company needs:	**I have:**
Strong VB.NET skills	Strong VB.NET skills
Experience with ASP.NET	3 years ASP.NET experience
Web skills	5 years web development experience

How my skills will help the company:

With my VB.NET skills and ASP.NET experience, I can help you create dynamic, intuitive web interfaces that are simple to use and cost-effective to update regularly. I'm already familiar with the latest web development tools, so I can have your site upgrades completed and online quickly.

See the difference? Example 1 offers a list of skills. It's up to the employer to figure out what those skills mean for the company. In Example 2, you give the employer exactly what he needs by answering his number one question: *What's in it for me?*

STAND OUT!
Focus on skills that will make you immediately productive.

But you're not done yet. Steps 1, 2, and 3 are important, but to really stand out, you have to take it further. It's one thing to list the "features" you offer. It's another thing to demonstrate the "benefits" you can give an employer. But even the powerful benefit statements listed above lose their effectiveness if you can't back them up with specific examples. So that's the next step.

STAND OUT!

Though providing examples of your work history is important, try not to overwhelm the interviewer with irrelevant statistics and trivia. Say enough to get the point across, but not so much as to be a bore.

4. **Provide specific examples from your work history that demonstrate your skills.** This is where bragging rights come into play without making you sound stuck up. You can talk about your accomplishments here because you're using them to demonstrate what you can do for your next employer. Like this:

   "My previous employer had a client who can only be described as terrified of technology. The client had a Website that needed to be updated daily, and he was tired of paying big bucks to an outside web design shop that was overcharging him. So I designed a VB-based application that let him use familiar Microsoft applications—Word and Excel—to make changes to his site and upload them with one click. And upgrading his basic HTML pages to ASP.NET meant that many of his updates were automated. We saved the client money, which made him very happy. So happy, in fact, that he referred us another $50,000 worth of business that month."

   You've now backed up your assertion of what you could do with a real-life example that shows how you did it already.

STAND OUT!

"As a recruiter, it is my job to screen out candidates for my clients. First the candidates must prove to me that they are qualified for the job. Then they must prove it to the employer."—Don Bernard, StarDot RPG, Inc.

Once you've come up with several strong asset statements, you may be tempted to relax and coast your way through the rest of your preparation. Don't do it. Go a bit further. Show the employer what sets you apart from other candidates. Take a look at your other skills, skills that aren't directly related to your job description, but that really make a difference in how you do your job. The skills you need to stress now are skills that may not be emphasized—or even present—in your current résumé. So take some extra time to review the following information, uncover those skills, and call attention to them.

Identifying Other Skills

If you've come to IT late in the job game, you may have a lot of experience in other industries. That's okay, as long as you know how to present your experience to your best advantage. Even if you've worked exclusively in IT, you may want to transition from one technology to another, or you may want to break into the IT department of a company in a highly specialized industry.

Before you discount your years of on-the-job learning as completely irrelevant, take a good look at how what you did before reflects on your overall ability to shine in the workforce. This experience makes you a balanced, experienced, *promotable* professional. Here are some examples of transferable, or "soft," skills:

Project Management Project management goes beyond learning Microsoft Project. Success as a project manager depends on your ability to define, plan, organize, control, and complete a variety of complex and interdependent tasks.

Communication Skills From answering the phone to writing an e-mail or putting together a proposal, how well you put your point across will affect others' perceptions of your abilities. Make sure each interaction paints an intelligent picture.

Presentation Skills Forget the horror of high school Oral Communications classes. These skills are a must for any situation such as running a meeting, pitching a product or solution, or justifying why you should get that raise. It doesn't matter how many are in the audience, every time you open your mouth you are using these skills. Make sure you're presenting the image that you want by mastering this skill set.

Selling Face it—regardless of whether your title includes "sales," you're always selling. Whether it's yourself, your project, or your next position, you're always asking people to buy in on something. Learn how to do it more effectively.

Running Meetings Learning how to facilitate meetings and manage group interactions is an important first step to becoming a team leader.

Leadership There are many keys to successful projects, including organizational buy-in, good project management, and proper resourcing. A strong leader understands these dynamics, harnesses the diverse energies within an organization, and pulls everyone together.

Problem Solving This is the skill that you are probably most familiar with. To some, problem solving comes instinctively. To others, it's not so natural. The key is to find a process that works and apply it.

Customer Service Yes, people are difficult. But when they're customers, they come first and they're always right. They need to feel valued and important. Just remember: if you don't treat them right, someone else will.

Self-direction This is the ability to do your job without having to be told how to do your job. It's extremely important because by the time your manager gets through telling you how to do it she could have probably done it herself.

Teamwork No man is an island, certainly not in IT where there just isn't room for egos. With so many different operating systems, servers, networks, databases, and other things that need to be coordinated, no one can do it alone. Here's where those skills that you learned in kindergarten come in: sharing, saying "please," and more importantly, "thank you." Play nicely with others, or take a time-out.

STAND OUT!

Transferable skills may be hard to identify at first. You can start off by asking to see a more experienced colleague's résumé to get some ideas.

Review this list, pick out the skills that apply to you, and try to create statements that showcase your specific strengths, as in the following examples:

- Able to assimilate large amounts of technical information quickly
- Able to quickly identify client requirements and develop a detailed project plan
- Proven history of improving operations and increasing profitability
- Able to coordinate many tasks simultaneously while remaining focused on company goals
- Excellent communicator with proven problem-resolving skills
- Team player committed to achieving overall department and company goals
- Comfortable working as a team member as well as independently
- Able to handle constant change and interruption
- Self-motivated, hardworking team player
- Able to motivate staff to meet project deadlines
- Excellent interpersonal skills; able to relate to culturally diverse customer base
- Able to prioritize and work proactively
- Proven ability to work in a fast-paced, challenging environment
- Exceptional ability to quickly master new software/hardware and apply its full range of capabilities
- Expert technical troubleshooter and problem solver

STAND OUT!

Do you tend to be too hard on yourself? Don't make the mistake of selling yourself short when taking stock of your skills. Before assuming you don't have adequate skills, make sure you aren't setting your standards too high. You don't have to be a world-renowned expert to say you have a particular skill.

Finally, if you really want to shine (and I doubt you'd be reading this otherwise), use the following questions to uncover your own special talents and skills. You'll be surprised by just how much you have to contribute to your next organization. Remember, the key here is to take the previous list of statements and turn them into asset statements that focus on benefits to the employer.

- Your boss always counts on you for something you're especially good at. What is it that he always counts on you for?
- Think of a problem that came up that had other people stumped, but that you were able to resolve. What did you do? What does that say about your abilities?
- What's your best "trick of the trade"? What do you do better than anyone else in your organization? What keeps you successful?
- When did you go above and beyond your job description, and more than earn your pay that day?
- If your friends were to brag about your skills, what would they say?
- If you felt totally comfortable bragging about yourself, what would you brag about? What are you most proud of?
- List ten qualities other people have that you most respect or admire. Go through the list and apply each of these qualities to some aspect of yourself or your work.
- If you suddenly had to leave the area for a while, how would your coworkers' jobs be tougher or less enjoyable when you're not there to help?
- What professional award would you most like to receive? For what? How close are you to getting it?
- How many of your professional goals have you achieved so far? Five years ago, did you think you could be where you are today?

STAND OUT!
Master a one- or two-minute commercial in response to "tell me about yourself" requests.

Putting It All Together

Once you've identified, developed, and perfected your asset statements on paper, it's time to put the show on the road. First, read the statements aloud several times until the words are familiar. Then work on making each statement into a story. Let your personality shine through. Make it conversational. Run through them over and over until you feel comfortable delivering each statement.

Extra effort takes, well, extra effort, but it does get results. Skip these steps, and you'll blend back into the background with the rest of the crowd. Are you content to settle for mediocrity? Or do you crave something more? Work smarter—it pays better.

Checklist

You may have noticed that the overwhelming theme of this chapter is preparation. And in keeping with that theme, I'll leave you with a checklist you can use to make sure your preparations are complete and you're ready to venture forth.

- ☐ Did you invest some time learning about the industry you're targeting?
- ☐ Did you research individual companies carefully, reviewing their unique points, corporate culture, leaders, and values?
- ☐ Did you use targeted Websites to dig up financial information and get the inside scoop?
- ☐ Did you move beyond online research to find additional information?
- ☐ Did you create asset statements to highlight specific employer benefits related to your various skill sets?

Chapter 5

Making a Great First Impression

In Chapter 4, we looked at ways to stand out at your interview. Now I'll cover something even more basic: the importance of a great first impression. Remember those deodorant commercials from the late 1980s? "You never get a second chance to make a first impression." It's the truth.

Superficial or not, most of us form impressions of people within seconds of meeting them for the first time. Someone rings your doorbell. You open the door, and the person standing there is well-dressed, neatly pressed, and has a nice car parked in the street. You'll probably be more receptive to him than you would be to, say, someone standing there in ripped jeans and a torn T-shirt with a jalopy still backfiring in your driveway.

Now, before you rush off to lease a Jaguar and tell your significant other that this book says you'll never get a job without it, hold off. I'll show you how to make a stellar first impression without expensive gimmicks. You'll learn

- What people notice about you and why
- How to overcome the jitters
- Secrets of successful scheduling
- How to go from first impression to lasting impression

Mirror, Mirror, on the Wall: All About Appearance

Appearance counts. Tough break, but it's the truth, and the sooner you accept it, the sooner you'll make it work for you. The no-brainer part of this, of course, is that your clothes should be clean and ironed, and your hair should be combed and preferably a natural-looking color (no green or purple).

STAND OUT!
Your appearance should reflect the standards of the industry and the job you are seeking.

Be sure your hands and fingernails are clean, smooth, and well-groomed. If you wear nail polish, make sure it's not chipped or peeling, and keep the color conservative. Now is not the time to try out new nail art.

"But what about my sense of style, flair, and individuality?" you shriek. "I got into IT so I could be part of a hip, funky culture. If I wanted to wear ironed clothes, I'd be a lawyer."

In a word: tough. Yes, a few years ago, if you were that mysterious animal spoken of in reverential tones as "an IT guy," you could get away with multiple piercings, shirts with writing on them, and pretty much whatever you wanted in a salary and benefits package. But those days have passed. IT professionals are just that—professional. If you want to stay in the game, you have to play by the rules.

STAND OUT!

If you're trying to obtain a job at a higher level than any you've held in the past, be sure your image is congruent with that higher level, even before you have the job.

Dress for Success

You stand in front of your closet crammed full of clothes, and as cliché as it is, you find yourself moaning, "I have nothing to wear." Before you head off to the mall, take a few minutes to figure out exactly what you need to wear to your interview.

You want to err on the side of caution, but you also don't want to go too far. If you have no idea what the dress code in the office is, go for normal business attire: suit and tie for men, business suit for women. If you're wildly uncomfortable in such clothes, make an extra effort: wear them for at least an hour a day every day until they feel natural. You'll look and feel much more at ease, and you'll be better able to concentrate on the actual interview.

Of course, you should have some clue as to normal office attire, because you'll ask about it when you're on the phone arranging your interview. That's right. When the Company of Your Dreams calls to offer you an interview, you'll be prepared, and you'll say, "What's your dress code? Should I wear a suit and tie [or a business suit, if you're a woman]?"

The person on the other end will either say, "Well, you'll be meeting the CEO, so you probably should wear a suit and tie," or "Oh, gosh, no, we don't let anyone in here dressed like that. Business casual is fine," or something else entirely. If necessary, you can always remove a coat or jacket and tie, but it is tough to produce these out of thin air if you have gone too casual. If you have the time, it might be valuable to drive by the facility during the typical employee arrival time in the morning and see what employees are wearing. Be sure to notch up one or two levels for your interview.

STAND OUT!

Remember: dress for the position you seek, not the one you have.

Here's a list of things to watch out for to make sure you project the right image for the position.

- Shirts with collars win out over shirts without, every time.
- Don't wear something you'd be embarrassed to let your mother see you wearing—nothing with obscenities written across it, regardless of the language of the writing.
- Don't wear clothes that are dirty or in need of repair.
- Make sure your clothes fit you. If they're too big, you'll look sloppy, and if they're too small, you'll look like you don't care about yourself. If you don't care about yourself, why would anyone imagine you'll care about your job?
- Avoid dousing yourself in perfume, cologne, or aftershave. Do feel free to use your favorite scent sparingly.
- Reevaluate your hair. Very long hair on men is still widely perceived as a sign of rebellion. Keep in mind that if an interviewer is over 50 years old, has served in the military, or was a law enforcement officer, he could have preconceived ideas about a prospective male employee with long hair. On the other hand, really short hair is often associated with hyperconservatism or "skinhead" attitudes. Don't let your hair style become a stumbling block that keeps someone from fairly evaluating your skills.
- If you have a mustache or beard, make sure it's neatly trimmed.
- Right before you leave, take an extra moment to give yourself a once-over in a full-length mirror. Fix anything that needs readjusting, and then try not to eat or drink anything besides water until after the interview is over.

Pack Your Bags

The other part of your appearance is your bag, whether it's a purse, backpack, or briefcase. And as you've learned by now, organization and preparation are what set you apart from the crowd. If you're offered a last-minute chance to interview for the job of your dreams, you want to be able to accept without hesitation. In addition, when you're organized, you appear more competent, and you're free to concentrate on the task at hand—getting the job offer.

Make sure you have a stack of printed copies of your résumé. Set up a form to keep track of when and where you sent your résumé and when you need to follow up. Include a column for notes you can enter after the interview.

Keep an interview folder in your bag. Include several clean copies of your résumé, pen and paper for notes, and copies of written references you might have. You should also have a comb and small mirror, tissues, and breath mints or a travel toothbrush and toothpaste. Check the contents of your bag regularly, and replenish when necessary.

APPEARANCE CHECKLISTS

Refer to the following checklists to make sure your appearance is appropriate for the interview.

Men

- No bulge in the pockets
- No five o'clock shadow
- No sagging coat lining
- No short or white socks
- No sandals or unshined or worn-down shoes
- No mismatching belts and shoes
- No ties too short or too long
- No wrinkled or soiled clothing

Women

- No heavy makeup
- No makeup on the collar line
- No provocative clothing (see-through, tight, super-short skirts)
- No flashy jewelry, dangling earrings, or ankle bracelets
- No strappy shoes, sandals, or stiletto heels
- No big hair
- No chipped or unusual color nail polish
- No hosiery runs
- Either bring a purse or a briefcase, but not both

For Both

- No visible body piercings
- No tinted glasses
- No fad watches
- No visible body art (tattoos)

> ***STAND OUT!***
>
> For women only: You can count on panty hose running at the most inopportune time. Carry a spare pair in your bag.

Ideally, turn your PDA and cell phone off during the interview. Even if you have it set for vibrate, this can interrupt your concentration. Also, if you have a PDA with your calendar, be sure it is freshly synced with your current meeting info and bring it along in case a second interview needs to be scheduled. Just be certain that it has any audible event alarms turned off so there won't be any disruptive beeping to inform you that you should be at an interview right now. If you are using a nonelectronic planner, bring that along.

Be very careful not to let your bag become a catch-all for clutter. Clean it out every night. You don't want to wade through wadded-up tissues, leftover lunch remains, and 27 receipts from the gas station while you tell a potential employer about your superior organizational skills.

Overcoming "First Date" Jitters

It's natural to be a little bit nervous as you head into your first interview, or even your first interview at a new company. And a little nervousness can actually be a good thing—it keeps you on your toes. But don't let fear overwhelm you and prevent you from selling yourself effectively.

Remember, you've taken the time to prepare properly. You know what you're doing, and you *are* ready for this opportunity. Need some reassurance? Here are a few little exercises to help you ease your nerves just before an interview:

- Close your eyes and concentrate on relaxing each muscle in your body. Start with your toes and work you way up, moving on to the next set of muscles only after the previous set is relaxed.
- Breathe in deeply and hold your breath for a count of five. Exhale. Do this four more times.
- Think about something else. Distract yourself by reading a magazine in the waiting area or by simply chatting with the receptionist. The key is to focus on something other than yourself.
- Visualize a successful outcome to your interview. Imagine your first day on the job as you meet your new coworkers and they anxiously await your contribution to the team.
- Practice focusing your discussion on the employer's needs. Show that you understand those needs, that you possess the specific skills to handle the job, and that you are in sync with the company culture.

Psych Yourself Up

Remember all those asset statements and accomplishments you wrote up in your résumé? Look them over, and take the time to read them aloud. Hearing such statements spoken is a powerful ego-booster. Envision yourself on the job, solving problems, participating in staff meetings, accepting an award from the company president. If you believe you're the best person for the job, it'll be that much easier to convince the interviewer.

You can even carry a small index card with some of your greatest life achievements recorded on it. Review it immediately before an interview for an instant kick in the seat of the pants.

BEHAVIORS TO WATCH OUT FOR

Many of these behaviors are very natural and you may not even be aware of them. When you are nervous they can become more pronounced as your body seeks a way to relieve the stress. This is where an honest friend and a video camera can really help. It is a moment of real humility and course correction when you realize that you said, "Um" 20 times in 10 minutes! More nervous habits to avoid include:

- Tapping feet
- Twirling, pulling, or rearranging your hair
- Jingling change in your pocket
- Folding your arms
- Fidgeting
- Not maintaining eye contact
- Chewing gum
- Mumbling
- Interrupting
- Slumping
- Playing with your pen or other objects

In addition to watching your physical behavior, get control of your voice as well. Some words and sounds to avoid include:

- Um
- Uh
- Yeah or yup
- Y'know
- Like
- Okay
- I guess
- Kind'a

Practice Makes Perfect

Would you ever get up at a recital and attempt to play a difficult piano piece you'd never seen before? Of course not. The same goes with any performance—and an interview is your chance for an Oscar.

Rehearse your spiel. Out loud. In front of a mirror. If you're really ambitious, set up a video recorder or have a friend watch you and offer suggestions. Go through the questions in this book and plan your answers to all the relevant ones. Yes, it's a lot of work. No, most people don't bother. But *you* bothered. *You're* willing to go the extra mile. What company wouldn't want to hire you after that?

Timing Is Everything

It happens. You have the world's greatest idea. You're the perfect person for the job. You've got it all figured out—but the timing is off. Sometimes, no matter what you do, things just aren't in sync. It works the other way around, too: you can be in the right place at the right time and snatch up a job almost effortlessly. How can you make that happen? By exercising a bit of scheduling savvy.

Never set up an interview for a Monday. People are pressed to start the week and get some work done. Or they're depressed that the weekend is over already. Either one puts them in the wrong frame of mind to discover how great you are.

Don't plan on Friday interviews either. Many people take off—mentally or physically—right after lunch on Friday. You don't want to be the reason your interviewer can't leave early to start her weekend in the Hamptons, right?

You're left with Tuesday, Wednesday, and Thursday, all prime interview days. Try for a morning appointment when people are likely to be fresher. Right after lunch is the worst time of day—everyone's tired, yawning, and ready for a nap. If you can set up a middle of the week appointment for 10:00 A.M., your timing should be perfect.

Doing the Detail Work

If you've gone to the trouble to time your interview perfectly, don't blow it by showing up late for your appointment. The day before the interview, make sure you know exactly where you're going and how to get there, the name and phone number of the person you'll meet, and what time your meeting is. Always allow at least 20 minutes extra travel time. You should arrive about 10 minutes early. Put your favorite music on and enjoy the drive, thinking about how well things will go at the interview. Now is not the time to be trying to cram company facts into your brain or memorize questions you want to ask. These things should have all been done before the interview. If you have done your homework now is the time to be confident. You are going to get this job. Remember that the worst thing that will happen is you will get some practice at interviewing and go away with lessons learned for the next one.

Plan to arrive very early so if you have misjudged the traffic or have a car problem, you will still arrive in plenty of time. Find a restaurant near the business or interview location. Relax and gather your thoughts over your favorite (non-alcoholic) beverage, being careful not to spill it all over yourself! The last stop at the restaurant is the restroom. There may not be one easily available at the interview site.

Be sure your car is clean. If the interview has gone well, you could get a lunch invitation and think of the embarrassment if your car is a mess inside and out. If you get to the place half an hour early, read a book in your car or at a coffee shop within walking distance. Don't sit in the waiting room and put pressure on the receptionist and the person you're waiting to see.

Make sure you know the parking situation ahead of time. Is there a visitor parking area? If the parking area is full of employees' cars, is there a public lot nearby? Will you need to pay for parking? Exact change only? And don't wait until you're about to leave to get gas. Fill up your tank the night before.

If you'll be taking public transportation, double- and triple-check your route and stops. Do you have the money you'll need? Do you know exactly which stop you need and how frequently the line runs?

Security concerns have compelled many larger companies to carefully screen every visitor to their physical plant. You might need a photo ID to be issued a temporary visitor badge. Be sure you have your driver's license or other photo ID ready in case you are asked to present it at the security desk. It could be a long walk back to your car to retrieve this from the glove compartment. You may need to be escorted by an employee while you are in their building complex. This is another case for making a restroom stop before you arrive. It can be pretty embarrassing to have a security guard or employee escorting you to the bathroom facilities.

Success is often in the details. Don't let your failure to anticipate them keep you from making the right impression.

Who's Who and Where's Where?

Remember, you have to find more than the right building. You've got to get all the way to the person who's doing the interview. Large companies may have several buildings with several entrances and hundreds of floors of offices. Do you know precisely where you need to be?

Of course, you need to write down the name of the person you're meeting, and you should take a phone number (and a cell phone) as well. If all your correspondence has been by e-mail, call ahead to find out the pronunciation of the person's name. Try calling his or her office after hours, when you are most likely to get voice mail.

Make Your First Impression a Lasting One

If you're all about flashiness, you may make a splash when you enter the room. But will anyone remember you when the excitement of your visit has passed? You want to make a great first impression, but you want it to be all about substance, not just style. That way, the interviewer will remember you tomorrow, next week, and when it's time to make a hiring decision.

So how do you do it? How do you make your first impression last? It starts from the moment you walk into the room. Start off by giving the interviewer a genuine smile, making eye contact, and offering your hand. Give a firm handshake; don't crush his fingers, but let your handshake demonstrate your confidence. If you have a hard time with names, you can repeat the name back out loud as you shake his hand and make eye contact. You will need to remember it long enough to get that recorded on your notes after you are seated.

STAND OUT!

For men only: Avoid shaking hands extra gently with women. Soft handshakes are considered to be patronizing or chauvinistic.

Wait to be offered a seat. If you are being interviewed by more than one person, try to arrange the chairs so that you can keep everyone in your line of vision. That's much easier than swiveling your head back and forth the whole time. If you need to rearrange the chairs in the room and can do so without too much trouble, go for it. Just say, "I'd like to be able to see you both, if you don't mind, so I'm going to move over here." What are they going to do? Stop you? Unlikely. It's much more likely, in fact, that they'll note your initiative as a positive character trait. If there are multiple individuals at the table, write down their names so that you can easily recall who is sitting where, what their job function is, and what their role is in the interview process. This information will likely be given during the introductions. You might be handed business cards that will aid you in this process. As you are seated, get your notepad out and get this information down before you forget it. In some corporate settings, employees will be wearing ID badges. If you have forgotten any names, you can briefly glance at the badges to jog your memory. This will be the last time you should look at their badges. It can be very annoying and awkward if you are staring at someone's badge instead of giving them proper eye contact.

If you're offered a drink, accept. Everyone rushes to say, "No, thanks, I'm fine." When you accept the drink, you indicate that you feel comfortable and confident. You can take sips to buy a few seconds while you think about your answers. (Of course, I mean coffee, tea, water, or a soft drink. Never, never, never drink alcohol at an interview, even if it's a lunch or dinner interview, and even if your host is drinking.)

If you're sitting down and someone else enters the room, stand up when you're introduced. It's a sign of respect. Unless you're specifically asked to do otherwise, always address interviewers by their title and last name, for example, "Mr. Smith."

STAND OUT!

For recent college grads only: The most important characteristics that college recruiters look for are enthusiasm, communication skills, self-confidence, a well-groomed appearance, and technical knowledge.

Listen Carefully

Everyone loves to talk. Make sure that you give the interviewer a chance to talk. The more carefully you listen, the more you can tailor your responses. If you're really good, you'll pick up on words and phrases used in the interview and offer them back in your answers. It's a subtle way to indicate that you already fit in.

Never interrupt your interviewer, even if you're sure you know the answer. Always let him or her finish speaking. Make sure you're really hearing the question. Don't spend the whole time thinking about what you're going to say. Just listen. You'll have plenty of time to formulate your response once the interviewer stops speaking.

Also, show your interviewer that she has your full attention by looking at her while she speaks. Don't glance at your watch or go through your notes. It's okay to take a few notes while your interviewer speaks, especially during a technical interview, when you may need to solve problems on the spot. But taking notes means jotting a few words down to remind yourself of something later on, not asking her to repeat what she said so you can write it verbatim. Repeat back any questions to be sure you understand what they are asking. It is one thing to look like you are listening intently. It's another to be able to accurately repeat back questions and use phrases that the interviewer has just said. The most precious words a person hears are her own words being repeated back to her.

Say It with a Smile

When it's your turn to talk, don't rush it. Take a moment to collect your thoughts, then say your piece. Smile when it's natural to do so. Make eye contact as you speak. When you've said everything you have to say, sit back and shut up. The old proverb says, "Even a fool appears wise if he remains silent." Don't get yourself a job and then lose it by saying too much. Don't be afraid of silence, and don't weaken a strong answer by tacking an "Uh..." at the end of it.

Confidence Is Catching

The following chapters will prepare you for the specific questions you can expect at your interviews. But this is the first step. If you've taken the time to prepare yourself physically and mentally, it will show. You won't just *feel* ready, you'll *be* ready. You'll project your ability to do the job well, and interviewers will notice.

Building Rapport

Rapport means bonding. It's the magic that happens when you draw the interviewer into what you're saying. How do you do it? Check out the following exchange:

You: What do you see as your greatest need in increasing the productivity of the helpdesk?

Interviewer: Our challenge is increasing the accuracy of the responses the helpdesk technicians provide on the first call.

You: I understand. Working together, *we* could solve that problem. In my previous position at Thompson University, through training and working with the technicians, I was able to increase the initial call close rate by 75 percent. I believe that *we* could apply some of those same solutions here.

The words *we*, *us*, and *our* are extremely powerful in helping the interviewer envision you solving his problems. These words convey inclusion, cooperation, and alliance. The following is a list of words that convey the idea that you're a team player and contributor to the workplace:

Collaborate	Synergy
Cooperate	Team
Good listener	Together
Open mind	Work together

If you want to give an impression of accomplishment, use some of these words:

Achieve	Leverage
Analyze	Organize
Automate	Persuade
Create	Proactive
Document	Produce
Enhance	Reduce
Extend	Revitalize
Grow or growth	Self-starter
Implement	Succeed
Leadership	Visibility or high visibility

Checklist

Dozens of candidates apply for IT positions every day. Out of the stack of résumés hiring managers receive and review, only a few are chosen to interview. If you've made it to that level, the company wants to hire you. Whether or not they choose you depends almost entirely on how you fare at the interview. Review this checklist to be sure you're ready to make a great first impression—you won't get another chance.

- ☐ Did you take care with your appearance?
- ☐ Do you know exactly where you're going, how you'll get there, and what time you're due?
- ☐ Do you have a well-stocked "interview bag" ready to go at all times?
- ☐ Did you schedule your interview at an optimal time?
- ☐ Do you know how to listen well and really hear what the interviewer is asking?

Part III

The Interview

In This Part

Chapter 6

The Questions Everyone Asks—and Answers That May Surprise You

You're settled into your chair. Your breath is fresh, your back is straight, and you've passed the handshake test. The interviewer smiles, you smile back. And then it begins: the questions fly fast and furious. Are you ready to answer them? You will be, if you understand what the interviewer really wants to know. Every single question posed to you serves a greater purpose. The interviewer is always asking one of four things:

- Can you do the job?
- Will you fit in?
- Do you want the job?
- How much will you cost?

Once you accept that your answers must go beyond the questions you're asked while also addressing these needs, you'll be in a much better position to tell the interviewer exactly what he needs to hear.

Can You Do the Job?

Clearly, your ability to get the job done is crucial. Your interviewer needs to know that you have the skills necessary to do the job and do it well. So he'll ask a lot of questions designed to elicit information about your technical expertise. You might be asked, for example, any of the following questions:

- Why are you looking for a new job?
- Why did you leave your last position?
- Why have you changed jobs so frequently?
- What are your greatest strengths?
- What's your biggest weakness?
- How did your last boss get the best out of you?

- What makes you stand out among your peers?
- How do you build a team that you are responsible for?
- What do you consider the biggest accomplishment in your present (or past) job?
- Think about something that you consider a failure in your business life, and tell me why you think it occurred.
- What have you done to save your company money or time?
- How adaptable to change are you?
- How flexible in the way you work are you?
- Where do you need to improve?
- Do you have any questions for me?

> **STAND OUT!**
> **When asked why you're looking for a new job, never blame your former boss. It's bad form.**

When you answer these questions, you need to be careful. Avoid blaming other people or circumstances. Instead, focus on your ability to do the job at hand, and demonstrate your talent by providing specific examples. That means don't say you're looking for a chance to make more money, get away from your wacko boss, or you want to work with people who appreciate the genius of "Spy TV." This may all be true, but it won't get you hired.

So what should you say? Start off by letting the interviewer know that you are excited about the chance to grow. One possible answer:

> "I love to be challenged. I'm looking for a position that will give me a chance to put my skills to the test."

Or:

> "Your company offers so much growth potential. That kind of environment suits me perfectly."

If you really have changed jobs frequently, be sure to offer the interviewer some reassurance:

> "I was tempted by the promise of working with cutting-edge tools. But the company ultimately chose not to migrate to the newest technology, and I saw that I wouldn't have the opportunity to explore the latest frameworks like SOA. You're already using it here, and that's the kind of forward-thinking I'm looking for."

> **STAND OUT!**
> **Turn your weaknesses into your strengths. Interviewers don't want to hear that you're going to cost them money or be unpopular and demanding.**

When you discuss your weaknesses, of course, you need to play up the positive. Always offer a balanced answer. For example, if you say the following, it's unlikely anyone would ever want to hire you:

> "I don't handle stress well. I go crazy when a project is due, and I spend the whole time worrying about it."
>
> Instead, say something like:
>
> "I'm obsessive about deadlines. I love to schedule projects out to the last deal and work with my peers to get things done on time, but I tend to be more directive at the end of the project to make sure we roll out releases on schedule. I guess I become intensely focused, but I almost never miss a deadline.

After you've introduced your "weakness" this way, you can follow up with a specific example that turns it into a strength:

> "At my last job, I was responsible for overseeing the rollout of our new software suite. There were five products, and I had five separate teams to direct and manage. I made each team leader provide weekly updates, and I conducted random spot-checks on the programmers to make sure their work was on schedule. They might have felt I was micromanaging them, but we met our target release date, which was crucial, because it was timed to coincide with our industry's major expo. We were there, in full force, and with a product that was ready to go. We wound up exceeding revenue expectations by about 25 percent."

When it's time to talk about your strengths, be prepared with specific examples that showcase the qualities you're discussing:

> "I'm very good at supervising my peers and communicating with management. My team had a major project due, and we ran into a snag. The client hadn't made the necessary adjustments to their legacy systems, and data migration was going to take an extra three weeks. I split my team into two groups and had one group tackle the migration issues while the other continued on the current project. It meant super-careful delegation and some fancy footwork on my part to oversee everyone, but it worked. And I kept management informed of our progress every step of the way. In the end, we actually finished the project a week early and saved the client about $25,000. They referred us another $2 million in accounts last year."

Follow these rules when discussing past achievements and failures, too. Never, ever list what you believe are your real shortcomings. If you tell the interviewer that you made a mistake that cost the company millions in lost revenues, but you felt really bad about it afterwards, guess what? Your honesty won't get you the job. Take a different approach:

> "I miscalculated the amount of time a major upgrade would require. I was new, and I hadn't yet learned how to make those kinds of technical estimates. I did warn my supervisor that my estimate was very rough, but it was translated to the client verbatim. When we couldn't deliver on time, I got a great lesson in the fine art of simply telling my employer that a particular task is beyond my area of expertise."

And follow up immediately with a specific example of success:

> "Of course, now that I have several years' experience under my belt, I know how to better gauge how long a project will take. In fact, all of my projects have come in on time—or even a few days early—for the past three years."

Likewise, when you're asked about areas you could improve, focus on short-term, easily attainable goals:

> "I haven't yet had the opportunity to work in a .NET environment as much as I'd like to. I really want to immerse myself in it. In fact, I just got a textbook the other day, and I started reading it last night."

When you describe what sets you apart from your peers, use anecdotes that show your commitment and direction:

> "I define myself by the high quality of my work. I'm not happy with code that's just workable, or even with code that runs 'just fine.' I like my code to be clean, well organized, properly commented, and well documented. That way, if we go back to make upgrades later on, or if I'm not immediately available, anyone else who works on the project can immediately get a clear picture of what's needed."

PLAYING TO WIN

When you prepare anecdotes about your work history, remember that every word counts. Always use active verbs—they signify accomplishment and create a strong, lasting impression in the interviewer's mind. Instead of saying, "I came up with a system that saved us a lot of time on data entry," say, "I created and implemented a time-saving, data-entry system." See the difference?

Think you'll sound phony? Remember, practice makes perfect. Take the following list of Ten Winning Words and write up an anecdote for each one. Then practice telling the stories—to your dog, your roommate, your mother—until the words feel natural to you.

Ten Winning Words

Achieve	Persuade
Analyze	Produce
Create	Reduce
Implement	Revitalize
Organize	Succeed

To answer questions about how your actions saved your company money and/or time, you want to show the interviewer that you take pride in your work and you view the company's success as a reflection on you, and vice versa. When you're committed to your job, you take it personally, and that's something employers love. Make sure your answer is complete, though. Don't just say that, as a helpdesk technician, you wrote a FAQ that answered the 50 most common tech support queries. Take it a step further: how did that help the company?

> "I realized that our technicians were bogged down with the same series of questions again and again. I created a FAQ that provided customers with answers to the 50 most commonly asked questions. It didn't cost us anything to include the document on the installation CD, and it cut tech support calls by 40 percent. As a result, we were actually able to reduce our tech support hours with no negative effect on customer satisfaction. In fact, because people had the answers they needed right on the installation CD, we actually saw a 65 percent increase in customer satisfaction. And we're saving about $125,000 a year because we don't need as many support technicians."

As you've noticed, specific examples that illustrate your strong points and back up the buzzwords are the key to answering questions that address your ability to get the job done. If you spend some time crafting answers that work in anecdotes from your employment history, you'll be able to answer these questions with confidence—and you'll show the interviewer that you're perfectly capable of handling the task at hand.

Will You Fit In?

Your technical ability is obviously important, but it's also crucial that you fit in to the corporate culture. If you're looking for a job with a major automotive company in Detroit, for example, and you are vocally car-free by choice, chances are you won't be hired. But it's also important that you merely get along with your coworkers. Team projects move much more smoothly if team members speak a common language.

When the interviewer is looking to find out how you'll mesh with the rest of the IT group, you might hear some of these questions:

- Tell me about yourself.
- Give me a little background information about you.
- Tell me something that's not on your résumé.
- Tell me how your approach to working with coworkers has changed from the way it was ten years ago.
- What kind of people do you find it difficult to work with?
- How do you influence people to accept your ideas?
- How much direction do you need to get the job done properly?

- What has been the most difficult decision you have had to face in your professional life, and what was the outcome?
- What makes you most valuable to your current supervisor?
- How many hours do you have to put in to get your job done?
- What would be the next step for you at your current job?
- What are the rewards you expect from a job?

Many candidates get too personal with these questions, or make them the focus of the interview. They're not. Your answers should be succinct, yet have enough personality to reassure the interviewer that you're normal and will fit in. Aim for about three minutes, maximum.

You can talk a bit about how you first came to be passionate about technology. Did you take apart an alarm clock in the second grade? Build your own Speak'n'Spell when you were eight? Share an anecdote that demonstrates why you love what you do:

> "My mother isn't at all surprised that I became a network engineer—she couldn't tear me away from my computer as a kid. All the money I earned went into modding my computer."

STAND OUT!
It's okay to be human. If you don't have a life outside of work, that's typically a sign of trouble.

Do show the interviewer that you have a life outside of work. Are you a sailing fanatic? Writing a novel? Do you collect antique horseshoes? Just remember, when you talk about your passions outside of work, moderation is the key. It's okay to say you're a *Star Trek* fan. It's not okay to speak Vulcan. Try something like:

> "On the weekends, I love to get outside. I hike, run, or just play sports—any kind of physical activity that lets me enjoy the outdoors works."

If you want to demonstrate that you can keep up with younger coworkers, or that you have the maturity required to fit in a professional workspace, try a variation of this:

> "Part of what makes teamwork so enjoyable is having the opportunity to hear multiple points of view. It's great when more experienced developers share tricks and save me from reinventing the wheel, and the fresh perspective college hires have is often just what's needed to find a new and innovative solution."

Do you make life easier for your boss by taking on supervisory responsibilities? Are you easy to get along with? Do people find it easy to take direction from you? Say so. Try something like:

> "My boss oversees a team of 20 engineers, and she has her own development work to do as well. I keep my eyes open for ways I can lighten her load. When one of our new hires, Jim, inadvertently insulted Dave, a more senior member of the team, by criticizing the online

filing system Dave had developed, I was able to diffuse the situation. I took Jim aside and explained that Dave had come up with the system on his own time, and that while it might not be completely intuitive, it served the department's needs adequately. Jim understood and later mentioned to Dave that once he saw the system in action, he recognized its merits. What could have been a tense and awkward work situation was resolved quickly and without the need to involve my supervisor."

Of course, you want to let your interviewer know that you get along famously with everyone. And the only people you have trouble with? Slackers. You can say:

"I have a hard time dealing with people who shirk responsibility. It frustrates me to see a team suffer because of one or two individuals."

It's important, though, to indicate that you also recognize that people come from different places and that you need to get inside their heads when you approach them. Say something like:

"I do try to put myself in other people's shoes when I present ideas or suggestions. I try to work from their perspective, because it's far more effective to do that than to talk blindly without considering their feelings."

Some questions have no right or wrong answers. When an interviewer asks, for example, how much direction you need to get the job done properly, she's trying to see if your style meshes with hers. If you like a lot of direction and she likes to toss off one-word assignments, you have a problem. But if you have similar styles, things will be easier.

Likewise, when you're asked about how many hours you'll need to work to get the job done, tread lightly. You should have some sense of the corporate culture where you're interviewing. At start-ups, for example, people tend to work long hours; leaving at 5:00 P.M. is generally frowned upon. In contrast, at a large, established company, it's common to see the place empty out after 5:00. If you're the kind of person who typically works 12 hour days, you might not fit in.

STAND OUT!

Honesty earns you trust. We're not talking about coming out of the closet, but if you have other commitments that you must honor, let the interviewer know. At the same time, let them know that these have not interfered with previous employment.

If other commitments—night classes, a second job, children—prevent you from working past a certain hour, no matter what, you need to say so. It doesn't do you any good to lie and then lose the job later. But if you're fairly flexible, offer an open-ended answer:

"I've worked for companies that kept a rigid 9 to 5 schedule, and I've worked for companies where everyone pitched in and worked longer hours to get things done. I'm comfortable in both environments. What's the norm here?"

You're throwing the question back to the interviewer, engaging her in conversation, and demonstrating flexibility. That's a winning answer!

It's natural for an interviewer to ask what your next step at your present company might be. He's trying to find out if there's something preventing you from moving up. Are you politically unaware? Do you lack specific technical skills or the ability to demonstrate those skills? The question is designed to elicit information about how you "play the game" at work. It's all about fitting in. Reassure the interviewer by addressing the underlying question in your response:

> "The next step for me would be project manager, the position I'm applying for here. I've felt ready to take this step for several months now. But as you know, the company I work for is small. There simply isn't a need for another project manager, and it could be another year or two before such a position opens up. That's why I've starting looking elsewhere. I love the people I work with, but I'm ready for more responsibility. I've honed my technical skills and my management skills, and I'm eager to contribute more to a company."

When you talk about the rewards you want from a job, remember to put the company before yourself:

> "I like to excel and to know that my work directly affects a company's success. I like to know that my hard work is paying off for the company that hired me. I get an incredible amount of satisfaction from knowing that I've put my very best work out there, and that it's getting results."

When you're that dedicated, who will be able to resist hiring you?

Do You Want the Job?

It might surprise you to know that interviewers work very hard to find out if potential candidates really want the job they're interviewing for. Yes, we know you want *a* job, but do you want this one? Will you leave next month for greener pastures, right after the company has invested in your training? Will you come in every morning ready to work, or will you leave your enthusiasm at home in bed?

Your job is to show the interviewer how much you want this job. You don't want to come off as desperate, but you do want to display a moderate amount of excitement and desire. Be prepared for questions such as:

- What are your career goals?
- Where do you see yourself in five years?
- What are the reasons for your success in this profession?
- What aspect of your job (or past job) do you consider most crucial?
- Why are you the best person for the job?
- What are you looking for in a position?
- What do you know about our organization?

If you're genuinely enthusiastic about a job and a company, let it show. Don't be afraid to talk about career goals. You don't have to pretend you're after the interviewer's job, but you shouldn't be afraid to say that you have aspirations. The key is to first address the position at hand, and then talk about growth opportunities:

> "I've been looking for a position that would offer me the chance to develop in a J2EE environment. My primary goal was to find a company that is using that platform, like yours is. I know that I have some learning to do, but I hope that in a year or two, I'll be the person everyone comes to with questions. And I look forward to managing projects when I have a little more experience."

When you're asked where you envision yourself in five years, the interviewer is really asking about your commitment to the company and the job in question. Even if you hope to be retired on a desert island by then, you should instead focus on your willingness to help the company with its long-term goals. When you phrase your answer, concentrate on the position you're applying for, but indicate your desire for broader responsibility. If, for example, you're applying for a position as a Unix administrator, say:

> "In five years, I'd expect to have gained an even greater understanding of Unix networks. I'd hope to administer LANs at multiple locations of the company by then—for example, here and in your Phoenix office—and to take on more extensive troubleshooting responsibilities as well."

Then follow up by asking the interviewer:

> "Where do you hope I'd be in five years?"

The interviewer's answer will likely provide valuable insight into the company's growth opportunities.

Give credit where credit is due. If a mentor played a significant role in your success, say so:

> "I'm not afraid to ask questions. At my old job, I actively sought out a mentor. Having someone experienced I could turn to for technical advice really helped me. In fact, after seeing what a difference the program made, I found a junior developer to mentor."

Highlight the specific technical skills that set you apart from the pack. If you interned at NASA and used cutting-edge modeling technology, say so. The interviewer only knows as much—or as little—as you tell her. You may well be the best person for the job, but if you don't share that information, you'll take it with you to the unemployment line.

It goes without saying that when the interviewer asks what you know about the company, you've prepared an intelligent answer. But don't just spout off facts from their last annual report—personalize it:

> "All semiconductor companies intrigue me. But when I read about the liquid conductors you're using on your new chip, I was hooked. I read that your focus is shifting toward small wireless apps, like cell phones and PDAs, and that the liquid conductors allow you to increase

circuitry in smaller spaces. How does it work, exactly? Do you just spray it directly onto the PCBs?"

Here, you've demonstrated that you really are interested in the company and its products, you're well-versed in technology, and you engage the interviewer with a question, opening up a chance for a real dialogue.

If you're very brave, you can follow up that question with:

"Is there anything that makes you hesitant about hiring me that I could address now?"

This question gives the interviewer a sense of your seriousness, and it offers you a chance to stave off any misconceptions that might otherwise affect your offer.

How Much Will You Cost?

Yep, money matters. It's the way of the world, and there's nothing to be done about it. Your interviewer wants to find out if the company can afford you. Your goal is to get the best possible offer. We'll cover salary negotiations in depth later on. For now, you need to know that when the interviewer asks about money, he'll most likely be very direct:

- What salary are you expecting?
- What kind of money are you looking for?
- What would it take to get you over here?
- How much money do you want?

Your answer, of course, will require slightly more finesse.

Always try to avoid talking specific numbers until there is an actual job offer on the table. You don't want to price yourself out of the running before they've had a chance to fall in love with you. Likewise, you don't want to lock yourself into a low number that will leave you feeling resentful in the morning.

First, try to deflect the question with an answer such as:

"I'm happy to entertain any reasonable offer that takes my experience and ability into account."

But don't expect it to end there. The interviewer will almost certainly press you for specifics, and you can respond by saying:

"I'd really like to wait until there's an offer on the table before we talk about money."

If the interviewer persists and you're asked to give your magic number, counter by asking what the offered range for the job is. Factor in your own experience, and choose a number somewhere in that range. Check this number with others to be sure you are in the ballpark.

If the entire range is too low, you've got a problem. Either you haven't done your market research properly, or the company is living in dreamland. If you've prepared (you have prepared, right?) according to plan and you know your worth, say so:

> "I'm sorry, but the typical range for mid-level software developers in Los Angeles is $62,500 to $80,000. You're offering $55,000, which is more suitable for a junior programmer. Are you sure that you really want someone with more experience? If you're looking for someone more experienced, you'll need to come up a bit."

Never tell the interviewer that the money isn't important to you and you'll take whatever they're offering. You're essentially saying that your work isn't really worth that much—or that you're completely naïve about the market.

Remember, it's best to wait until the last possible moment to talk about money. You're in a much stronger bargaining position if you sell yourself before you show your price tag.

Checklist

Remember that once you land an interview, whether or not you get a job offer is largely up to you. Your technical skills have prequalified you for the position, and at this point it's all about presentation. If you can show the interviewer that you have the answers to the four primary questions on his mind, you're that much closer to getting hired. Each time you're asked a question, take a moment to think about what the interviewer really needs to know. Then make sure your answer reflects your understanding of the underlying concern as well as the superficial question being asked. Think you're ready? Let's see:

- ☐ Did you prepare specific anecdotes that demonstrate your ability to get the job done?
- ☐ Do you know how to talk about your weaknesses in a way that turns them into strengths?
- ☐ Did you prepare questions to ask the interviewer?
- ☐ Did you research the company and the industry to demonstrate your interest?
- ☐ Have you determined your worth and carried out salary research?
- ☐ Can you listen to a question and hear the interviewer's underlying concern?

Once you can honestly answer yes to all of these questions, you're ready to move on to the next step: overcoming objections.

Chapter 7

Mastering the Sticky Questions

Didn't think there could possibly be so many questions to be prepared for? Think again. We haven't even gotten to the job-specific questions yet! Those are coming in Part V, the "Interview Encyclopedia." But before we get there, let's pause and review the possible problem areas in your résumé.

We all have them, those areas that potential employers tend to find the most interesting, but which we'd most like them to stay away from. These include:

- "You got the certification, but where's the on-the-job experience?"
- "Yesterday you owned your own shower installation business, today you're a network engineer?"
- "Three jobs in one year! Bad year or dot-com bust?"
- "Six years to get an associate's degree in communications. Trouble deciding what your major would be?"
- "Took a few years off to explore the world?"

Do any of these sound familiar? Do you fear having to explain any of them? Fear not. In this chapter, I'll address these and more. I'll take it from the employer's perspective, and show you what the IT manager is really thinking. This chapter covers:

- Strategies for overcoming objections
- Recent college graduates
- Paper certifications
- Job veterans (over 50)
- Career changers
- Job hoppers
- Layoffs and other terminations
- Questions you don't have to answer

ON THE RECORD

An IT Hiring Manager on Finding Good Candidates

The focus of this chapter is developing strategies for representing yourself as a V(IT)P. We asked Brian Jaffe, an IT director in New York City, what he looks for in a candidate and his suggestions on how to handle some of the sticky spots in your work history. Here are his thoughts:

Brian, first of all, how do you normally find the people to fill your positions? For the most part, I've relied on agents [recruiters]. They will place ads in the newspapers, search their databases, and post the position on various job Websites. The agents I use are ones that I've known for years, ones that I enjoy working with, and ones that I believe make the task easier for me.

What are the ways in which an IT candidate can make a favorable impression on you? At the top of the list are good communication skills and professionalism. When the candidate is answering my questions, I'm not only listening to what he says, but how he is saying it. I'm trying to make an assessment as to what kind of person and worker he is. I ask myself, "Will others enjoy working with him? Will he be responsible and dedicated? Is he motivated and eager?"

What are the automatic ways in which IT candidates lose favor with you? There are several ways that a candidate can lower his chances of getting hired.

I always start by reviewing a candidate's job history. Job hoppers don't stand a chance. If a candidate has a history of staying two years or less at his past few jobs, he is immediately disqualified.

I also have little tolerance for people who show up late to the interview. When being late is absolutely unavoidable, the very first words out of the candidate's mouth should be "I'm sorry I'm late." I've had a few candidates who show up late and don't even mention it. Perhaps they were hoping I wouldn't notice.

While it is a faux pas, I don't get too bothered by a typo on a résumé. But when I see a series of spelling or grammatical mistakes, I assume the candidate either doesn't know the language or doesn't pay attention to detail.

Candidates who are over-confidant or over-eager won't be invited back. While I look for confidence, too much of it can cross the line into "cocky" and "attitude." Those who are too eager make me think they are desperate and lacking in confidence.

Aside from the technical capabilities of the candidate, what are the characteristics that you're looking for? I look for applicants I believe will be reliable and responsible. I'm looking for people who see IT as more than just their job, but something they enjoy during their off hours.

The candidate has to be someone I believe people will enjoy working with as well. This includes not just the users, but peers, staff, and of course me, as their manager.

What makes a résumé stand out? When I review résumés, I don't look for a laundry list of technologies. I look for accomplishments. What has the candidate done with his technical skills? Does the employment history show growth or has he essentially been doing the exact same thing over the past few years?

I also recommend not going overboard with formatting. I've seen résumés with all kinds of graphics and colors. Just deliver the facts in an easy-to-read format.

On a scale of 1 to 10, how prepared is the typical candidate that you interview? Most candidates that I interview rate about an 8. Most have read the job description that I gave to the agent. Some have researched the company. But at times, these efforts have only been cursory.

In the candidates that you interview, what are the most frequent mistakes made? The most serious mistake is not knowing when to say "I don't know." I've had candidates make up answers that have just hurt their credibility. I'll respect you more for knowing when to say "I don't know."

Another frequent mistake is behaving too casually during the interview. I had one candidate who received (and responded to) two e-mail messages on his Blackberry while he was being interviewed. If he's going to interrupt the interview to respond to a page, he should at least excuse himself.

Another faux pas is when the candidate seems to be acting like he's doing me a favor by being interviewed.

Lastly, there is the candidate who proactively demonstrates that he hasn't done his homework by asking a question like, "What business is this company in?" At the very minimum, visit the Website before you come in to interview.

The Strategies

Despite what other résumé or interviewing books might say, there is no such thing as the perfect résumé or the perfect interviewee. That's because there's no such thing as the perfect candidate. There's only the V(IT)P candidate as we built him or her up in Chapter 1, or the candidate who best fits what the hiring manager is looking for at the time.

Some of us take longer than others to decide on our career paths. We have to decide what type of organization and industry we best fit in. There is absolutely nothing wrong with starting a brand-new, post-50 career in IT. Older workers bring with them maturity, people skills, and organizational knowledge that younger techies have yet to acquire. Your skills are an asset, not something you have to defend.

Strategy #1: Never Get Defensive

The number one strategy for handling some of the questions that interviewers will pose is *never get defensive*. Whether you're talking about your education (or lack thereof), life choices, or employment history, don't ever defend yourself. Banish all of the following phrases from your vocabulary:

- "But it wasn't my fault!"
- "The organization didn't see my vision."
- "I tried my best."

All of these will raise a red flag in the employer's mind. Your history is your history. You can neither change it nor negate it. You can, though, *downplay* it so that it is not the first thing that grabs the interviewer's attention.

Strategy #2: Don't Arouse Suspicion

Your résumé will direct the types of questions that your interviewer will ask you. You can downplay any red flags such as frequent job changes, missing degrees, and terminations or layoffs by how they appear on your résumé. *Ace the IT Résumé!* offers some excellent suggestions on how to effectively represent any potential problem areas on your résumé. Here are some quick suggestions:

- A strong qualifications section provides you with the opportunity to highlight your strengths. Ensure that you don't use language that inadvertently points out a potential issue, such as no hands-on experience.
- Combine technical and soft skills under the qualifications section to demonstrate maturity and well-roundedness.
- If you were employed by a company for less than 12 months, represent your dates of employment using year ranges only, rather than point out the number of months you were with them.
- Consider using a skills-based résumé format rather than a historical résumé to focus on your accomplishments instead of the length of employment.
- Do not include any reasons for leaving your past jobs as a part of your job summary.
- If you did not receive your college degree, simply list the name of the institution with the dates you attended. You may mention "Coursework toward web development" if you have enough courses to substantiate it.
- Do not include unrelated job experience or educational courses unrelated to IT.
- If your age could hurt your odds of being considered for the position, including getting called in for the interview, de-emphasize your age by not mentioning such things as your 24-year experience in the workforce. One strategy is to include only 10 to 15 years of your work history.

- If you have an employment gap between positions, represent employment dates with years only.
- If you have too many jobs in a single year, by your own choice or because of economics, you may choose not to include all your positions as a part of your employment history. Choose the ones where you gained the most experience and incorporate additional skills into your technical skills section or as a part of another position.

The important thing here is to understand that the interviewer doesn't have a crystal ball that gives them access to your permanent record. You are in control of what the employer learns about you. Master the art of résumé writing to ensure that you are putting your best foot forward, especially when your résumé is what will get you the invitation for an interview.

Strategy #3: Address the Hiring Manager's Hidden Needs

At all times, hiring managers are trying to assess four things about you:

- Can you do the job?
- Will you stick around?
- Will you fit in?
- What will you cost?

With this in mind, all information you present and how you present it should be to convince the interviewer that:

- *Yes*, you can do the job because you have either the skills or the ability to acquire the skills.
- *Yes*, you will stick around because you have demonstrated unquestionable commitment to your previous employers or you have finally found the right match with their company.
- *Yes*, you will fit in because you are personable, friendly, and someone with whom people enjoy working.
- *Yes*, the company is willing to pay your worth because you have demonstrated that you are a solutions-driven employee.

In other words, you are a V(IT)P!

Strategy #4: Seek First to Understand

Undoubtedly, the interviewer will find something to lock in on. Should this happen, it's crucial to understand why the interviewer is asking the questions. Is he just plain nosy? Not likely. Is he looking for inconsistencies, ulterior motives, hidden information, or does he just want to see how you react in uncomfortable situations? Probably not.

If you understand what the interviewer wants to know, you'll know how to approach the question. In the following sections, I'll address several common situations, the typical questions you'll be asked to address, the motives behind the interviewer's question, and how to answer the question.

Recent College Graduate

Everyone has to start somewhere, right? Having a college degree behind you is an important start to a new career in IT. College graduates have a leg up on others entering the IT field, as they have a solid foundation for career advancement.

The hardest part of being a recent college graduate is getting hired for that first job. Entry-level jobs in IT typically come in the form of PC technician/desktop support, helpdesk, quality assurance, and (if you're lucky) programming positions. These positions provide newbies with the corporate experience to learn business and IT departmental processes. They are the stepping stones to better programming, network engineer, and systems analyst positions.

Unfortunately, as a recent college graduate, you're competing with other IT professionals with newly earned A+ or Microsoft certifications. They may have more hands-on experience with current technologies than you. Their advantage? They can assimilate faster within the prospective company. Their disadvantage? They don't have the solid foundation in systems analysis, processes, and project management. They have never heard of project management, software life cycles, or quality assurance testing. You will rise faster through the ranks and get the better jobs faster. The question is often asked if certifications are more or less important than a college degree. These are obviously both important. In many companies, the lack of a college degree could limit your potential to make the interview cut. Even experience might not rescue the non-graduate résumé from the trash. A college degree says that you have stuck with something for two to four years, and you now have an independent institution that vouches for you that you are indeed teachable. The commitment and ability to learn new content is exactly what employers are looking for.

An important note for recent college graduates as you apply for jobs: no one expects you to have the experience of a 10-year veteran. Don't worry about your lack of real-world experience. Focus instead on the skills you've learned and the knowledge you've attained.

Also, despite what some may tell you, your first IT job will play a significant role in shaping your IT career. It's much better to start off in an entry-level position with a good, solid company than to go for the glory of a job with a better title with a little-known company. Why? The name recognition of your first company will open doors for future jobs. Being the small fish in a big pond allows you the anonymity of learning a lot under the radar. You get exposed to larger organizations and how they are run, more sophisticated business processes, the benefits of larger IT budgets, and increased development opportunities, including training and mentoring. You'll go farther when you work in a larger organization at the start of your career.

What Is the Hiring Manager Thinking?

Primary concern:

- Will you fit in?

Secondary concern:

- Are you trainable?

Fitting in means that you can work effectively as part of a team and efficiently on your own individual assignments. You can follow directions and get things done on time. But it has nothing to do with whether you know *how* to do the actual job of programming in Java, for instance. The chancellor of a state university system recently asked a group of prominent businesspeople what skills the state's college graduates most sorely need. Their answer: the ability to work as part of a team.

Everything within an IT department is done as a team. Systems are interrelated, programmers must work with project managers and users to develop the right systems, and helpdesk technicians must work together to solve problems for their users. Entry-level jobs are utterly dependent on teams in order for new hires to learn the corporate culture, processes, and systems. In any job, your fellow team members will teach you more than any other training materials, seminars, or managers.

Hiring managers also understand that what is taught in college courses has little application to day-to-day tasks. But your college career *is* an indicator of how you will perform on the job. See the questions in the following sections for insights.

Your Strategy

Your overall strategy is to present yourself as a mature individual who has a base set of IT skills. You want to demonstrate that:

- You are a team player who will easily adapt to a new work environment.
- You are trainable.
- You are hardworking.

I'm a Team Player

The most important trait for you to get across is that you are a team player. IT managers don't have the time to deal with prima donnas who think too highly of themselves and end up sabotaging stable work environments. Hiring managers value teamwork so highly that I recommend incorporating teamwork into your asset statement to differentiate yourself from your competition.

To substantiate your asset statement, you will be expected to provide examples of how you have worked cohesively as part of a team. Think back to your college days and provide examples of when you:

- Were a member of a sports team
- Worked on extensive group projects to complete your major
- Were a member of a school association, fraternity, or sorority

You should also be prepared with specifics on the project, the group dynamics, how you came together as a team, and the results. The following page lists some questions to be ready for.

- What were the benefits of working as a team rather than completing the project alone?
- How did you pick the group leader?
- How did you divide the roles and responsibilities?
- What were the challenges of working as a team rather than as individual contributors?
- How did you overcome conflicts?
- What was your most important contribution to the team?

If it's been a while since your organizational behavior class, here's a refresher on the characteristics and benefits of working as a team. A highly cohesive group is characterized by increased communication, greater trust among team members, greater exchange of ideas, more creative thinking, greater productivity, better solutions, and generally more accomplishments by team members. All this results in projects getting done faster and the caliber of the result being a higher quality. Any time that you can point to these benefits you will score points.

After all this talk on teams, don't forget to ask the interviewer about the kinds of company teams you could be a part of.

I Am Trainable

Remember, employers don't expect recent college graduates to have the experience that a more experienced IT professional would have. It's unrealistic to even imagine that this would be the case. So relax. Take a breath. You'd be amazed to find out that employers actually seek out recent college grads because they have a clean slate—no bad habits or misaligned expectations. This is great news! What's the catch? Along with that clean slate comes one important characteristic: being trainable.

Being trainable means many things. It's the ability to learn technical topics quickly. It's the ability to adapt to change. It's having an inquisitive mind. It's also maintaining a self-directed and highly motivated approach to one's work and career. It's seeking to contribute to an organization.

Your ability to demonstrate these traits is what will convince your potential employer that you're the right person for the job. The following statements—along with specific examples from your past—will help get the point across:

> "My education has not only provided me with valuable job skills, but has also helped prepare me to learn new skills throughout my career. In learning a base set of programming languages, I now know how to quickly pick up any new language, its logic, and its expressions."

> "The best part of my education was how it expanded my mind and opened me up to new ideas or perspectives. For example, by learning what makes teams function more effectively, I learned how to provide feedback that will be better received by members of the team."

> "Through my education, I learned the analytical and logic skills that I now use every day as I work on my programming projects."

EFFECTIVE TEAM BUILDING: FORMING, STORMING, NORMING, AND PERFORMING

No team ever comes together perfectly. Instead, all teams go through established phases. Here's a brief description of each so that you can recognize the patterns of team development for the teams that you've participated in.

Forming

Forming is the orientation period. The team is not sure what its task is, and members are not well-acquainted with each other, nor have they learned what sort of a team leader they have. Team members want to be told what to do. They tend to respond to the leader's requests and express negative feelings either very politely or privately.

Team members are generally excited and enthusiastic.

Storming

Storming is the phase when team members feel more comfortable expressing their opinions. They may challenge the team leader's authority and recommendations. Some members may become dissatisfied and challenge not only what the team is to do and how it is doing it, but also the leader's role and style of leadership.

Team members are frustrated by lack of information, low cohesion, and early project challenges.

Norming

Norming is the third phase and builds on what was learned in phase two. Team members begin drawing upon their cumulative experiences to work out problems and pull together as a cohesive group. This process should result in the team establishing procedures for handling conflicts and decisions and methods for accomplishing team projects.

Performing

Performing is phase four and should be the payoff. In this phase, the team has achieved harmony, defined its tasks, worked out its relationships, and begun to produce results. Leadership is provided by the team members best suited for the task at hand. Members have learned how to work together, manage conflict, and contribute their resources to accomplish the team's goals.

Ways to increase team effectiveness:

- Team members listen and pay attention to one another.
- People discuss the subject at hand and are willing to work through conflict as opposed to avoidance of conflict.
- Members know and use problem-solving steps.
- Members are clear about group decisions and are committed to them.
- Frequent feedback is given to help members stay focused on team goals.

The key is to demonstrate that you have a solid foundation in IT that will easily transfer to any specific operating system, database, programming language, and network architecture. Don't believe it? Pull out your college transcript. Look for processes, architecture, design, and analysis theory that you were introduced to and now use as best practices. For example, read the following course descriptions in your old college catalogs:

- Introduction to Management Information Systems
- Introduction to Computer Science
- Operating Systems and Computer Architecture
- Programming Fundamentals
- Relational Databases
- Software Engineering Object-Oriented Development
- Systems Analysis
- Networking Essentials

While you have your transcript out, take a look at your grades. Which courses were you better at? Which ones did you enjoy the most? These should give you a better understanding of the type of work that you will excel at after college. Did you like logic? Perhaps look into a job in programming. Did you like hands-on hardware and software courses? Try network engineering. Did you like leading groups? Consider a career in project management.

The result of this reflection will prepare you for the questions that the interviewer will most likely ask you:

- Which courses were your best?
- What type of job do you see yourself doing in three years?

Of course, if the courses you mention for the first question are those that best meet the requirements of the job, so much the better. As for the next question, you can draw on what your education has taught you about career progression, knowing full well that your first two years in any position will be spent building the necessary skills to do the job well.

Last but not least, showing your enthusiasm for your education and future career is extremely important in conveying that you're the right person for the job.

I Am Hardworking

During your interview, you also need to demonstrate that you are a hardworking, dedicated prospect. Downplay your lack of experience and showcase your abilities by discussing your student jobs, co-op education, and internships or unpaid work with campus organizations or nonprofit organizations. You should

- Talk about your leadership ability and how it transfers to what you hope to accomplish in your career as a team member, lead, project lead, or manager.

- Emphasize goal-oriented activities or groups that you belonged to and are proud of.
- Only mention fraternities and sororities in the context of leadership activities and doing good works.
- Mention all elected offices you have held.
- Discuss the self-motivation required to get through school despite any financial or personal challenges.

Unless interviewers frequently speak with recent college graduates, they have a hard time relating to school activities. So make sure you focus on how your school activities translate into company benefits.

Questions

Here are some possible interview questions you may encounter. Take the time to consider your answers for each question. Remember, preparation is the key to a successful interview.

- How has your education prepared you for this position?
- What do you like the most about the career you're seeking?
- What do you like the least about the career you're seeking?
- Why did you choose the college that you attended?
- Why did you select the major that you selected?
- What aspects of your education will assist you in the job you are seeking?
- How will your degree help you succeed in the job you are interviewing for?
- What was the most complex assignment you have had? What was your role?
- Give an example of how you applied knowledge from previous coursework to a project in another class.
- Describe a situation in which you found that your results were not up to your professor's or supervisor's expectations. What happened? What action did you take?
- Describe a situation where others you were working with on a project disagreed with your ideas. What did you do?
- By providing examples, convince me that you can adapt to a wide variety of people, situations, and environments.
- Describe a situation that required a number of things to be done at the same time. How did you handle it? What was the result?
- Give an example of when you had to work with someone who was difficult to get along with. Why was this person difficult? How did you handle that person?

- Give a specific example of something you did that helped build enthusiasm in others.
- Tell about a difficult situation when it was desirable for you to keep a positive attitude. What did you do?
- Give an example of a time you had to make an important decision. How did you make the decision? How does it affect you today?
- Describe a time when you got coworkers or classmates who dislike each other to work together. How did you accomplish this? What was the outcome?
- Which of your courses will contribute the most to your effective performance in this job?
- Describe a specific problem you solved for your employer or professor. How did you approach the problem? What role did others play? What was the outcome?
- What was the single most important lesson that you have learned in school?

Over Fifty

Recent grads frequently think they can't get a break. But the group on the opposite end of the spectrum—experienced job-seekers over 50—also believe they are often overlooked. This group, experienced as it may be and protected by a federal law, does encounter discrimination. Although employers should not pose questions about your age, some believe that age is a legitimate concern and will do anything they can to ferret out the number of your birthdays. Sure, it's unfair, but if you're a near retiree, you have to deal with it.

Remember that your age can work for you. Older employees have better people skills and more life experience, are more stable, and can set a good example for younger employees with their better work ethic. Employers are seeing more applicants who took early retirement or were laid off from other fields and are now seeking IT jobs as a second or third career. These folks can bring a wealth of life experience into the workplace.

Age prejudice most typically happens in line positions, including team leads and first-level management positions where experience is necessary. If you're looking for an entry-level position and you're over 50, you should be especially prepared to encounter resistance. But persistence and preparation are your best defenses.

What Is the Hiring Manager Thinking?

Primary concern:

- Will you fit in?

Secondary concern:

- What will you cost?

Get inside the hiring manager's head for a moment. Regardless of how badly you want or need this job, his concerns are legitimate and genuine. He's worried that you might not fit in with his team. Can you keep up? Are you ambitious and motivated? Will you get along with everyone else? You'll most likely have to overcome some of the following myths associated with older workers, especially in IT:

- Older people don't "get it" as quickly as Gen Yers.
- Older people can't work odd shifts and long hours (or as long as younger IT professionals who frequently pull all-nighters).
- Older workers aren't as creative as younger IT professionals.
- Older workers take fewer risks than younger IT workers.
- Older workers are stuck in their ways and have a hard time learning new things.
- Older workers take longer to adapt to change than younger IT workers.
- Older workers will question direction more frequently than younger professionals.
- Older workers will not have the same drive as younger workers.
- Older workers are uncompromising and inflexible.

Another concern hiring managers have with hiring older workers is the cost of employment. Literally, this translates to your salary expectations. Do you expect to earn more than the going rate just because you are older and may have additional financial obligations? Often, hiring managers decide for you that the going rate won't cover your basic living expenses, and they'll automatically disqualify you. It's up to you to address these concerns, even if they are unspoken.

Your Strategy

When you think an interviewer's judgment could be influenced by age concerns, emphasize the positive aspects of your age in your behavior and your conversation. Try the following strategies.

I Have More to Offer

With age comes experience. Focus on what you bring to the company. If you do this well, you won't bring inordinate attention to your age, and the interviewer will think of you as an experienced candidate, rather than an older one. Qualities to emphasize:

- Commitment to a career—maturity breeds responsibility
- Proven success and verifiable track records
- Dependability—maturity develops reliability
- Stable work ethic
- Not likely to voluntarily change jobs soon
- Lower turnover and absenteeism rates
- Realistic expectations
- Positive attitude—glad to be working

As you look through the list above, be prepared to back up your claims using storytelling techniques with ample examples. Above all, project yourself as cheerful and flexible, and back up that beaming personality with concrete proof of your skills and success. Here are some examples of how to do so:

> "Over the course of my career, I have constantly sought out more responsibility. For example, at my last company, I went from managing individual departmental development projects to managing company-wide systems integration projects. The decisions I helped my teams make and implement affected all the business systems within the company."
>
> "My previous managers have always rated me highly on my reliability and dependability in accomplishing the tasks assigned to me. My tenure within the organization contributes to my understanding the impact of my projects on the overall effectiveness of the business."
>
> "At this point in my career, I am seeking a position that allows me to apply my team-building and analysis skills to mentoring a group of junior developers."

You'll also want to show how you can use your experience to benefit the company in solving long-term problems, building profit, reducing costs, or assisting in other departments. For example:

> "I am particularly effective in reducing telecommunications costs across multiple sites by bringing together purchasing decisions and negotiating with a single company for the best service and best price."

I Fit In

Fitting in doesn't mean that you have to look like everyone else in the group. It means bringing something to the group that is valued. Your experience, stability, reliability, and day-to-day continuity are qualities valued in any situation. Explain how you are an anchor in providing these qualities and move any discussion away from the other qualities associated with younger team members: tardiness, lack of structure, haphazard work ethic, moodiness, and individual contributions over group contributions.

To address the issue of whether you will work as hard by staying late or working weekends, express your commitment to the job and stress your flexibility and willingness to work extra time in order to keep the project on schedule and under budget. Provide concrete examples of times you've worked long hours to properly complete a project. You can also point out that your analysis and project management skills—which have been honed over time—will significantly reduce the amount of overtime required to complete projects.

I Know What I'm In For

Career changing is an opportunity to start fresh, but how do you deal with it at 50? It's a double whammy. You may have two strikes against you: age and lack of experience. Of course, every hiring manager will think you're crazy—working a helpdesk at 50? But you know how it beats trucking across the country every week. So how do you deal with this situation? Head on.

Don't ignore the elephant in the room. Instead, confront it immediately. Be honest. What made you jump ship? Tell your story:

> "I spent 15 years managing a fleet of moving trucks. When we built our Website six years ago, I discovered the Internet, and I was fascinated. I read everything I could get my hands on and started taking computer classes. I've been spending my nights and weekends programming, and I'm ready to make it my day job, too."

Explain why you've decided to make a career change at this stage in your life, and express what this new career means for you professionally and personally.

If you're just not where most people would expect you to be at this stage in your career—for example, you're 50 and you're applying for a helpdesk position—then explain how this fits into your overall career strategy. Where do you expect to be in five years? Examples of what you enjoy most about this position in comparison to your previous jobs will be particularly powerful.

For additional recommendations, see the section coming up on career changers.

Appear Young

IT is undeniably youth oriented. Though you can't turn back the hands of time or take a magic potion to strip away the wrinkles, there are things that you can do to appear younger. Physical strength and stamina are a part of feeling young. Exercise, eat properly, get plenty of rest, and stay emotionally engaged with life, and you'll retain more of the health that employers value in youth.

Transmit energy. Make the interviewer perceive you as a vibrant presence, and you'll deliver a highly positive impression. Keeping yourself fit and presenting yourself as such are crucial.

Paper Certifications

Paper certifications—certificates awarded by Microsoft, Cisco, and other hot companies on the basis of exams only without requiring any real-world experience with the technology—are a hot issue with IT professionals. If you spent the last nine months earning your certifications by day, night, or on weekends, you're hoping that a high-paying job awaits you. The reality is a splash of ice-cold water from a very big bucket. Overzealous training providers have often added to these unrealistic expectations. Employers pay high dollars for experience, not certificates.

When you confront objections, remember that certifications *are* a good thing and they are valuable in the job market. You will gain formal technology education—crucial knowledge that often cannot be attained any other way. Like the college graduate, you have proved you are teachable and you have the discipline to see a commitment through. All you have to do is demonstrate that you *do* have valuable real-world experience that employers can use.

Here's a peek inside the hiring manager's mind.

What Is the Hiring Manager Thinking?

Primary concern:

- Can you do the job?

Secondary concerns:

- How do you stack up against the other candidates who may have the job experience but may not be certified?
- Can you be trained to do the job?

The overriding concern for any hiring manager is whether the job candidate can do the job, certification or no certification. Remember, hiring managers want to lower their risk factor by feeling comfortable that you have done this job or something similar somewhere else. With paper MCSEs, CNEs, or CCNAs, the red flag goes up immediately—they've seen the résumés of hundreds of recently certified professionals in the past. Their bad first impressions make it more difficult for you to even get your foot in the door. Needless to say, your résumé must seriously mask the lack of formal job experience to even get past the screener.

IT managers will consider your certification an important credential if it's in a new technology, or if they don't already have someone certified. For example, CCIE, MCSD, and CISSP are top-rated certifications at the moment. These hot certifications will stand out and can put you at the top of the qualified list.

Hiring managers do consider certification a sign of good things to come. First, your certificate demonstrates that you are trainable and open to learning new technology. And in IT, new technology comes out about every 30 seconds, so this is a very good thing. If you funded your own training, you're also obviously committed to your own self-development. Employers can count on you to stay up to date.

A caveat: If you don't have hands-on credentials, employers believe they'll have to train you, and they may be reluctant to consider you for anything beyond an entry-level position. They think they'll need to invest more time in getting you up and running to be productive. So you may find yourself fielding a job offer at a lower salary than you originally anticipated.

Your Strategy

Your strategy for handling this situation is a four-pronged approach. You must:

- Demonstrate that you have a solid foundation in the knowledge and skill set required to do the job for which you are interviewing.
- Present your education as work experience.
- Demonstrate that you are trainable.
- Call upon your transferable skills to demonstrate your overall value to the organization.

I Have the Skills to Do the Job

First, you must demonstrate that you can directly apply the knowledge and skills you learned through certification and outside the classroom to the position at hand. Start off by reviewing all the details of the position and asking as many questions as you can about the job before you start talking about your own experience. This is one way you can drive the interview process. It enables you to form more articulate responses to any questions regarding your skills and capabilities.

For example, if you are being interviewed for a PC technician job and you have an A+ certification, you will want to find out about:

- Types of PCs you will be supporting
- Network environment
- Operating systems and applications
- Remote access systems
- Printing environments

Then you can tailor your responses with specific examples of troubleshooting PC models similar to those within this organization, building PCs using the same OS and applications, and providing helpdesk support for remote users similar to their user base. Use your examples to keep the focus on project experience. You don't have to mention that it comes from class, internship, or volunteer work.

If you want to give an example of your work in information security—a hot topic in any server room—detail-specific examples of how you (or an organization you were working with, such as your training center) were affected by the latest virus. Detail what steps you had to go through to ensure data integrity and overall protection of the organization's intellectual property stored on its servers. Many operating system certifications steer trainees toward server support, and yet there are few situations where newbies are placed in server support roles without lots of time proving themselves in a desktop support position. Be very careful about implying in interview comments that all you want to do is server support. It is unlikely that any newly certified employee will be ushered into the server room and given an administrator position. Instead, talk about your overall operating system familiarity.

The more you know about the position for which you are interviewing, the more detail you can give when you describe your skills and experience. Your goal is to paint a picture so vividly that the interviewer cannot help but envision you on the job.

I Have Work Experience

By the time you finish telling your story, the hiring manager just won't care about the chronological order of your employment history, right? Perhaps, but just to be on the safe side, you should have a well-rehearsed project list that you can talk about.

First, run down your relevant paid experience. If you don't have any, you may want to try the following line:

> "Most of my hands-on experience comes from my work on various projects while earning my certification. Let me tell you about those..."

You probably had some experience before earning your certification. Start there. Try something along the lines of:

> "I always worked with computers in my previous jobs. My hobby quickly became the opportunity for a new career after I bought my first home computer and hooked it up to the Internet. I now have a home network for myself, my wife, and my kids that consists of four computers, a whole graphics setup, a DSL line, and a multiport router. I found myself hooked even on family vacations when I couldn't stay away from e-mail. I decided that I wanted to pursue this full time, and earning my A+ certification was the first step."

I Am Trainable

A trainable employee is open to change, a highly regarded quality in the IT department. And getting certified is hard work. It means you take your career seriously and are willing to invest the time. Should the interviewer try to gloss over your certification credentials, try some of these reminders on him to refresh his memory on the value of certification and trainability, and show him what you can bring to his organization.

> "My Network + certification provided me with a solid foundation in networking architecture that I can build on, regardless of the networking operating system I'm working with."

> "Because I was on an accelerated study program to earn my certification, I developed my own approach for learning new software and ramping up very quickly."

> "For me, funding my own certification has increased its value in my mind. I have a real appreciation for the time and financial investments I made. It's great motivation to stay current."

> "Earning my certification in six months demonstrated to me that I had the capacity for this work and that I would succeed."

> "My education has not only provided me with the skills for this particular job, but it has also prepared me to learn new skills throughout my career. It has expanded my mind, opening me up to new ideas and perspectives through working with different technical instructors who shared their excellent field experience."

It also doesn't hurt to reiterate that today, lifelong employability comes with the price tag of constant vigilance in keeping your skills up to date.

I Can Provide Value to Your Organization

Helpdesk technician today, helpdesk manager tomorrow. Okay, your certification is recent. You have limited technical skills. But you've got more than that to offer, and you need to make that clear. For example, suppose you've just earned your A+ and Network + certifications, but you also have five years' experience managing entry-level employees. Your additional skills—even those outside the technical arena—will improve your chances of making the cut, *but only if you talk about them*. In this case, your promotability and management skills translate to added value to the organization. You might start as a helpdesk technician, but you're someone who could easily be promoted to helpdesk manager before long.

What other skills can you call upon here? Take a look back at Chapter 3 and review this list:

- I am able to coordinate many tasks simultaneously.
- I have strong communication skills.
- I am able to prioritize and work proactively.
- I am a team player with the ability to effectively coordinate.
- I am devoted to excellent service and customer satisfaction.
- I am very detail oriented with excellent analytical and project-tracking skills.

Questions

The questions that you should be prepared to answer if you find yourself in this situation include:

- Why did you decide to pursue your certification?
- Who financed your certification?
- What was your primary objective in earning your certification?
- How has your certification prepared you for a job as a network engineer [or other position]?
- What skill sets do you bring to the table?
- How do you plan on keeping your certifications current?
- Why did you choose to pursue certification over a college degree?

Career Changers

Making a dramatic career change, such as moving from a blue-collar job to becoming a programmer, takes time. In many ways, career changers are in the same position as recent college graduates, with perhaps a newly granted certification or degree, but very little practical experience. But unlike a new grad, you probably already have a family and financial obligations. So the pressure is on to find a good paying job as quickly as possible.

You also have to face your own expectations of the jobs available to career changers. You're looking to IT for the opportunity to earn a good salary, enjoy job security, and have plenty of jobs to choose from. This is all true, but the common disclaimer applies: your results may vary. If you've just earned your certification and want to switch careers, you'll be up against some tough competition, and you won't have hands-on experience to back you up.

Doctors go through a residency period before they are allowed to go out on their own. The same is true with IT professionals. Your first job will be tough. The money may not all be there, and the hours will be grueling, but you will learn what you need for your next job. Don't be fooled by the thousands of job openings. Take a look at your local paper to see what's really available in your area. Most likely, the job openings are mid-level IT positions for workers with at least two or three years of experience. If you are aware of this reality and have planned for it, you won't be disillusioned and will have a more successful time with your job hunt.

What Is the Hiring Manager Thinking?

Primary concern:

- Can you do the job?

Secondary concerns:

- Are you too old to do the job?
- How long will it take for you to be productive?
- Will you fit in?
- Will you accept an entry-level position?

This situation is actually a combination of paper certification and over-50 issues. Combined, these objections can be tough to overcome. The hiring manager's overriding concern is that a career changer will not have adequate practical experience and will need extensive ramp-up time.

If you're over 50, the hiring manager will also worry about how you'll fit in at the organization. Changing careers in midlife is not an easy thing. You'll be working with mostly younger colleagues. (The average age of IT professionals within many organizations is 30.) You'll be an entry-level employee, probably reporting to someone younger than you. Talk about a blow to the ego!

Will you be able to mesh with the existing team? Can you work long hours and odd shifts and be a team player? The hiring manager is betting you can't.

Can you pick up on new concepts and technology and keep pace with younger team members? You know you can, but you've got to convince the hiring manager of your ability.

Although there are laws against age discrimination, it still exists. There is, unfortunately, a serious bias against older workers who have recently joined the IT ranks.

Your Strategy

Your strategy when changing careers is to create a bigger picture of what you can offer the organization. Make sure that your asset statements truly reflect what you bring, through your current skills as well as the skills you have from your previous career. Let the employer know you're aware of what you're getting yourself into with a career change at this point in your life. If you are open and forthcoming, you will put the interviewer at ease and he'll be more receptive to your possibilities.

I Can Be Productive on Day One

Your first strategy is to demonstrate that you can hit the ground running. Review the previous sections entitled "I Have the Skills to Do the Job," "I Have Work Experience," and "I Am Trainable" for important pointers on how to overcome the stigma of not having the skills and experience to do the job. Next, focus your efforts on demonstrating the additional skills that you bring to the table based on your other career experience. Remember, you want to make it easy for the hiring manager to say yes to hiring you.

What's important on the first day (or week) on the job and why it's important:

- Ability to prioritize tasks and responsibilities, so you can figure out what your primary responsibilities are, who can coach you while you pick these up, and who can answer all your first-week questions.
- Previous experience working in a large organization, so you can quickly recognize requests from the CEO, COO, CFO, and CIO and their admins, and respond to these immediately.
- Solid foundation in networking, troubleshooting, and customer support, in order to recognize the difference between the phone and the network jacks, and to know to ask whether the computer monitor is turned on.
- Ability to apply existing knowledge to new technology, because regardless of how well they prepared you in technical school, the company you're going to work for won't have the same versions of software you're certified on.
- Ability to learn quickly, because everything changes so often, and you know users will never be satisfied with the currently "IS-supported" software.
- Ability to assess needs and requirements, because sometimes the user at the other end of the phone doesn't clearly diagnose his own problem. With a few key questions under your belt, you'll be able to get to a resolution quicker.
- Self-sufficiency, because sometimes there's simply no one else around.

When you talk about skills you bring from your previous career, be thorough. Here's a sample of skills you might have:

Real Estate People skills, negotiating, selling, resourcefulness, ability to work independently, ability to meet goals

Construction Management of a team, keeping projects on schedule, working hard, cost containment, working under deadlines, common sense

Finance Managing varying work loads that come with cyclic business, protecting sensitive data, ensuring approvals are correct allowing work to be performed

Manufacturing Understanding of processes, safety awareness, teamwork, managing teams, operations management

Retail People skills, sales skills, needs analysis, communication

Homemaking People management, scheduling, prioritization, persuasion, budget management, juggling multiple projects, resource planning

Trucking Optimization of resources, scheduling, planning, forecasting

Food Services Managing multiple tasks, working in a fast-paced environment, customer service

Teaching Mentoring, explaining difficult concepts, presentation skills, uncovering problems and issues, thinking on your feet

I Fit In

The key here is to have the hiring manager see you doing the position that you're interviewing for—not any past positions on your résumé. So, do the job! This job. Ask as many questions as possible about the job up front. Then tailor your professional background and educational history to the tasks that are important. Sometimes, the ad may be more extensive than the actual position and what they are willing to pay to fill it.

Fitting in also means knowing what role you will play on the team. Find out as much as you can about the individuals that make up the team and then ask to meet them. Just don't expect them all to fall in love with you right away. Whenever a new member joins a team, turmoil ensues. Stave off some of the chaos by making allies even before you are officially asked to join the team.

When you meet the team, be humble. This is not the time to demonstrate what a hot shot you are at programming. Save that for the formal interview. When you meet the entire team, practice these bonding techniques:

- Use a firm handshake.
- Listen attentively when they speak.
- Look the other person in the eye when they are speaking.
- Smile.
- Make an extra effort to say and remember their names.
- Recognize how busy they are and thank them for their time.

It's easy to make people like you. The secret is letting them see that you like them as well.

Questions

The questions to be prepared for if you find yourself in this situation include:

- What are your long-term goals?
- How do you plan to achieve these goals?
- How would you describe your ideal job?
- Describe a situation in which you were successful.
- What do you think it takes to be successful in this career?

- Describe why you think of yourself as a team player.
- Provide an example where you have demonstrated that you handle conflict well.
- With your limited experience, why should we hire you?
- Tell me about some of your recent goals and what you did to achieve them.
- What major problem have you had to deal with recently? How did you handle it?
- Do you have any plans for further education?

Job Hoppers

Objections about your employment history are the most common concerns interviewers raise. At the top of the list is frequent job changes, also known as job hopping. It's natural for employers to question frequent job changes. After all, recruiting, hiring, and training are expensive and time consuming. No employer wants to make that investment in an employee who won't stick around.

The charge of job hopping should not take you by surprise. You yourself know whether you have changed jobs too frequently and should be ready to explain why you had multiple jobs in one year.

The best defense is a good offense. Job hopping should not stand out on your résumé. There are plenty of techniques to ensure that it doesn't. Here are a few refreshers on how to downplay job hopping on your résumé:

- Use a skills-based résumé format that focuses on accomplishments and skills.
- Use a year format rather than a month/year format to describe length of employment.
- Consider leaving out employment dates.
- Name-dropping can be a good thing. If you have had a short-term gig at an influential employer location, be sure that is included.

You will spend a lot of time preparing your résumé. Make sure you review it from the recruiter's perspective before you send it in. There are legitimate reasons for several short-term positions. But don't let job hopping be the most interesting part of your résumé. If you had three jobs in 1999, prepare a solid defense for why you left each one. Then use the techniques above to mask your job hopping, but be ready with your defense in case you're cross-examined.

What Is the Hiring Manager Thinking?

Primary concern:

- Will you fit in?

Secondary concerns:

- Will you stick around?
- Are you worth the investment?

Hiring managers use past performance to forecast future achievement. When they see frequent job changes, they get suspicious. They seek employees who are committed for the long term, who will see projects through, and in whom they can invest for the long haul. Many successful companies continue to promote lifelong employment.

When the hiring managers detect a job hopper, they want to know two things:

- Your capacity for making long-term commitments
- Whether this opportunity will satisfy your long-term needs

It's natural, then, that they want to know your reasons for leaving your previous employers.

Your Strategy

Your primary strategy for handling any objections regarding your job longevity is to be prepared with acceptable, verifiable reasons for your job changes. So what's a verifiable, acceptable reason? Well, it's not, "Because I didn't like my manager." Beyond that, there are plenty of acceptable reasons, including not having a clear direction of where you wanted to take your career.

I Left for a Legitimate Reason

Stuff happens. Project-oriented work ends, companies downsize, and departments shut down. Sometimes you simply realize that you're in a dead-end job and there's nothing left to challenge you.

If the reason you were employed for a relatively short period of time had to do with time-defined project work, make sure your résumé clearly identifies project or contract work as such. Even if you were hired full time by the organization but with the understanding it was simply to handle a project, indicate so on your résumé by adding "Contract" next to the job title. This will eliminate any unnecessary questions regarding the length of your employment, especially during the initial résumé screening process where you may otherwise be weeded out because of short-term work assignments.

Use the same strategy if you worked for an outsourced skills company that hired you out by the project.

Other legitimate reasons include layoffs or departmental shutdowns. I cover how to address these issues in the next section.

I Was Seeking Additional Opportunities

It's okay to look for better opportunities. After all, employers want people they can motivate with new responsibilities, increased accountability, and the promise of promotion. But presentation, as always, is everything.

At all costs, avoid statements like, "My old position had no room for growth." All hiring managers read this as, "I was bored, tired, and unmotivated." Here are better ways to present yourself:

Reason	Example
Desire for increased responsibility and accountability	"After three years as a senior helpdesk technician, I feel that I am ready to manage a helpdesk team of my own."

Reason	Example
Desire for a career in a more satisfying and financially lucrative area	"After years as an administrative assistant, I decided to get certified and become an applications instructor."
Seeking a loftier scope of operations	"After six months with this start-up company, I realized that they would not be able to deliver their original promise that I would direct a team of 15+ programmers."
Aspiring to have greater impact on the organization	"Having originally joined the organization in an entry-level position, I quickly realized that I would not have the opportunity to work in activities that directly impact the bottom line. I am now seeking to use my buying and negotiating skills more usefully in a position to cut costs within an IT department."
Willingness to join an organization experiencing high growth that may offer opportunity for superior financial or career growth	"Like many others in 1999, I jumped at the opportunity to join a fast-growing dot-com. Unfortunately, it grew so fast that its money supply ran out in the middle of 2000."

Your goal is to convince the interviewer that you left previous positions only after you realized that moving on was the only way to increase your responsibilities and broaden your experience.

Better yet, refocus your response on why you want to move to the prospective employer. See how it's done below.

I Had Difficulty Defining My Career Goals

After four years of college, with little experience in the corporate world, how could you be expected to know exactly what type of position is your perfect match? It's not atypical for recent college graduates to go through six or more positions in four years. What's important in your interview process is to represent yourself as having figured it out—regardless of where you are in the process—or no one will hire you.

This means confessing if you had difficulty defining your career goals at first. Of course, you want to follow it up with stating how sure of your direction you are now.

Here's a clever way to present yourself at the interview:

"All through college, I was convinced that I wanted to be a programmer. But after a few months at my first job, I found that I was unhappy. Naturally, I blamed the company and the job. So when an opportunity opened up at a local bank, I grabbed it. Once the novelty of the new position and company wore off, I again realized I was unhappy with the job responsibilities."

"I recognized, though, that I did enjoy one component—user applications. So when I heard about the job in end-user computing at Tricon, I went for it. I learned a lot there, but it was a small firm with limited projects and challenges."

"I was recruited for the applications position at Hidall, and I got the job because of my experience at Tricon. The work has been terrific. But once again, I find that I'm a one-person department."

"Your position offers the opportunity to manage a department and interact with programmers and applications specialists on the cutting edge of technology. Throughout my career, the one thing that has remained constant is my love for learning. This job would certainly challenge my programming and managerial skills and would be my chance to contribute my own experiences."

Layoffs and Other Terminations

If a voluntary move from one job to another is eyed with suspicion, what about layoffs? Strictly speaking, getting laid off is not your fault; it is loss of a job because of circumstances beyond your control. Nevertheless, some employers will feel that had you really been valuable to your former employer, the company wouldn't have dumped you. Fault or no fault, you've got some negative baggage to deal with.

If you were laid off from a job that was part of a larger reduction in employees, indicate that. Saying "I was laid off" is a lot different than saying "I was laid off along with our entire department" or "The contract we were working on was completed and our entire team was laid off."

If you were fired, you certainly shouldn't volunteer this information, and nothing on your résumé should indicate that this was the reason why you left your last position. When the interviewer asks why you left your last job (at this point we all know he will), you might explain that your approach differed from management's. Unless you can make an airtight case that you were fired unjustly, never blame other people for what happened to you. Demonstrate that you understand you failed and, more importantly, how you will avoid repeating the failure. You learned from your experience, and the prospective employer will reap the benefits of what you learned.

What Is the Hiring Manager Thinking?

Primary concern:

- Will you fit in?

Secondary concern:

- What's wrong with this individual?

Layoffs and other terminations have to be the hardest for hiring managers to get past. As managers, interviewers clearly understand that terminations are a part of being a manager. They understand that business realities cause companies to reduce staff size and eliminate perfectly great performers. They also understand how these decisions get made. There are layoffs and then there are reductions in individuals who probably should have been terminated a while back and it's now convenient to do so.

In their minds, they go back to the last round of layoffs that they personally went through. They'll remember how they made their decisions—perhaps each department had to terminate a certain number of employees. There may have been any number of ways that they came up with who would be the ones to be let go:

- Least seniority
- Least important project
- Least impact on customer service
- Project was being eliminated altogether
- Personality didn't blend in with the group
- Most days off work
- High maintenance
- Least productive
- Most disruptive
- Least well-liked regardless of performance

As you can see, they may start off with perfectly legitimate reasons, but progress to the not-so-good reasons. And that's just on the layoff side. We don't need to go any further in the case of being fired.

Their primary concern is going to be to identify whether your termination was beyond your control or a firing under the guise of a layoff. That's tough.

Your Strategy

Your strategy is to shoo away all the negativity associated with any sort of termination by the employer. There are two components to this strategy:

- In the case of a layoff, demonstrate that you were one of many to be affected.
- In the case of a termination, plead the case that your approach was different from management's.

Beyond My Control

To prepare your defense, you need to start off with all the facts regarding your layoff:

- What prompted the layoff? (Missed revenues, downturn in product demand, over-capacity, merger or acquisition, etc.)
- Was there a formal announcement put out by the company?
- How many people were involved?

- What departments were affected?
- What methods were used to determine who would be released?
- How many people survived the cut?
- How many rounds of layoffs did you survive prior to being released?

It is important to have all these facts to substantiate that you were in fact one of many. What works in your favor?

- Being part of an entire unit that was eliminated.
- Surviving several prior reductions in the workforce.
- Large numbers of employees being released at one time.
- A public announcement regarding the reduction and the reason for the reduction in the workforce.
- Seniority as the method for selecting the released staff.
- The company only kept a core set of people to keep the business afloat.

Remember, you want to demonstrate that there were circumstances beyond your control that affected the decision to lay you off.

My Approach Differed from Management's

This is a sticky situation by all means. Let's first define "approach." It can be anything from the processes by which you did your job, to the architecture you used in designing your projects, or the amount of time you spent on each customer service call. Your goal is to shift the focus away from why you did things differently from the way management wanted, and move it to what your own approach is. For example:

> "I truly believe that every customer deserves the best customer service experience that I can provide, even if it means being on the phone a bit longer than the rest of my colleagues. My customers don't have to call back again—their issues are resolved. At times, going this extra mile may affect call times on the helpdesk."

This is one way to cast a positive light on your involuntary termination.

You can also consider telling the truth. People make mistakes. Mistakes result in learning and growth. Employers are willing to forgive and forget. If you own up to your mistakes and present the lessons you've learned, you may be able to make lemonade from lemons.

Questions

The questions you should be prepared for if you find yourself in this situation include:

- Could your layoff possibly have been related to your performance?
- Was anyone laid off immediately after you were? If so, how many and which departments?

- Do you feel that the decision to let you go had anything to do with your interpersonal relationships with your boss or any of your coworkers?
- How many people survived the cut?
- How many waves of layoffs did you survive before you were let go?

Questions You Don't Have to Answer

Employers are forbidden by law to make hiring decisions based in any way on marital status, sexual orientation, age, ethnic background or national origin, race, religious beliefs, gender, or disabilities. There are exceptions where a *bona fide occupational qualification* can be demonstrated, but, in general, these personal characteristics and attributes are protected by law.

The following is a list of the questions that an employer can't and can ask.

AGE

What They Can't Ask

- How old are you?
- When were you born?
- When did you graduate from college/high school?
- Are you near retirement age?
- Aren't you a little young to be seeking a job with this much responsibility?

What They Can Ask

- Are you over 18?

CITIZENSHIP

What They Can't Ask

- Are you a U.S. citizen?

What They Can Ask

- Can you legally work in this country?

ETHNICITY

What They Can't Ask

- What's your native language?
- Where were you born?
- Where were your parents born?
- What kind of accent is that?

What They Can Ask

- Do you know any foreign languages? (If it's relevant to the job.)

SEXUAL ORIENTATION

What They Can't Ask

- Are you straight?
- Are you gay?
- Do you have any roommates?

MARITAL/FAMILY STATUS

What They Can't Ask

- Are you married?
- Do you live alone?
- Do you live with your parents?
- Have you ever been married?
- What does your husband/wife do?
- Do you have any children?
- Are you a single parent?
- How do handle childcare?
- Do any of your children not live with you?
- Do you plan to start a family?
- My wife (husband) hates me working weekends. What about yours?
- Will travel be a burden on your family?
- Are you pregnant?

What They Can Ask

- This job involves some travel. Would that be a problem?
- This job requires overtime. Would that be a problem?
- Would you be willing to relocate?

RELIGIOUS AFFILIATION

What They Can't Ask

- To what religion do you belong?
- Where do you worship?

NON-PROFESSIONAL AFFILIATIONS

What They Can't Ask

- What associations outside of work do you belong to?

APPEARANCE

What They Can't Ask

- What is your height?
- What is your weight?

HEALTH AND DISABILITIES

What They Can't Ask

- How is your general health?
- How is your family's health?
- Please list your medical history.
- Do you have any disabilities?
- Do you have HIV, AIDS, or AIDS-related syndrome?
- How many days were you sick last year?
- Were you ever denied health insurance?

What They Can Ask

- Can you perform this job?

MILITARY

What They Can't Ask

- Were you honorably discharged?
- In which branch of the military did you serve?

What They Can Ask

- What training did you receive in the military?

ARREST RECORD

What They Can't Ask

- Have you ever been arrested?

What They Can Ask

- Have you ever been convicted of a security violation (or other crime associated with the position)?

How to Handle These Questions

So what do you do when such a question is asked? Take offense? Call the police? Technically, you can do anything you want. It depends on how much you want the job. You certainly won't win friends or score high marks with the interviewer by saying, "It's illegal to ask me that." In general, there are three ways to handle illegal or inappropriate questions:

- You can answer the question.
- You can evade the question.
- You can openly object to answering the question.

Let's try out different scenarios.

You Can Answer the Question

In general, if you feel comfortable answering a question—even an illegal one—by all means answer it. You might not mind if the interviewer knows you are married or what your native language is. There is nothing wrong with answering these types of questions as long as you don't see a way for your responses to be used against you. Interviewers typically want to find out as much about you as they can. They may actually have no intention of discriminating against you. Use your judgment to determine the spirit in which the question is asked.

You Can Evade the Question

If you would prefer not to answer the question, try out the "Ifs" technique. For example, to the question "How old are your children?" you might reply:

"I'm not sure what you wish to learn from that question. If you're concerned with how I handle my childcare arrangements, I can assure you that I take my professional commitments seriously and my family respects these."

Other examples of "Ifs" that you might want to address in a similar way include:

"If you are concerned whether starting a family will make me unreliable..."

"If you are concerned that my religious affiliation will interfere with a normal workload..."

"If you are concerned that I will not be properly motivated because of my age..."

"If you count my husband, two cats, three dogs, and tank full of fish, then I have 17 children."

"If you are concerned that my wheelchair limits my productivity..."

You Can Openly Object to Answering the Question

If a question is blatantly discriminatory, offensive, or just plain stupid, you might want to respond in a more direct manner. For example, you may want to respond, "Does my religious affiliation have any bearing on my ability to do this job?" The key is to not act defensive. Let it go and don't make a big deal about it. Interviewers ask illegal questions simply because they don't know any better. If you let them off the hook graciously, it may just be taken into consideration.

If you're wondering what to say, try these simple phrases and then move on:

"I don't think this question is appropriate."

"I'm not sure I understand the relevance of the question."

"I'm sorry. I don't intend to discuss that."

"I like to keep my religious beliefs separate from my work, and I respect that right in the people with whom I work."

What Should You Do?

So what do you do if you were asked an inappropriate question and didn't get the job? Well, first ask yourself whether you really want to work for unethical people. Then, if you decide that you want to pursue the matter, you can file claims with the appropriate state agency and the federal government's Equal Employment Opportunity Commission. It may take a while to hear back from these agencies. Don't be too hopeful. The burden of proof will be on you to demonstrate that you were wronged.

Checklist

No candidate is perfect. We all have problem areas in our résumés, and hiring managers don't really expect you to be perfect. Your job is to ensure that you're prepared when they ask the tricky questions. Think you're ready? Run down this checklist to be sure:

- ☐ Know your rights. Brush up on the questions that employers should not require you to answer. Practice your evasion techniques and how to politely refuse to answer a question.
- ☐ Be prepared. Some interviewers will throw you curve balls. Your best way around them is to know what to expect—understand what their primary and secondary concerns are.
- ☐ Don't let an interviewer intimidate you based on your age. Focus on how you can fit in and be productive starting on day one.
- ☐ Understand that all hiring managers are trying to assess whether you can do the job, whether you'll stick around, how you'll fit in, and what you will cost. Knowing this, you can better prepare for any interviewing situation.
- ☐ Practice your responses!

Chapter 8

Special IT Interviewing Scenarios

If you are reading this chapter, you've probably either found out that your interview will be held somewhere other than the employer's offices, or discovered that the interview will consist of more than just a question-and-answer session. In this chapter, I'll cover special IT interviewing situations that you might run into, including:

- Telephone interviews
- Interviews at job fairs
- On-campus interviews
- Interviews over meals
- Video conferencing interviews
- Skills tests

Interview Settings

Obviously, the number one place that interviews are conducted is in the employer's office. Though this provides the interviewer with a home-turf advantage, it is probably your most comfortable interview setting as well. After all, you can see the company in action, have access to all the important players, and get the best feel for the company. However, there are a number of other interviewing alternatives.

Telephone Interviews

During your job-hunting, you will run into telephone interviews a lot. Some call them the toughest of the interviewing situations, but have you tried actually enjoying an interview over a meal? Yikes. If it's not the spinach stuck between your teeth, it's the tomatoes rolling off the plate. Now, those are sticky situations. So when you're faced with a phone interview, you can always be grateful it's not the meal interview. (How to handle the meal interview comes later in this chapter.)

Phone interviews all have the same purpose. They are the initial screener used by HR specialists, managers, and recruiters. They come in three flavors:

The cold call You initiate the phone call to a hiring manager, and they are interested in your background.

The call-back Typically, you get these when you least expect them and are least prepared.

The set time You've prearranged a time to be interviewed.

Rarely will you be able to win the job on the telephone, even if you have the best "telephone voice." So don't worry if you get off the phone without a job offer. The objective is to land an in-person interview. Recruiters use phone interviews as the next screening tool after they've reviewed a pool of résumés. From here, you'll be passed on to the next round of interviews, usually in-person interviews with the hiring manager. Phone interviews are typically scripted to ensure that recruiters cover all the bases and confirm your qualifications.

Most people don't prepare as thoroughly for telephone interviews as they do for in-person interviews, and the casualty toll is heavy. Some recruiters seek opportunities to catch you when you may be off guard and most genuine, exposing your unrehearsed thoughts and feelings. They like to evaluate how you think on your feet.

Preparing for Your Telephone Interview

The advantage of a telephone interview over a face-to-face interview is that the interviewer can't see you. This doesn't mean that you should take your interviews in your bathrobe and bunny slippers. How you present yourself on a phone interview will come across on the phone. Be and dress your best so that all the interviewer gets are positive vibes.

Another advantage of a phone interview is that you have considerable flexibility in how you prepare and present yourself. Consider telephone interviews to be like open-book tests—with the right set of resources (web bookmarks, crib sheets, and scripted answers) you'll get through with flying colors.

STAND OUT!

Be prepared with:

- Your résumé
- Your asset statements
- Questions you want to ask
- Information on the company/interviewer

You need to be prepared at a moment's notice. This means having all your materials handy, well organized, and ready to go. Your "Cliff Notes" include not only your résumé, but also your asset statements and compelling examples of how you've made a difference on the job in the past. It can also include a prep sheet on the company, any information on the person you'll be meeting with, and the questions you'll want to ask the interviewer.

This preparation goes a long way. No matter how many papers you have flying on your end of the phone, you always want to come across as well-informed and well-prepared.

Here are some additional tips on how to prepare for your phone interview. Remember, you never know when the phone is going to ring.

- Make sure your résumé is always handy. The best way to ensure this is to tape it to a wall near the phone.
- Create a cheat sheet—a list of anticipated questions and your answers. Include a list of points about your skills and achievements that you want to mention.
- Organize yourself. Keep all of your employer research materials within easy reach of the phone. Keep individual folders for each employer or recruiter.
- Keep your calendar nearby for scheduling future meetings.
- Have a notepad and pen handy to take notes.
- Smile! Monitor your smile by keeping a mirror close to the phone. People can hear when you smile.

STAND OUT!

Before getting on the phone, make sure you have eliminated as many distractions as possible. Put the dog outside, turn off call waiting, and shut doors to create privacy.

If you have a scheduled time for your interview, here are some additional things to consider:

- Avoid calls from the office, if possible. If you are calling from the office, shut your door. If you work in a cubicle environment, see if you can schedule a meeting room or borrow an office. Remember that the risk of being accidentally overheard looking for employment elsewhere is extremely high if you are calling from your existing job.
- At home, go to a quiet room and place a "Do Not Disturb" note on your door.
- Turn off your stereo, TV, and any other potential distraction—including your pets. Though they don't come with "off" switches, put them in the yard or in another room where they can't jump on the phone and introduce themselves.
- Have a glass of water handy.
- Make sure you take a bathroom break before your call. You never know how long you'll be on the phone.
- Turn off call waiting on your phone.

SPEAK AND STAND

Here is a simple technique to increase your enthusiasm and the positive image that you project over the telephone: stand up. Whenever you are talking with a potential employer on the phone, simply speak standing. It gets your blood flowing, improves your posture, and improves your response time.

It's interesting to note that many telemarketing companies have come to realize that standing while talking with customers can actually improve their sales, so they often provide the telemarketers with hands-free headsets that allow them to stand and pace back and forth. It helps give an action perspective to an otherwise passive activity. Apply this technique in improving your telephone presence.

Don't Forget the Basics

Don't be thrown off by telephone interviews. They are your gatekeepers to the face-to-face interview. This means being prepared for any questions the interviewer might ask as well as having questions that you should ask the interviewer. At the start of the conversation, get the caller's name, title, company, address, e-mail, and telephone number. You'll want to follow up with an e-mail or letter, and you want to make sure that you get their name right.

Practice listening. Now is the time to become an expert listener. Unfortunately, you won't be able to tape your interview (taping phone conversations without the other person knowing is illegal). Because you won't have the same physical cues as in an in-person interview, it's important to pay attention to the details of the conversation. Take notes and demonstrate that you are listening by feeding back what the interviewer says, such as, "In other words, the candidate must have a great combination of technical and people skills."

Remember, the phone interview is a screening tool. Always push for a meeting. As the call winds to a close, say to the interviewer, "I know that your time is limited today. I would like the opportunity to discuss my qualifications for this position in person. I can be at your office tomorrow morning. Would you be available at 10 A.M. or is there a better time for you?"

Don't forget your manners—express your appreciation for the time spent with you and don't forget to put your thanks in writing via e-mail or a personal note.

STAND OUT!

Rehearse your response to the salary question. You can go as far as to print it out and tape it to your wall.

A word of caution: beware of being asked about your salary expectations. This is an overused screening tool used by recruiters and HR specialists to get a ballpark of whether they can afford to continue recruiting you. Dodge this question on the phone interview by saying, "I would expect a salary commensurate with the position. Since I don't have the particulars of the position I would prefer to hold off on salary requirements." From there you can always turn the tables around by asking the interviewer for specifics on the range for someone with your qualifications.

Meal Interviews

So you've made it past the phone interview. That wasn't so bad, was it? Now on to the mealtime interview. Here's the good news: being asked to lunch or dinner is a very, very positive sign. The employer is willing to invest in at least an hour and a meal. That's more than they invest with most candidates.

The bad news is that the mealtime interview can catch you off guard. Actually, it's designed for exactly that. Questions that would be blatantly inappropriate in the office seem to creep up over a meal. These include casual conversation about your spouse, kids, where you live, your hobbies, politics, and religious beliefs. You've got to be prepared to handle these without taking offense and without embarrassing the interviewer. After all, there are just so many technical questions they can ask you.

Here are some dos and don'ts to help you through an interview over a meal.

Dos

- Wait to be seated until your host sits down.
- Place the napkin in your lap as soon as you are seated.
- Remember your table manners. That means no elbows on the table.
- Order something easy to eat, like a salad or a sandwich. Remember you'll be answering questions through most of the meal so you may not be able to get through whatever you order.
- Order something similar to what the interviewer is eating or ask for a recommendation.
- If you are in the middle of a mouthful, finish chewing, take a sip of water, and then proceed.
- Be polite to the waiter.
- Thank your host for the meal as you are leaving the restaurant.

Don'ts

- Do not order alcohol.
- Do not order the most expensive or the most inexpensive thing on the menu.
- Do not complain about the food or send it back.
- Do not smoke. No exceptions.
- Do not open your menu until your host has.
- Do not begin eating until everyone is served.
- Do not attempt to pay the bill or split the cost; it will be covered by your host.
- Do not order a doggy bag.

Video Conferencing

Video conferencing is common when interviewing for upper-management positions. High-paid recruiters use video conferencing as a way of saving a cross-country flight for both you and them. Typically, these are screening interviews before sending you along to the hiring manager.

Here are some general recommendations when it comes to interviewing before the camera:

- Get directions to the video conferencing location and arrive early. Many FedexKinko's offer video conferencing services, so you might not have to go far.
- Arrive early to ensure that the system is properly set up and functioning.
- If you are new to video conferencing, ask the attendant to demonstrate how to use the video controls.
- Wear solid colors and avoid bright or heavy jewelry, especially clanking jewelry whose noise will be picked up by the microphone.
- Men: Make sure you are clean shaven. Women: Don't go overboard on the cosmetics. Check your appearance before the camera goes live.
- The interviewer will appear on a large monitor. Maintain eye contact with his image rather than with your own image (if the system has Picture-in-Picture). Turn off PIP if you are uncomfortable with watching your own image.
- Sit up straight. Don't lean forward.
- Don't fidget. Don't wave your hands. Too many movements will start to get irritating.
- Be aware of time delay. Though speech is typically transmitted over a conference phone, there may be a time delay with image transmission. This may cause jerky movements.
- Prepare for an online interview just like you would for any other type of interview.
- Breathe.

Job Fairs

Job fairs are always a great place to learn about the job market. In fact, many people go to job fairs to window shop for new opportunities. Up to 50 percent of the people you run into at job fairs are not seriously looking to change positions. Job fairs do tell you whether it's a recruiter's market or a candidate's market. If the job fair is packed with recruiters and companies, it's definitely a candidate's market. Unfortunately, in the last year, the ratio of candidates to employers has dramatically increased. A job fair may not offer the best opportunity to find your dream job, but if you've recently been downsized, it's a great opportunity to see how the job market is doing and what employers are looking for.

STAND OUT!

Whenever you leave your résumé "on file" with a company or recruiter, check in periodically to ensure that it hasn't made its way to the great circular file.

Job fairs also provide long-term networking opportunities whether you are in the market today or may be in the future. By meeting hiring managers from organizations in your region, you can start building your rolodex (or PDA) of contacts for when you are ready to move on. You never know when the right opportunity might come along. The key is to maintain these relationships so that you remain at the forefront of a manager's mind. It's also a great way to network and gather contact information for leading local companies. Even if they don't have a need for someone with your skill set today, you just never know what tomorrow will bring.

Interviewing at Job Fairs

You can basically consider your entire attendance at a job fair an interview. You will get noticed—from how you approach the organization's booth, to standing in line, to introducing yourself. It's all one great interview. So you want to ensure that you're at your best the entire time.

With that said, you will run into three distinct interview types when you have the opportunity to meet with a recruiter or company representative. As you watch and listen from the sidelines while others interview, you have the opportunity to identify different interviewing styles and modify your approach accordingly. You'll find: the screener, the mini, and the full interview.

The Screener

Talk about power interviewing—the screener usually lasts no more than two to three minutes and is usually conducted by companies whose main interest is gathering résumés. They base their decisions on moving to the next step on initial impressions. You've got to impress them fast or you won't make it. Your strategy:

- Quickly point them to the key areas in your résumé that reflect their needs. What needs? The needs they enumerated six candidates ago when you were standing off to the side as another candidate naively walked up and asked, "So what is your company looking for?" You need to fill the company's list of requirements or you will never see the light of day at the next level.
- As quickly as they've asked you to introduce yourself, ask the recruiter for a business card so you can follow up.
- Ask the recruiter about the next step. Thank them. Next!

The Mini

You can actually get two full sentences in on this type of interview. It usually lasts five to ten minutes and is conducted at the employer's booth. Your strategy:

- Focus all your attention on the recruiter you are meeting with.
- Use your asset statements to position yourself as someone who fits their company needs.
- Elaborate on the information contained in your résumé. This means knowing your résumé inside and out! Be prepared to comment on each and every item on it. Be prepared to give a full explanation of what might be only a single-line bullet item on the résumé.
- Be prepared to answer the question, "So why are you here today?"
- Ask for a business card and inquire about the next step.

Full Interview

You've made it. The full interview usually takes place behind a curtain or screen at the employer's booth, or it may be in another part of the hall altogether. Most employers use the full interview only as a secondary interview. In other words, you have to be invited to the interview based on the previous screening interview or mini-interview. Be prepared for 20 minutes or more, but probably no longer than 30 minutes, since most companies have a tight schedule to keep. Consider this interview the same as you would any full-length interview. Here's your strategy:

- Be aware that you may actually be interviewed by technical or line managers.
- You will be asked a great number of qualitative, open-ended questions and will be expected to elaborate on your answers.
- At the end of the interview, if you are truly interested, let the interviewer know and ask what the next step will be. Assume that he or she is also interested.

STAND OUT!

Don't be discouraged if you only made it through the screener or the mini interview. The key is to know what the next steps are and to follow up!

Unless you are certain that the company is conducting secondary interviews, do not consider it a negative if all you went through was the screener or the mini. It can be discouraging to spend two quick minutes with a recruiter after a 30-minute wait, but that is the reality of job fairs. Just make sure you know what the next step is and follow up.

Finding Job Fairs

There are plenty of job fairs out there. They all serve the same purpose: to bring recruiters and candidates together. The following Websites provide you with the latest calendars for job fairs:

- www.careerbuilder.com
- www.monster.com
- www.nationalcareerfairs.com
- www.employmentguide.com/browse_jobfairs.html
- www.psijobfair.com/
- www.jobexpo.com/
- www.careerfairs.com/
- www.jobweb.com/

You can find additional career fairs by searching your local newspaper. Often, these job fairs are sponsored by the newspaper itself or by the local chamber of commerce. If you can't find information on an upcoming job fair in the paper, visit its Website, which often keeps this information on hand.

Online Job Fairs

Imagine attending a job fair in your pajamas! Well, you can with online job fairs. A virtual job fair is simply a Website where a number of companies provide their recruiting information. Instead of sending a representative to a physical job fair or a campus, companies post their company information, including what they are looking for in candidates, on a Website and candidates can apply over the Internet. It is similar to providing information on career opportunities on their own company Website. The nice thing about how companies provide their information on online job fairs is that they make an effort to sell the company to candidates by concisely presenting the benefits offered, reasons for joining, and more specific information about the available positions and the types of candidates they are looking for. Virtual job fairs are popular for entry-level positions.

For an example of an online job fair, visit www.jobweb.com/employ/fairs/.

On-Campus Job Fairs and Career Days

Most college students get their first introduction to the job market through their on-campus job fair. Larger schools may offer multiple job fairs for different disciplines. To be successful, mark your calendar ahead of time and find out what the requirements are for participating. Your career placement office will have this information. Remember, you can't just show up unprepared and expect to be hired. You have to create your résumé (and read this book!).

Also note that many campuses offer a career day at the start of the fall semester as a predecessor to the actual job fair in the spring semester. Career days help you get acquainted with companies who will be at the job fair. Typically, companies will send a recent graduate of the school to speak to seniors about career opportunities with the company.

Getting Noticed at a Job Fair

Job fairs are not for everyone. You've got to do your homework and know how these things work. You have to have a strategy to make the most of your time and to get noticed.

Consider the facts:

- Recruiters see 100+ new faces in the six to eight hours they are there.
- Fifty percent of the people who attend a job fair are just window shoppers checking out the job market.
- If you're lucky, you will have 10 to 15 minutes with a recruiter.
- Recruiters you will be meeting are seldom the actual hiring managers.
- Recruiters are professional screeners.

Your Strategy

You have to have a strategy for increasing your success at a job fair. It should consist of:

- Preparation, which means researching companies you are interested in meeting with and what they are looking for from candidates
- A plan to maximize meaningful time with a recruiter

- A solid introduction
- Knowing how to make a lasting impression

STAND OUT!
Preparation is the key to success.

Preparation

If there's one thing you should get out of this book, it's how preparation is the key to all success. (And believe it or not, to 99 percent of success in life.) You always need to be at your very best. With such a short amount of time to grab the recruiter's attention and make them want to hear more about what you can do for their company, you've got to have all your ducks in a row. Consider every moment with the recruiter part of the interview! Make sure you:

- Understand what the company's all about—do your research before you arrive.
- Know the minimum requirements for getting hired by individual companies.

STAND OUT!
Recruiters are screeners.

Meeting with an HR recruiter is different from meeting with hiring managers. Recruiters have to be able to confidently recommend you for further interviewing. They don't want egg on their face when someone they've recommended turns out to be a dud. They are looking to screen you out, not qualify you in. Your objective should be to show that you not only have all the necessary basic requirements, but are also an appropriate candidate for their work environment. Consider *their* focus. Ideally, they should be able to visualize you as someone who could eventually become part of the team.

How to Strategically Maneuver the Job Fair

Use the following tips to create your job fair strategy:

- Get there early to give yourself plenty of time to check in.
- Scout out the place. Take a walk around the job fair to get a feel for who's there. Make a list of the companies you want to meet with. Spend your energies on them rather than wandering from booth to booth.
- Check out job openings for each company of interest, typically found on a listing sheet. Or use a computer, if provided, to look up individual companies.
- Before approaching a company, walk around their booth and pick up literature on the company and its hiring needs. Read through these before you approach a recruiter.

- Listen from the sidelines as recruiters talk with other candidates. Try to pick up on what they are looking for and use this to your advantage. You should also be able to pick out who the senior person is at the booth.
- Try to talk to the hiring manager or senior member of the team whenever possible. Recruiters can be helpful, but the hiring manager is the one you want to impress.
- Be ready with your asset statements. They should be concise and effective. Try them out *before* you get to the job fair. Make sure they represent something unique about you to differentiate yourself.
- Try to get a name or business card from anyone you talk to so you can use the name as a reference when you follow up.
- Plan to spend the entire day at the job fair. Get there early to avoid long lines. Take some time off during the midday crunch. Return to the job fair floor in the late afternoon for follow-ups and to make a lasting impression with the companies that truly interest you.
- Wear comfortable shoes. Job fairs typically involve waiting in long lines. You can avoid lines altogether through proper planning. If there's a long line at your top company, go visit the next company on your list. Return to the first company later in the day.
- If you do decide to stand in line, make use of the time to read company literature and to ask others around you, "What brings you here today?" and "What companies have impressed you the most today?" Needless to say, plan on visiting those companies.
- Stay upbeat and energized. Try to make an impression through your enthusiasm about the work.
- Follow up by sending a letter and another copy of your résumé to human resources and the hiring manager. Mention that you talked with them, or a company representative, at the fair. Tell them how excited you are about the position. Thank them for taking time to meet with you. Reiterate why you feel you would be an outstanding employee for their company. Mention that you would appreciate the opportunity to speak with them further, and that you will call the following week to arrange a meeting to discuss how your skills can benefit their organization.
- Needless to say, follow up in a week or so with a phone call inquiring about the position and the hiring status.

Try not to be overwhelmed by the size of the job fair or the number of job-seekers in attendance. There are plenty of window shoppers at job fairs. Don't be discouraged if you don't go home with a job offer or formal interview lined up. This should be just one step in your research and networking process. The new contacts can prove to be positive additions to your resources. Job opportunities sometimes come from the least expected sources at the most unexpected times.

What to Bring

Following are some of the things you will need to bring with you to the job fair:

Résumé Bring about 30 copies of your résumé. Make it count. Make sure your résumé fits on one page and is printed on quality paper.

Portfolio Be organized. Bring a portfolio for taking notes and storing copies of your résumé.

Briefcase You're going to collect a lot of brochures and pieces of literature. Bring your own briefcase. You'll appear far more professional than carrying around a plastic bag.

Dress Dress professionally regardless of the position. Image is crucial at a job fair—even more important than at a normal interview since decisions are made much more quickly.

Comfortable Shoes You'll be doing a lot of standing on concrete floors.

On-Campus Interviews

As a college student, entering the IT job market may be a bit intimidating. As you monitor the trade papers and read about downsizing, you may be wondering whether you made the right choice. Set your fears aside—IT is definitely the place to be, and on-campus interviewing is a great way to get your foot in the door.

On-campus interviewing brings the job market to you, and it's up to you to make the best of the situation. Even though on-campus interviews offer the most convenient way of entering the IT job market, you should not depend on them exclusively to guarantee you employment after graduation. There are far more companies than just those that are visiting your campus. Many of the best companies may not be visiting any campuses, so make sure you read Chapter 3 for additional resources to help you find your dream company.

On-campus interviews are screener interviews. They are fairly brief because the recruiter has several interviews tightly scheduled into the day. You're more likely to find the interviewer's approach to be traditional or behavioral rather than the stress or conversational style. They'll run all the interviewees through a list of the same questions. Be aware that companies often send their entry-level employees—particularly those who are alumni of the school where they're interviewing—so you may be dealing with an inexperienced interviewer. Even more reason to be ready to take control of the interview.

Right from the start you've got to set yourself apart. On-campus interviews are interview mills and the candidates start to blur together after a while. Try to schedule yourself for the last or next-to-last interview slots with the most important companies you wish to meet with. You stand a better chance of standing out in their minds if you are the last person they talk to.

There's more to on-campus interviewing than meeting with a half dozen companies and then picking the one you want to work for. Here is an easy formula for success with these types of interviews: first maximize both the quality and quantity of the interviews, and then maximize your interview efficiency. It is not enough to just show up for the interviews and hope that someone will miraculously offer you a job. You have to perform at your peak to gain any mileage from on-campus interviewing.

Performing at your peak includes understanding who your competition will be. They are the same folks who sat across from you in class and with whom you competed for grades. They will be there meeting with the same recruiters, competing for *your* job. But in an interview, it's not just about the grades. Companies are looking for people who can communicate as well as perform. If you're a 4.0 student, but can't hold a conversation, you will have a much harder time finding a job and getting past these recruiters. The key is differentiating yourself from these folks. Use your unique project or internship experience to help you leapfrog the other students.

How to Choose the Best Companies to Interview With

How do you choose which company to interview with? Year after year, students flock to the "household name" companies that come to campus (Exxon, General Motors, Ford, AT&T, IBM, General Electric), while some of the best employers go almost unnoticed, unable to fill their available interview slots. Why? Because few students take the time to do the research to find out about these companies. Often there are pleasant surprises when looking into the smaller companies, which can be more growth-oriented and offer better opportunities for career advancement.

A current trend at many schools is the invitational or "closed" interview, which involves forwarding the résumés of all interested students to the employer, who then selects those who will be interviewed. You can find out which companies will be holding closed interviews by checking with your career placement office well in advance of when the recruiters will be on campus. Ask for as much information as possible about each of these employers and the position requirements, including any minimum requirements for inclusion (such as GPA or major). Also ask when the screened résumé packet will be mailed to the employer.

It's important for you to do some research on your own as well. See Chapter 3 for additional tips on how to research companies. The way to differentiate yourself and get selected for a closed interview is to customize your résumé for each company. To tailor your résumé, you'll want to update your skills section toward the personal character traits, technical skills, and foundation skills that the company is looking for. If you don't know what technology the company uses, call the organization and speak with an IT manager. Mention that you will be meeting with one of their on-campus recruiters and you would like to find out as much as you can before the interview. Any IT manager would be impressed to have such a resourceful candidate.

Once you've customized your résumé, submit it to the career placement office for inclusion in the employer's résumé packet.

Additional Pointers

Timing is everything. Always request the last or second-to-last interview slot of the day. In addition to being easier to work into your schedule, these time slots carry the significant weight of being the most memorable time slots for the interviewer. If you want to be remembered, make it as late in the day as possible.

You'll want to make a great first impression. This means a professional appearance. Bring a portfolio/folder, two copies of your résumé, and copies of your top three letters of recommendation. Keep it simple. No need to bring a computer, no fancy PDAs.

One way to ingratiate yourself to the interviewer is to woo them with knowledge about their company. Bring any company information you have gathered with you to the interview. Keep it out so the recruiter can see you have done your homework. Most recruiters will notice immediately. Company information is available through your career placement office as well as on the Web. Make sure you know the information inside and out. This is not just a prop for show, since you will be expected to know more about the company if you have it. Be ready and willing to demonstrate your basic understanding of the company when asked. Good preparation will always impress an on-campus recruiter, whose day often consists of explaining, over and over, what their company does.

Testing What You Know

Imagine yourself in the shoes of this employer. Fingers-a-Walking, Inc. is migrating to new technology (let's say.NET) and is in urgent need of programmers with.NET experience. The only people they have on staff with.NET experience are folks who read about it in the latest *MCP* magazine. How are they to know whether they are hiring someone with the right skills?

Here's another scenario: BigBlue is a major systems developer whose most important resource is the developers it hires and cultivates to develop new firmware for its microprocessors. It uses its own proprietary software language. It relies on the untainted, moldable minds of recent college graduates. How does it determine whether someone has the aptitude for programming and is a good investment hire?

Certainly the face-to-face interview will play a very important role in their screening process, but it can be tough sifting through the thousands of résumés their HR department receives on a weekly basis. (Hiring managers typically spend about 45 seconds reviewing each résumé they receive. It would take them two full days of doing nothing else to review 1,200 résumés.) In these cases, they often turn to assessment exams to help in the screening process.

If you haven't already run into an assessment exam, the likelihood is high that you will one day be asked to take a pre-employment exam. Assessments have been popular for years outside of IT. You find them in other professions such as sales, law enforcement, civil service, and call centers. They go by others names like personnel tests, hiring tests, or pre-employment tests, and they test typing skills, integrity, personality, intelligence, and aptitude. Pre-employment tests have been slowly making their way into the tech world for the past five years.

In IT, there are two types of pre-employment tests that you might run into: technical aptitude and technical proficiency. *Aptitude tests* are used to identify those who have a better chance of succeeding in technical training, but who have little or no prior experience. These are primarily seen when recruiting for entry-level positions. *Proficiency tests* are used to identify the technical skill level of experienced IT professionals prior to employment. Some employers use them to test how much you really know. These tests are constructed to predict success on the job.

Technical Aptitude Assessments

Technical aptitude tests help employers determine whether they should make the investment in training you for a technical position. These tests are particularly important in very large organizations where recruiting new technical resources is a daily task. These companies include phone companies, the insurance industry, shipping companies, technology firms, and accounting and financial services organizations.

Aptitude tests reduce the time it takes to screen candidates, and they are by far more effective in identifying aptitude for areas like programming than any human screener. In fact, according to Keith Larman at Psychometrics Inc., there's a .5 to .6 correlation to the success of the individual as predicted by an aptitude test over a .2 to .3 correlation for the best interviewer. (The correlation numbers represent the likelihood of a "good" match between the candidate and the position.) Aptitude assessments actually work in the IT candidate's favor. IT professionals are not natural interviewers. Getting past the skillful recruiter is not their expertise. By scoring high marks on a technical aptitude exam, you've passed one hurdle. IT aptitude tests truly are a techie's dream, testing reasoning or logic—areas where they excel.

Using aptitude tests, employers can identify IT job candidates who will be able to learn new content and technologies quickly and be able to solve complex problems on the job. Technical aptitude tests evaluate your problem-solving ability, including numerical reasoning, verbal reasoning, symbolic reasoning, and visual speed and accuracy. The theory is that employees with higher technical aptitude learn technology more effectively and less expensively while being able to apply their skills faster than individuals with lower technical aptitudes.

Technical aptitude tests measure:

Numerical Reasoning Your ability to analyze logical numerical relationships and to discover underlying principles.

Verbal Reasoning Your ability to combine separate pieces of information and to form conclusions on the basis of that information.

Symbolic Reasoning Your ability to manipulate abstract symbols mentally and to make judgments and decisions that are logically valid.

Visual Speed and Accuracy Your perceptual speed and accuracy—the ability to compare numbers or patterns quickly and accurately.

Typically, aptitude tests exist for general IT-related positions such as computer operators, as well as specialties such as mainframe, client/server, and systems programmers. Aptitude tests originally came about when employers experienced unacceptable failure rates during training. Employers needed a better indicator of success than computer science degrees, which they had previously been using as their screening criteria.

Technical Proficiency

While aptitude tests predict the ability to learn a new skill, proficiency assessments predict success on the job. They are not certification exams, but rather, they assess how the test taker would react in a number of real-world situations.

Again, large organizations that attract hundreds of applicants for their job openings rely on proficiency exams to streamline recruiting by demonstrating the application of skills. These assessments do not measure definitional knowledge or syntax that can be easily memorized.

Proficiency assessments allow recruiters to concentrate on more subjective areas such as motivation, commitment, and enthusiasm. Proficiency exams are a techie's best friend as well. If you know your stuff, you'll do quite well. According to Keith Larman, he gets comments from his clients claiming that they interviewed someone they would never have considered before. Having information about their technical ability allowed them to see through a poor interview.

Some of the assessment tests you will run into in this area include:

Company	**Types of Assessments**
Brainbench, Inc.	Computer software
	Essential skills
	IT industry knowledge
	Databases
	Programming
	Networking
	Technical support, software testing
MeasureUp, Inc.	Networking proficiency
	Programming
	Security
	Technical aptitude exams
Psychometrics, Inc.	Programming proficiency
	Networking
	Systems analysis

Tips for Test Takers

For those of you who haven't taken tests lately, here are some quick tips to help you ace that assessment exam:

- Take the test cheerfully even if you are annoyed to be asked to take it.
- Pay close attention to the instructions and ask for clarification if you need it.
- Manage your time. Most assessment exams are timed.
- If you don't know an answer, don't just guess. You can improve your odds by eliminating answers.
- If you can, schedule your exam for Tuesday morning. Why Tuesday? It's still early in the week and you will have fewer unintended interruptions while studying. Even if your in-laws and friends come over during the weekend, there's still Monday night.
- The more hands-on experience you have with the products (operating systems and applications), the better you'll do.

- Invest in taking a Brainbench or SkillDrill exam. Both allow a candidate to take the exams as a professional credential. Get the feel for the environment. The more familiar you are with the testing environment, the better you'll score if your potential employer requests that you take one of the exams.

WHY ASSESSMENTS ARE AN IMPORTANT PART OF IT HIRING TODAY

Interview with Mike Russiello, CEO, Brainbench, Inc.

With more than 6 million registered users, Brainbench is undoubtedly one of the more popular sites for IT professionals. Here you'll find hundreds of assessment exams that allow you to test your skills against other IT professionals from around the world. I had the opportunity to sit down with Brainbench's CEO, Mike Russiello, to learn more about the role of Brainbench assessments in the recruiting process. Here's an excerpt from our conversation.

Assessments are really taking off. We conducted a survey of IT candidates to find out whether they were running into assessments as a part of their interviewing process and 50 percent of them said yes. Why are hiring managers and recruiters turning to pre-employment assessments from companies like Brainbench? The answer is quite simple; the IT space is changing so rapidly that hiring managers and recruiters can't keep up with the technology themselves in order to recruit the right people for their organizations. At the same time, the high rate of turnover within IT departments, coupled with the need to keep IT projects on budget and on time, is driving IT managers to look for professionals who can hit the ground running. This means having the skills specific to the project for which they are hiring.

These skills are something that the hiring manager or recruiter cannot typically evaluate themselves. They have a couple of choices: either have the recruit interview with one of their technically savvy employees or have them take a technical assessment. In the real world, a typical recruiting process involves a combination of both of these methods. Technically savvy employees typically have other jobs to do other than interviewing. Hiring managers don't want to distract them too long from getting the job done. Assessments, though, offer a more efficient way of initially screening the candidates whose résumés stood out. Face-to-face interviews can then be used for more subjective evaluations of candidates.

What type of companies use pre-employment assessments? It seems that more and more different types of companies are using assessments. Staffing companies use assessments all the time when they don't have the technical expertise on their staff to thoroughly evaluate candidates. They want to make sure they don't embarrass themselves by sending unqualified individuals to be interviewed by their clients. Since they are typically filling staffing requirements for all sorts of technologies, they need to ensure that their candidates fit the bill.

Continues on next page

Non-IT companies are increasingly using pre-employment assessments. These include companies in the financial services and insurance industries for whom the use of assessments has always played a role in their hiring requirements. These organizations are more culturally open to assessments and testing. In comparison, IT companies tend to have more technical people on staff who have a greater ability to interview technical recruits.

For an IT candidate, is there an advantage to taking Brainbench assessments before they are even asked to take one as a pre-employment requirement? In today's IT job market, an IT professional has to make sure they stand out. A Brainbench assessment provides you with an analysis of your strengths and weaknesses and a percentile against all the people who have taken the test. By demonstrating these credentials, it might just get you noticed and make the difference between an interview offer or no offer.

Brainbench assessments help IT professionals in another way. Many of our clients have told us about incidents when they would normally not have hired an individual based on their interviewing skills or appearance, but when they received their Brainbench assessment scores, they reconsidered. If interviewing is not your strong point, let your technical abilities get you the job by making sure that you show what you know. A Brainbench credential can help you here.

If You Apply for a Job at Microsoft or Google

Many of you aspire to work at premier technical organizations like Microsoft or Google. They are great companies to work for though some candidates report that their interviewing experiences can be a bit on the unconventional side. Google is rumored to even require candidates to sign a non-disclosure agreement about their hiring experience. *If* you're interested in getting a leg up on the competition be sure to Google "Google interview question" (OK, you can MSN as well). You can never be too prepared, right?

Checklist

Feeling a little intimidated about all the different interviewing scenarios? You don't have to be. Here are the keys to ensuring your interviewing success regardless of the situation.

- ☐ Preparation, preparation, preparation. Know as much as you can about the company, position, and interviewer.
- ☐ Be ready at a moment's notice. Whether it's interviewing on the phone or on the spot, organization is key for projecting a professional image.
- ☐ Understand what you're getting into. Know the rules of the game whether it's phone interviewing, interviewing at job fairs, or taking a pre-assessment exam.
- ☐ Breathe. It will help you relax and be in the moment. It will help you be more successful.

Chapter 9

"Do You Have Any Questions?"

This is a question that occurs at the end of nearly 99 percent of all interviews. In fact, most of the time its appearance pretty much signals the end of the interview. So what should you do? Do you ask your list of 100 questions that you've carefully prepared based on your pre-interview research, or do you let the interviewer bring the interview to a close?

Well, it depends on the clock and the interviewer's body language—but you never, ever answer no! Even if you can pretty much tell that the interview is over and this is just a rhetorical question, ask a quick one and then say you have many more but you want to respect the interviewer's schedule.

There's always the possibility that the interviewer wants to structure the interview by having you ask the questions. You should always be ready for any situation and with this chapter you will be. I will focus on the questions that you should ask the various people with whom you will interview. These people include:

- The human resource specialist (or the gatekeeper)
- The hiring manager
- Other employees who work there (or group interviewers)

The End Already?

Job-seekers dread getting to the point of the interview when they hear, "So, do you have any questions for us?" It can be difficult to come up with questions to ask because many will have already been answered by your pre-interview research or throughout the interview. This is particularly true in a conversational interview in which the interviewer may have told you everything you need to know about the position and the organization.

So how do you ask intelligent questions when you don't really have any in mind? Consider the following strategies:

- Avoid the problem altogether by asking questions throughout the interview rather than waiting until the end. If you've asked all your questions, a great way to finish is by asking, "When do you expect to make your decision?"

- Don't ask anything you should know already because it's easily available on the company's Website or through brochures.
- Don't ask about money and perks, such as salary, health benefits, vacation, sick leave policy, and other questions that should not be brought up in a first interview.
- Ask questions that will help you get a clear picture of what the day-to-day will be like.

Your questions should focus on three basic categories: the position, the organization, and the next steps in the hiring process.

CAN'T THINK OF QUESTIONS?
When you don't have any other questions (hopefully because you've been asking questions throughout the entire interview), you can always finish by asking, "When do you expect to make your decision?"

Why You Want to Ask Questions

It's easy to get caught up in the challenge of impressing the interviewer with your brilliant answers, but it's also important that you don't lose sight of the fact that you have a goal—trying to determine whether this situation is right for you, and whether this job is worthy of your talents and commitment.

The best way to assess the position is by asking questions throughout the interview process and of each of the interviewers. Asking questions is also a key way for you to get the upper hand in an interview situation. You have the ability to guide the conversation in the direction that you want to take it to showcase your particular skills and accomplishments. It's also a great way of filling in any awkward moments.

Asking questions also shows that you have done your homework on the company. It's a way of demonstrating your resourcefulness. But be careful, make sure that your research is thorough and that by asking questions you don't display your ignorance about the company and its initiatives.

You should be prepared with a list of questions that you can easily refer to and check off as you progress through the interview. Make sure you categorize the questions so you don't have to search for them rather than effectively using your time with the hiring manager.

Questions to Ask the Human Resource Specialist

In large organizations, the human resource specialist will typically be the gatekeeper or your screener. In smaller organizations, this role may be filled by the office manager or the administrative assistant to the hiring manager. This is the person who has thought enough of your résumé to give you a call and conduct a phone screen. Typically, the screener is running the show and you may have very little opportunity to ask questions. Not to worry. It just means that you have to be prepared with your quick list of questions at a moment's notice.

The following questions assume that the gatekeeper has allowed you passage to the next step—the in-person interview.

- Can you e-mail or fax me a copy of the job description?

  The formal job description will provide you with further details about the position so you can tailor your asset statements to the position and the organization's need.

- Who will be making the hiring decision?

  This prepares you for the face-to-face meeting. You want to be prepared to ask the right questions to the right set of people. There's nothing more embarrassing than discovering that you've just spent two hours talking to someone who wasn't the decision-maker.

- Has there been high employee turnover and, if so, why?

  This will allow you to start forming a mental picture of the corporate culture and prepare you for additional questions surrounding this culture.

- Why is the job available?

  You'll want to know whether you have some big shoes to fill. It will also allow you to start figuring out how you'll fit in, whether you'll be accepted, or whether you've got to measure up to someone else's standards.

- How long has the position been available?

  This can indicate several things: a picky hiring manager, something undesirable about the position, or unrealistic expectations of the candidates they've interviewed. In today's job market, beware of a position that's been available for more than 60 days.

- Besides the company Website, how else would you recommend that I familiarize myself with your organization?

  This can open up some additional insider information that may not have normally been available to you. If you've built up enough rapport with the interviewer, consider asking for the company employee newsletter. It will provide you with valuable insight into the company culture.

The questions you ask will open up additional opportunities and enhance your rapport with the interviewer. Remember, the goal is to be as prepared as possible for the face-to-face interview. There is no excuse for not being prepared!

Questions to Ask the Hiring Manager

When asking questions of the hiring manager, you have to strike a careful balance. On the first interview, the questions you need to ask fall into three categories: questions regarding the company, questions regarding the department, and questions regarding the position. Though there are hundreds of possible questions to ask the hiring manager, you do have to be careful that the questions you end up asking are appropriate for your position and the situation.

Let's take an example. You are applying for a helpdesk position. You're meeting with the helpdesk manager.

Inappropriate Could you tell me the company's compounded growth rate for the past five years?

Appropriate How has the helpdesk staff grown over the past five years?

Follow-up What has driven the increase in staff?

See the difference?

In general, you can follow these guidelines to determine the appropriateness of the questions you should ask:

- Ask questions that will clearly define your role in the organization.
- Ask questions that will provide you with insight into the characteristics of a successful hire.
- Ask questions to find out how the position or department is perceived within the organization.
- Ask questions to gain a better understanding of the current challenges within the organization.
- Avoid interrogation questions of irrelevant topics such as corporate officers' salaries and a "grueling" analysis of the financial statements.
- Avoid questions that deal with issues outside the realm of IT.

Questions About the Company and the Department

Again, make sure the company questions are appropriate for the position that you are applying for. The questions set in *italics* are optional; all others are "must ask" questions.

- How many employees does the organization have? Where are they located?

  This will provide you with a general idea of the scale of the position and how you might be supporting a distributed organization.

- How do you provide IT support to these employees?

  Use this question to assess whether there is an appropriate ratio of IT support staff to the number of people within the organization.

- What are the organization's challenges in supporting all the company employees?

  You want to uncover preexisting issues that may play a factor in your decision to join the company. For example, if the company says they can't get a handle on technical support issues with field sales reps, you'll want to assess whether there is enough support staff available to do the job. It would also give you an indication of how you'll end up spending most of your day.

- *How large is the IT budget?*

  Or

  Do you feel that the company has allocated enough resources to get all of the current projects accomplished?

Success comes from having the right resources available to get the job done properly. This means people, time, and money. A lack in one resource, such as time, will result in an increase in the need for one of the other resources, people or money. Sometimes organizations are in denial of the appropriate resources required to accomplish their objectives. It's good to know these things up front before you accept the position.

- *How does the organization rank in its industry? Has this position changed in the last five years?*

  This will help you determine whether the organization is on its way up or down. Another way to frame this question may be to ask, "Who does the organization consider its greatest competitor and how does it effectively position itself to meet this competitive threat?" Going back to our discussion on appropriateness, this may not be an appropriate question for entry-level positions.

- What are the challenges the organization faces moving forward?

  For entry-level positions, you may want to skip this question.

- What role does the IT department play in solving these challenges?

  Another way to ask this type of question may be, "What are the company's priorities for the coming year as they pertain to this position and the IT department?"

- How is the IT department regarded within the organization? By the end-users? By management?

  This question helps you understand the attitudes that may help or hinder you in performing your job. You will probably have to work with others throughout the organization and it's best to understand if they will support you in doing your job or if you will be swimming against the tide.

- *What are the company's leading product lines?*

  Understanding what the company does and how it makes its money is extremely important. This will help you prioritize your work once you get on board and are asked to support a project.

- *What are the organization's biggest initiatives for the upcoming year?*

  Understanding priorities is important and will help you assess whether they are priorities that you will be able to support.

- *What major problems or challenges has the company recently faced? How were they addressed? How does IT fit into these initiatives?*

  If this question is inappropriate for you to ask try, "What are the biggest challenges the department has faced in the past year?"

- Is the IT department growing or shrinking?

  This question provides an indication of room for advancement. With a growing organization there will be greater opportunity for moving up the ranks if you are a star performer.

- Describe the company culture.

  This is an important question to help you assess whether you will fit in. Remember, hard qualifications are not the only things to look for. You want to ensure that you will be happy and challenged in your position.

- Describe the IT department culture.

  Some additional questions along these lines include, "What hours do others in the IT department keep?" "Do you expect employees to work on weekends and holidays?" "What's the on-call policy?" "Is the department structured?" "Are there set procedures for documentation?"

- What has been the company's layoff history in the last five years? Do you anticipate any cutbacks in the near future, and, if you do, how will they impact my department or position?

  You want to get an indication of whether the department brings on resources for special projects and then lays them off after the project is complete.

- Does the company have a build or buy philosophy?

  This question is particularly important because the number one motivator for IT professionals, as you know, is staying challenged. Typically, when an organization chooses a build strategy, there's greater challenge for all IT resources. With a buy mentality, you tend to function more in the integration and support mode, which may leave you wishing for a bigger challenge.

- *What is the organizational reporting structure for the CIO?*

  You can ask this question to have a clearer understanding of organizational support for the IT department. It can also indicate where new initiatives may originate and the buy-off process for organizational changes, infrastructure improvements, budgets, salary increases, and overall accountability.

- *How is the department organized?*

  This question helps you assess your room for growth. The more layers of management, the greater the possibilities for vertical growth. The more management disciplines, the greater the room for lateral or cross-functional growth. Remember, areas of growth don't necessarily mean just up and down the corporate ladder.

Questions About the Position

The following questions pertain to all IT positions for which you may be applying. The questions set in *italics* are optional; all others are "must ask" questions. Make sure you rehearse how to bring these questions up in your interview.

- Is this a new position?

  You need to know what boundaries you are working with—do you have the opportunity to define the expectations associated with this position or are you filling someone else's shoes? It's always good to ask this question up front so you can better position yourself in the interview.

- Am I replacing someone or have additional resources been made available for hiring this position?

  This question helps you understand whether the group is expanding or simply in maintenance mode. The addition of resources is a very positive indication of a healthy company.

- Can I speak to others who hold this same position?

  If the response is yes, be prepared to ask the questions covered in the next section. You will want to assess the current skill level of others who hold the position and their openness to accept a new team member. How will they take having a new kid on the block, especially if this new kid has more experience?

- *Will I be part of a larger team? What's the mission for the team? What are their responsibilities and what systems do they support/work on?*

  Of course you'll want to find out as much as you can about the team you'll be working with.

- How does that team fit in with the overall IT department?

  An important part of fitting in is interrelating with other groups in IT. If you're a developer, you'll want to find out about the project management and Q/A teams (if these teams exist). If you're interviewing for a position on the helpdesk, you'll want to find out more about your escalation team (and ensure that one exists.)

- *How does the company view the position?*

  The worst situation to walk into is one where management recognizes the need for a role, but the rest of the group resents your presence—for example, being brought on to build a time management system to track developer time allocations. Yikes—are you sure you want the position?

- How has the job been performed in the past?

  Technology changes quickly, but the basic functions with an IT department don't change as much. Finding out how the tasks required for the new position were previously accomplished will give you an idea of the level of sophistication within the organization and their commitment to getting it done right. To gain further insight into the evolution of the role, you may also want to ask why there was a need to change how the tasks are accomplished.

- What can you tell me about the responsibilities of the job?

  Obviously, you want to ensure you know all the responsibilities of the job. You may want to have the written job description in front of you when you ask this question so you can clarify any roles.

- What skills do you think are most critical for this job?

  This question will help you take charge of the interview by having the interviewer list the important characteristics they are looking for. You can then tailor your presentation of your skill sets to this exact position and save the interviewer the trouble of interviewing any further candidates.

- What kinds of people are most successful in this job?

  Here is another opportunity to tailor the interview to show what you bring to the organization. You can incorporate the characteristics they mention into your own asset statements.

- What resources are available to get the job done (budget, training, mentors, and other associates)?

  Earlier I mentioned that to do the job right you have to have three types of resources: time, people, and money. Here's where you can assess whether there's one missing and how the other resources will be leveraged.

- What kind of training should I expect and for how long?

  No one expects you to walk in on day one and know exactly what to do, right? Well, you never know. Now's the time to find out before you quit your current position and can't turn back.

- *What significant changes do you see for the department in the future?*

This question will provide insight into organizational development. With change there is potentially further opportunity and that can include growing the department and developing new expertise. It is unlikely that the hiring manager will let you in on any organizational changes that are confidential, but he certainly might try to sell you on additional opportunities for growth.

- *How many people will I manage? What are their responsibilities?*

  This question assumes that you will be joining the organization as a manager. Certainly part of the job description will include the number and roles of people within the team.

- *Describe the team members. How do they relate to each other? How well did they relate to their former boss? When can I meet them?*

  This is a follow-up to the previous question. It provides you with greater insight into how the team interrelates and how open they will be to a new leader. You should always ask to meet future team members to provide you with perspective on team dynamics and whether this is a team you would truly like to lead.

- *What type of information systems, software, e-mail, and voice mail are in place?*

  This question provides general information about the environment you will be working in.

- *How do my qualifications look to you?*

  This is a touchy one, but if you've established a rapport with the interviewer, you may just pull it off.

- *Is there no one from the organization who is qualified for the position?*

  This question sheds light on the organization's promotional preferences. If the hiring manager says that they conducted an internal search but did not find anyone with the existing appropriate skill sets, you may take that to mean they are committed to promoting from within. If, on the other hand, the manager says they were looking for fresh blood, you may question whether they are providing career advancement for their employees. A follow-up question may be, "What career development paths do you offer your employees?"

- *May I ask what your background is?*

  Or

  What has your career path been?

  It's important to know how the hiring manager ended up in his current position. It will provide you with insight on his management style, the culture within the department, and his overall philosophy on technology and getting the work done. Managers who have been with the company for less than two years may have a more aggressive approach to getting things done in comparison to managers who have risen in the ranks. That's because they have had exposure to other working environments and they bring different best practices to the job. Managers who have been with an organization for a long time may be more complacent and stuck in their ways.

- What do you find most satisfying about working here? Most frustrating?

  You want to get an honest answer. There is no perfect working environment. A manager who is up-front about his own challenges and frustrations will go a long way in earning his employees' trust in order to resolve those frustrations.

- *How would you describe your management style?*

  Is he a micromanager? Hands off? What autonomy does he allow his direct reports? How does he empower his team leaders? How does he evaluate performance? Who takes credit for team accomplishments?

- *How do you communicate with your employees?*

  Is there a regular staff meeting? Are team members encouraged to share their ideas in solving problems?

- What might be the potential career path within the company?

  You want to know that the company develops its people. If the hiring manager takes too long to answer this question, you might question the company's or the manager's commitment to advancing its employees.

- *How could the new employee make your life easier? What are your most important concerns about this job and the new hire?*

  This is a great lead-in question to other questions that assess the hiring manager's priorities. It also gives you an idea of the areas where the hiring manager will be most interested in seeing results.

- Can you describe a typical day in this position?

  You want to know, as much as possible, what you're walking into when you accept the position. There's nothing better than an hour-by-hour description of what the job entails. If the hiring manager cannot provide these details, make sure to ask to speak with someone else in the role.

- What is the first problem that would need the attention of the person you hire? What other problems need attention now? Over the next six months?

  This is another way of asking what the departmental priorities are.

- What would you like to be able to say about the new hire one year from now?

  With this question, you can get the hiring manager to tell you what his vision of success is so you can work toward it.

- Is there a probationary period associated with this position?

  It might be good to know if they have a probation period and how long it is, as it might affect benefits.

- *Do I have to relocate for this position? Ever?*

  Just because the position today does not require you to relocate, sometimes there are expectations of relocation later on. The same applies for working from home.

Questions to Ask Others Who Work There

Peers tell you a lot about how the organization really runs. It's important to get this perspective, as a hiring manager may try to sell you on an ideal situation because he has a project to complete and needs warm bodies. Remember, you are looking for your ideal situation. You want to use as many resources as possible to assess whether this is the right fit. Many of the questions that follow are the same questions you would ask the hiring manager. What you're looking for by asking these questions of others who work there is whether their responses align with those provided by the hiring manager. Notice that all these questions are "must ask" questions.

- How long have you worked here?

  This lets you know whether this is someone who believes in the company and the direction it's heading or whether they were just in your shoes not too long ago.

- What made you join the company?

  Let the person sell you on why you should join by giving his or her reasons for joining.

- What positions have you held since joining the organization?

  This gives you an idea of how the organization feels about promoting from within. It also gives you an idea of what you might expect from a career with this company.

- How regular are reviews and promotions?

  You want to beware of companies that offer very little feedback on performance, promotions, and raises. You don't want to have to haggle for every raise.

- What is your direct manager's management style?

  You are looking to avoid a micromanager or abusive manager situation.

- How is morale?

  If you're making a change, you want it to be to a positive, growing company, not one that has to convince its workers to come back every day.

- What do you like most/least about the organization?

  This is another advertisement for the company.

- What is your day like?

  If you are in a salaried position, you could be asked to work many hours beyond normal work hours. If the employee you are speaking with is coming in at 7 A.M. and leaving at 7 P.M., six days a week, it is obvious this is not just a 40-hour work week they are expecting.

- What are your biggest challenges in performing your job?

  A positive challenge: lots of new and exciting projects. A negative challenge: turnover leading to lack of stability of services.

- Do you feel you have the resources to do your job successfully?

  You should be looking for the right equipment—both quantity and quality.

- What is the most exciting thing about working here?

  You should be looking for an answer that rolls off the tip of his tongue. That means he is actually thrilled to come to work each day.

- What do you expect your career progression to be?

  You are looking for a possible career path within the organization.

- Does the organization support training and promoting from within?

  Keeping your IT skills current is the best thing you can do for your career. An IT department should recognize the need for regular training.

- How often does the department reorganize?

  A department that is constantly in reorganization leads to lack of productivity because of FUD (fear, uncertainty, and doubt).

- What is the department culture like?

  Here you can discover things about the department that the hiring manager may not have told you, such as how effectively teams within IT work together.

- How do others within the organization perceive the IT department?

  The IT department may not have the best reputation. You want to find out before you join the company. Being the object of contempt can be a very negative working environment.

- How regular are raises?

  The important thing to determine is whether they are given out as part of a regular review cycle. If the company hasn't given raises in multiple years, stay away or negotiate a good salary up front. The likelihood that you'll get one soon is very low.

- Are there any outstanding benefits you have taken advantage of?

  Some benefits might be overlooked in the regular interview. An employee might tell you about educational reimbursement, cell phones, laptops, PDAs, and other benefits for you to factor in when you are given an offer.

Closing the Deal

If you are at a loss for words when you hear the dreaded "Do you have any questions?" an excellent way of bringing the interview to a close is to ask questions about when and how the hiring decision will be made. The following set of questions will help you find out additional information. The questions set in *italics* are optional; all others are "must ask" questions.

- When do you expect to make a decision?
- *How many candidates do you expect to interview?*
- When do you need someone to start in the position?
- Is there anything else you need from me to have a complete picture of my qualifications?
- *Before you're able to reach a hiring decision, how many more interviews should I expect to go through and with whom?*
- How many candidates have been interviewed? How many more candidates will you be interviewing before you make a decision?

Checklist

Are you prepared to maximize your time with the interviewer? Being prepared with questions to ask the hiring manager is an important way to find out whether this is the right job for you.

- ☐ Do you have a strategy for incorporating your questions into the interview process rather than waiting until the very end when it may be too late to ask them?
- ☐ Have you identified the most important questions for you to ask the hiring manager?
- ☐ An excellent way of responding to "Do you have any questions?" is to inquire about how and when the hiring decision will be made.

Part IV

Closing the Deal

In This Part

Chapter 10

Staying on Top

The interview is over. Your heartbeat has returned to normal. Your sweaty palms have dried, and in the safety of your own home, you've had time to replay every moment of that tense hour in your head. So, that's it. Now you just sit around and wait for them to call and beg you to come work for them.

Or not.

Yes, the interview is over, but your chance to impress them isn't. In this chapter, I'll talk about the importance of follow-up, including:

- How and why to write a thank-you e-mail
- Scheduling your next steps
- Preparing for the second interview
- Checking up on your references

Yes, you've still got a bit of work ahead of you, but the really hard part is over. Don't let that fool you, though, into thinking you can skip the follow-up. Remember, as I've stressed throughout this book, success is in the details.

The Art of Follow-up

It's one thing to go out on an interview. It's another thing to turn that interview into a job offer, and follow-up is often the key. Many candidates discount the etiquette of following up after their interviews and then are stunned when the offers don't roll in.

So what's the trick? For starters, follow-up is more than calling to ask for a status report. In fact, a status report doesn't help you at all. You'll hear something like, "We're still interviewing candidates," or "We're going to make a decision sometime soon." This is not useful information. It doesn't help you, and it doesn't give you a chance to help the interviewer.

When you finished your interview and left the building, time didn't stop. You only went on one interview, but the interviewer saw many candidates. Some who came after you may have raised issues the interviewer never considered until that moment. He may suddenly be confronting specific problems and tasks that the new hire will need to address. But you never presented your ability to handle those tasks, because they weren't part of the position when you interviewed. You could be out of the running without even knowing it.

But you can prevent this from happening. You'll set the stage in your follow-up thank-you e-mail (I'll cover that in depth in a moment). When you call a few days later, you won't just say, "So, where do things stand?" You'll say:

> "I know that this position may still be evolving as you interview more candidates. Are there any new questions or concerns you have that I can address?"

In essence, you're allowing the interviewer to acknowledge the dynamic in play, and you're engaging him in a continuing dialogue. You're becoming a part of the hiring process, rather than standing by as a Mack truck plows through your dream job.

Thank You Very Much

Remember back in grade school when you had a birthday party? You opened up everyone's gifts, and your mom wrote down what everyone gave you. Later that night, before you could play with any of your cool new toys, you had to write thank-you notes to all your friends.

Turns out, Mom's pretty smart. She knew what she was talking about. Thank-you notes aren't just a social nicety. They're an unavoidable and important part of life. Think about it: the last time your brother came through town and you rearranged your schedule to pick him up at the airport at midnight, stocked the fridge with his favorite beer, skipped out on poker night with the guys, and got up at 5:00 A.M. to take him back to the airport. How'd you feel afterwards? A little put out? Now, imagine that when little brother left, you found a pair of tickets to the next Bulls game and a thank-you scribbled on the back of his used boarding pass on the unmade bed. You'd probably invite him back next time he's flying through, right?

Your interviewer took time out of his day to meet with you. Maybe he skipped lunch with a friend or stayed late to make up for lost time. When you send a thank-you note, you're saying, hey, I appreciate the trouble you went to on my account. You indicate your respect for his time. Respectful people make good employees and team members.

Thank Goodness for E-mail!

Luckily, these days, hiring managers aren't expecting a paper thank-you card but they do expect you to acknowledge that you took up their time. Looking for what to say? Here's your cheat sheet.

Sample Thank-You E-mails

When you write your message, take your cues from the interview. Did you address the interviewer as Ms. Jones? Then write, "Dear Ms. Jones" in your note. Did she tell you to call her Jane? Then address her as "Dear Jane" when you write.

Once you're past the salutation, what you say depends on how the interview went and what you're hoping to accomplish now. If the interview went well and you're writing the note for form's sake, a basic thank-you letter should suffice:

> *Thank you for taking the time to meet with me yesterday to discuss the open software developer position at AVT. I enjoyed the opportunity to hear about the company firsthand, and I appreciate the time you took to show me the various labs you have onsite.*
>
> *I know we discussed my technical abilities in depth yesterday. I also want to let you know how enthusiastic I am about working with your staff—everyone I met impressed me as hard-working and team-oriented.*
>
> *I look forward to speaking with you in the next few days. If you have any more questions for me, please don't hesitate to be in touch.*

If you forgot to mention something specific at your interview—relevant experience, for example, or something else that might put you ahead of other candidates—a thank-you e-mail can address that as well. Try something like:

> *I meant to mention yesterday that during my NASA internship, I had the opportunity to work with 3-D modeling equipment. I had to learn the software on my own in about two weeks, and I was able to master it well enough in that time that I could render my models without additional help from the very busy staff engineers.*
>
> *I know that you and your staff are under a lot of pressure to roll products out on time, and I want to stress that I am a quick study, and I'm not afraid to learn on my own.*

Occasionally, you might leave an interview feeling like you didn't make a good impression. The interviewer wanted specific skills you have, but couldn't articulate. Describe these in your note:

> *I want to clarify something from our interview yesterday. You expressed concern at my lack of experience in project management. It's true that I haven't served in the official capacity of project manager, but I have frequently taken the reins and run projects when others were unable to do so.*
>
> *For example, several months ago, my project manager was unexpectedly placed on emergency bed rest, and my team had an important deadline to meet. I contacted our remote groups via e-mail and made sure that everyone stayed on track. I also coordinated with our Q/A teams in the home office, and made sure that tests were conducted on time. I kept the project manager up to speed with frequent phone calls and e-mail updates. My quick decisions and ability to step up kept the whole project from derailing.*

Another approach is to actively demonstrate your enthusiasm for the company and its projects and entice the employer. Like this:

> *I've been thinking about our interview all evening. We only spoke briefly about the new FTR software release, but I have several ideas that I believe will greatly enhance the next version of your product. Specifically, these changes—which could all be implemented on your current development schedule, ensuring a timely rollout—would allow you to significantly broaden your user base by making the software extremely attractive to the lucrative higher education market.*

When you sign off, use the closing that feels right to you. "Sincerely," "Yours truly," "Respectfully," "Very truly yours," and even "Best always" are all good choices. The most important thing is to e-mail the thank-you note *within 24 hours of your interview.*

Tips for Great Thank-You E-mails

Be careful not to sabotage your effort by making a crucial mistake. Follow these quick tips for success:

- Make sure you spell the names and titles of your interviewers correctly. Ideally, you got their business cards at the interview. If you have to call to verify spelling, do so. If you do have to call to verify spelling, also verify the pronunciation on any names that you are having a hard time remembering. After you get off the phone, repeat these out loud several times so you will be prepared for the follow-up calls.
- Don't let spelling mistakes mar the rest of your message, either. Use spell-check.
- Remember to thank the interviewer for his time and attention, and remind him why you're the right person for the job.
- Always personalize your message, especially when you're sending multiple messages within an organization.

The Next Steps

Once the thank-you e-mail has been sent, you can move on to the next phase of your follow-up. Your strategy is twofold: you want to keep your name in front of the employer so that you're on his mind when he makes a decision, and you want to be an active participant in the hiring process.

Of course, proper organization will help you immensely as you plot and track your follow-up. You can keep a file that records when your thank-you was e-mailed, the results of your follow-up calls, and any follow-up interviews you schedule.

Phone Follow-up

It's best to wait about three to five days after the interview to call, unless the interviewer indicated otherwise. This way, your e-mail will have arrived, and the interviewer will probably have spoken with other candidates. Remember, based on those interviews, the company may have reevaluated its needs. Be sure to address this possibility by saying something like, "Are you still looking for the same skills we discussed? Or have your needs changed?" If the interviewer admits they need something slightly different, ask him to elaborate. Then show him that you're still in the running by pointing out your abilities in the new area:

> "I see. We didn't talk much about my networking experience at the interview, but you'll notice on my résumé that I did set up and maintain cross-platform networks for several departments at my college. In fact, I also do network troubleshooting on the side—I have several local clients who use me on a contract basis."

To keep yourself in the game, use this phrase or a variation of it:

"Is there any other information I can give you that might help alleviate any reservations you have about hiring me?"

When you've answered all the questions you can, ask again for a timetable. "When would you like me to check back with you?" or "When do you think you'll be making a decision?" Both work well. If the interviewer refuses to be pinned down, call once a week.

Tips to Prevent Crossed Wires

When you call, keep these tips in mind:

- Call early in the morning or late in the afternoon. You're less likely to be screened by a secretary or assistant.
- Introduce yourself and remind the interviewer who you are. He may have interviewed dozens of candidates.
- Don't harass people with daily phone calls. Once a week, or on the interviewer's timetable, is enough.
- Always be impeccably polite. If you burn your bridges, you will eventually regret it. Things change quickly in IT and you could be the top candidate for the next opening if you leave the door open.
- Always ask the interviewer if he has a moment to speak with you, and always thank him for his time.

Double Take: The Second Interview

The phone rings, and it's your interviewer. Your heart races with anticipation—your long-awaited offer is finally here! Well, almost. Actually, the interviewer would like you to come back for a second interview.

Second (and even third and fourth) interviews aren't uncommon. Put yourself in the interviewer's shoes: if the position has evolved, he needs to be sure that his top candidates are still on top. And it's easiest to make that determination in person.

A second interview can also be a trial run of sorts—a chance to introduce you to the team and see if you fit in. Remember that if you've been asked to come back for a second interview, the odds are considerably more in your favor than they were before. The company likes you and wants to be able to hire you. You just have to make it easy for them to offer you a job.

In some cases, the first interview might not have been very technical, and you might have thought they liked you so much you were going to escape a technical grilling. This sequence can be reversed, but usually the first interview will cover your work history and other general topics, and reveal if you might fit in. The second or subsequent interviews will likely be more technical. When you receive the phone invitation to the second interview, the attendees and specific contents of that interview may be discussed. The hiring manager might actually give you some information on the types of technical questions they will be asking. It is possible that you will be sitting with the manager you would be working for, and possibly one of his staff who is highly technical and has been brought in specifically to probe your knowledge.

Don't get too confident, though: the competition is now stiffer than it was earlier. You're up against all the best people the interviewer saw. So you still need to stand above the rest of the crowd.

What to Expect

You'll probably start off by having a brief discussion with the person who interviewed you. Then you'll be introduced to the team you'd work with, and you may be interviewed briefly by one or more team members. Finally, you'll meet some upper-level managers, and possibly even endure a panel interview.

None of this is done as a formality. People are busy, and they don't ask you to participate in interviews because they enjoy torturing candidates. They have a real reason for introducing you to certain people or asking specific questions. You might not know exactly why they're putting you through these tests, but they do. So keep a smile on your face, and keep your snide comments to yourself. No sense in sabotaging yourself when the prize is in sight.

You may suddenly find yourself in a group situation where a problem is offered and possible solutions are bandied about. Don't waste a lot of time psychoanalyzing yourself or the people around you. Simply behave normally. Don't ever be afraid to speak up, though. If you have an idea you think will help, say so. It could easily make a difference, and it just may get you a job offer.

If you are invited to a panel interview, position your chair somewhere that allows you to keep all the interviewers in your line of sight. Don't be afraid to physically move your chair. You can simply say, "I'd like to be able to see everyone, so I'm just going to move my chair over here." It's unlikely that anyone will object. On the contrary, they'll note your initiative as a positive trait.

If one member of the panel, or any of the interviewers you encounter, seems bent on disagreeing with everything you say, don't take it personally. He could be having a bad day (or a bad life). He could be testing you to see if you stick to your guns and stand up for yourself, how you handle pressure, or if you're likely to overreact. Stay calm. Smile. Repeat your answer, and back it up with information. If you're really feeling harassed, excuse yourself for a moment and take some deep breaths. But try not to resort to this tactic—part of what the interviewer wants to know may be whether you have what it takes to make it in a high-pressure position. If a few tough questions throw you for a loop, what will you do when a major project is on the line and a client throws a wrench into the works?

Be the First Choice at a Second Interview

Obviously, you did something right at your first interview, or you wouldn't have been invited back. So should you be exactly the same at your second interview? Yes and no.

Just as the company will now prepare a second, more in-depth round of questions for you, you should also go to the same trouble. Take the time to prepare a list of any questions about the company that went unanswered (or unasked) in the first interview. Type them up if you want to look really professional.

You'll also want to do some extra research on the company. When you're asked back, inquire if there's anything specific you should prepare. Then ask if you can get any more material on the company. Scour their Website again, and do Internet searches on the company and every person you spoke with at your first interview. You might discover a shared interest you can casually bring up at your second interview.

If you have a contact who has been interviewed by this company previously, he may be able to tell you more details about the second interview, what it consists of, and how technical it might be.

If you wore a suit and tie to the first interview, do so again, even if everyone at the office was in shorts. The only exception is if they say to you, "Please feel free to dress casually." Even if they say that, casual means clothes that have been laundered and ironed, and shirts with writing are almost always inappropriate. It's very likely you'll be meeting some higher-ups this time around, so you want to dress to impress them.

Many companies schedule multiple second interviews for the same day, so their staff can meet everyone at once. You need to work hard to stand out. Remember to smile and shake hands with every person you meet. Get names, repeat them, and ask for business cards. Make up your seating chart again, just like the first interview. Take your own business cards as well so you have something to offer in return.

Responding to Offers

You may get an offer at the end of a second interview. Not all companies do this, however, so don't think you're out of the running if you go home empty-handed. If you do walk away with a job offer, don't commit to an answer on the spot. Always ask for time to consider the offer properly. You don't want to seem too eager. You also don't want to jump to accept an offer that might not be right for you.

Most companies won't insist that you accept or reject an offer before you leave the premises. If they do, this could reveal a major drawback about the company. A company that treats employees disrespectfully before they are even employees might force people to make other employment decisions in a rushed manner, such as transfers, raises, and promotions. No matter how much you want the job, don't be pushed into a quick response. I'll cover salary negotiations and evaluating the overall offer in the next chapter. For now, thank the company for the offer, and tell them you'll get back to them shortly. Try not to give a definite date. Take at least 48 hours to evaluate all offers, and aim for about a week.

When You Don't Get an Offer

There will be times when you're certain you'll get the job—you've received great positive feedback, the interviewer introduced you around as the newest member of the team—but then the offer never comes through. Every time you call to follow up, you're given the brush-off. You're almost tempted to go down and stake out the employee parking lot to find out whether the interviewer was hit by a bus.

Here's how to prevent this situation from happening. Most likely, they indicated their interest in you personally, but you forgot to qualify the actual employment opportunity by asking the following very basic questions.

- Has this position been approved?
- Who else must I meet with as part of the recruitment process?
- When will you be making your decision?
- When do you need this position to be filled?

Though you can never fully prepare yourself for the letdown with these situations, it does help to remain detached on all interviews. Don't get emotionally involved until you have a written offer letter in your hand. More on offer letters in Chapter 11.

When You Don't Make the First Cut

Another situation that sometimes happens is you don't come in first place. The full-time position is already filled by the time you respond to an opening or you're not the number one candidate. Often, employers have additional needs—temporary contract-basis needs. There are a number of ways to look at this situation. If you are currently unemployed, like the company, and don't have better offers, why not take the position? It's certainly a way to get your foot in the door and earn some additional experience as well as cash.

If you are currently employed and want to consider the position, you really need to weigh the pros and cons of the situation. Contract positions typically do not include benefits such as vacation time, sick time, medical insurance, 401(k) plans—all the things you may be taking for granted at your current position. Is the salary enough to cover paying for these benefits yourself? What about taxes? Self-employment taxes can be a pain in the neck. Are you truly prepared to go out on your own?

Any Questions?

Of course you have questions to ask your initial interviewer. But you should also have at least one question ready to ask everyone you meet at your second interview. To get you started, here are some sample questions you can ask the different groups of people you might encounter on your return visit to a company.

If your original interviewer is part of the second interview process, ask him:

- Has the definition of this position changed since the last time we spoke?
- Do you have any new questions or concerns I can address?
- What kind of timetable are you working on at this point?
- Is there anything specific you'd like me to elaborate on?

If you are introduced to potential coworkers, ask them:

- What do you like best about working here? Least?
- What's a typical workday like?
- What kind of promotion potential is there?

- What are your normal hours?
- How often are you expected to work overtime?
- How much of your work is independent? With teams?
- What kind of management style is used?
- How much do you interact with management?
- How long have you worked here?
- Do you feel like your job is secure?

Some questions to ask your potential boss include:

- What would be my primary responsibilities?
- How long do you think it'll take me to get up to speed?
- What would I be expected to accomplish in the first week here? The first month? The first year?
- What are the projects I would be working on?
- What would I need to learn on my own? Who could I go to with questions?
- How much contact would I have with you?
- In your opinion, what makes an ideal employee?

When you talk to the hiring manager, ask her:

- What drew you to this company?
- What do other employees like best about the company? Least?
- What's the most common reason for employee turnover?
- What's the rate of employee turnover?
- How long has this position been vacant? Why is it open?
- What kind of orientation do new employees receive?
- Is the company under a raise freeze? Have you ever been?
- How often are raises and promotions given?
- How often are performance reviews given?
- What are the long-range possibilities for this position?
- What is your benefits package like?
- How long do benefits take to kick in?

Second Thoughts? Other Things to Consider

It's exciting to be asked back for a second interview. But don't fall into the trap of thinking that everything is absolutely rosy at the company. You don't have to suspect the company's motives, but you should be careful to temper your excitement and carefully evaluate the total picture presented.

Use your second interview to your advantage. Take the time to really look around. Can you see yourself fitting in here? Do these people share your values? Do you want to help this company's bottom line for a living?

Ask yourself:

- Are the people who work here happy?
- Do they seem to enjoy what they do?
- Are they nice? Helpful? Moody? Unkind?
- Are people enthusiastic about the job? The company?
- Do you feel welcome?
- Do you like the people?
- Do you like the atmosphere?
- Do you think you could be happy here?

It's okay to decide that you don't really want this job. There will always be another one that's more suited to you and your needs.

Take Two: Second-Round Follow-up

Guess what you have to do after your second interview? That's right, now is when you send thank-you notes to everyone you spoke with *again*. It's not okay to let it slide, even if you're one hundred percent sure you don't want the job.

If you met with an entire department, you do not have to write individual e-mails to everyone there. You can pick someone you connected with and ask him to forward your e-mail to the rest of the team.

Follow the tips offered earlier in the chapter when composing these notes, but make sure each one is personalized. If you're still interested in the position, say so:

> I really enjoyed having a chance to meet with you personally to hear about your vision for the company. I hope that I can be a part of the team that realizes that vision with you.

Sincere enthusiasm is always welcome. Employers like people who want to help the company succeed.

Again, wait three to five days after your second interview, then call the interviewer to touch base. Always try to find out a timeline: how soon will a decision be made? When should you call again? See if there are any new issues you can address. If you're part of the process, you're poised to become the company's solution.

Checking Up on Your References

When you offer your references to a prospective employer, what happens? Typically, they call or e-mail the people you've indicated and ask them several questions. They're not going to pick apart every bullet point on your résumé. Rather, they're going to try to gauge an overall impression of you as a person and as an employee.

The people you choose as references should obviously be people who like and respect you. It's okay to include one coworker who is at your level, but you should definitely include your supervisor or project manager, and if you can also include a higher-level manager, so much the better.

Always ask permission to use someone as a reference. While you're at it, ask for a letter of reference, typed on company letterhead. If you can get such a letter, make several dozen copies and save them to distribute when necessary.

If you're still using references from three jobs ago, keep tabs on people. Call your references yourself every few months. Say hello, verify that people are still reachable at the same numbers—and network.

If someone provides a particularly glowing reference, send a nice thank-you note or a small gift, such as flowers or candy. Remember: take good care of the people who take good care of you.

Checklist

Follow-up is a crucial part of your job hunt, and an integral part of the interview process. In fact, many interviewers believe that candidates who don't bother to follow up don't really want the job. After all, how often do you hear people speak negatively about someone who aggressively goes after a dream job? Not often. But we've all heard stories about people who let their dream job slip away.

Keep this checklist handy to make sure your follow-up doesn't fall through the cracks.

- ☐ Did you send a thank-you e-mail within 24 hours of your interview?
- ☐ Did you call three to five days after your initial interview to offer to answer any additional questions?
- ☐ Did you get a sense of the interviewer's hiring timeline so you can schedule your next follow-up phone call?
- ☐ If you were invited to a second interview, did you prepare properly?
- ☐ Did you send second-round thank-you notes?
- ☐ Did you make second-round follow-up phone calls?

After all that hard work, you should have an offer or two to show for your trouble. Continue to the next chapter to find out how to make sure the offer you get is the best one out there.

Chapter 11

Evaluating Offers

When that first job offer comes in, it's like manna is raining down from heaven. It's difficult to control your elation, and you're tempted to accept the offer on the spot. Wait! Don't do it. You've worked hard and come so far, it would be a shame to throw everything away by rushing to accept an offer that may not be right for you and can certainly be improved.

This chapter will give you vital information on:

- How to objectively evaluate an offer
- How to negotiate the best possible offer
- How to get the highest possible salary

Pay close attention. Absorbing the information in this chapter could put you in a higher tax bracket. Follow my advice, but only if you're ready to get a great offer and lots of money.

Getting the Offer

"We're going to send you An Offer." You can hear the capital letters over the phone, and if you're like most people, you're properly awed. But listen a little more closely, and what do you notice? They didn't say they were sending you their *final* offer. They said they were sending *an* offer. It's their *opening* offer, their first move. *Their first move.* What most job-seekers don't know or can't accept is that *no one expects you to take the first offer.*

In fact, if you do take the company's first offer, you can start yourself off on a lifetime of being underpaid and undervalued. A quick lesson in human nature: for better or for worse, the more expensive something is, the more value we associate with it. A Jaguar costs more than a Toyota. Is the Jag a better car? Maybe, maybe not—but there's certainly more prestige associated with it.

The In-Person Offer

Occasionally, a company will make you an offer in person, and they may use all sorts of tactics to try to get you to respond on the spot. This is a huge warning sign. You should never be pressured into accepting an offer. Do they have something to hide? If not, why are they trying so hard to get you to sign on the dotted line?

THE "BUY SIGNALS"

You will identify the most appropriate time to negotiate salary by recognizing positive signs or "buy signals" from the interviewer. If, toward the end of the interviewing process, you start experiencing these signals, then you're in. Feel free to negotiate away.

- Interviewer asks, "When can you start?"
- Interviewer questions you to see if you really like or want the job.
- Interviewer tries to obtain details about your non-competition contract and how much notice you must give to leave your present job.
- Interviewer tries to find out if you have other job offers.
- Interviewer shares confidential files with you.
- Interviewer describes the fringe benefits of his company.
- Interviewer tells you he's shared your résumé with a key person in the organization.
- Interviewer mentions you are one of only two candidates still under consideration.
- Interviewer starts using "when" instead of "if."
- Interviewer introduces you to future subordinates.
- Interviewer's assistant becomes friendlier.

So what do you say when you receive an offer in person? First of all, thank the employer. Next, if you have not received a formal offer in writing, ask for it. For example, if the employer says:

> "We'd really like to have you on board. I'd like you to join our team. Could you start on the first of the month?"

You can respond with:

> "Thank you. I appreciate all the time you've spent with me and how thoroughly I've gotten to know your company. Do you have a formal offer package I can look at?"

Rarely, the employer will press the issue:

> "Well, yes, we'll do all that official paperwork later. But will you come work for us?"

You need to stay pleasant but firm. Blame a spouse or significant other:

> "You know, if I made a decision like this without talking to my [wife/husband/fiancé], I wouldn't have a place to live anymore. I need to show him (or her) something in writing."

Explain to the employer that an important decision deserves careful consideration:

> "I really need a few days to think about this. Accepting this job isn't something I take lightly, and I'd like to make sure I give your offer the proper thought."

If the employer absolutely refuses to give you time to think about the offer or refuses to put an offer in writing until you accept, run, don't walk, to the nearest exit. Fortunately, most employers are not crazy, and they know full well that they need to give you a formal, written offer and adequate time to consider it.

Always try to get at least a week to consider an offer. Some employers say things like, "This offer is good for 48 hours," or "We really need a response by Friday morning." If it's not enough time, ask for more. If you ask for six months, you won't get it. But it's perfectly reasonable to say:

> "I appreciate that you want to move forward quickly, and I do, too. But my wife is out of town until Thursday, so I really can't give you my answer before Monday."

Or:

> "I don't like to make important decisions in a rush. I'd really like to have a full week to consider your offer. Is that all right?"

The employer will most likely realize that he'll look unreasonable if he turns you down, and your request will be granted. If you make your decision early, you can give it to them before your deadline, but if you do need the extra time, you'll have it.

You can do the same for offers made over the phone. Simply request that the employer e-mail or courier a written offer to you, or arrange an in-person meeting to pick up the offer package.

Written Offers

If an offer arrives in writing, immediately reply using the same medium (e-mail, fax, or courier) with a short note thanking the employer for the offer and indicating that you will consider it and return a reply within the agreed-upon window. Again, if the employer indicates that you must respond within less time than you feel comfortable with, simply say so in your note:

> "Thank you for the offer package you sent via FedEx this morning. You indicated that you would like a response by the end of this week, but I'd really like to take the weekend to think it over and give your offer the consideration it deserves. Would it be all right if I called you with my answer on Monday morning?"

As before, refusing your request puts the employer in an awkward position, so you probably don't have anything to worry about.

Evaluating the Offer

Now you have time to think it over. So what exactly are you supposed to be thinking about? You'll want to consider several things.

First of all, what are your overall impressions of the company and what it does? Did you like the people you met? The people you'll be working with daily? Obviously, if you vehemently disagree with the company's major philosophies or hated everyone you met, you shouldn't work there. But if you think you could be happy working there, you can go on to evaluate the rest of the offer.

Of course you need to consider the rate of turnover at the company, and in the position in particular. If the last three people who held the job left after three weeks, think very carefully before accepting. Examine closely any company with a high rate of employee turnover.

You'll also want to look at growth opportunities, for yourself and for the company. Is the industry one that is thriving? Is the company large enough to offer the responsibilities you hope to take on? If you're thinking of going to work for a start-up, do they have enough capital to carry them through the next two years? Be wary of any new company that says their funding is in the bag but won't offer any tangible proof.

What will your commute be like? Will you have to spend an hour and a half in traffic—each way—every day? Will the wear and tear on your car, and the cost of gas, be worth it to you? Will you have any time left over for the rest of your life?

It's important also to consider travel requirements. If you'll have to relocate, of course, make sure that you're happy with the location and that the rest of your family is, too.

Even if the job isn't your dream job, think carefully before rejecting the offer out of hand. Could this job be a stepping-stone to something better? Will it offer skills and experience you need to get your dream job? It may be worth your while to put in some time doing less-than-glamorous work for a year or two while you soak up information and technology training that will serve you well for the rest of your career.

Ideally, you should first truly and honestly answer all of the above questions before you move on to consider the salary package. It's important for you to know whether you really want the job in question. If you do, you can probably get the company to pay you what you're worth. If you really don't want the job, you shouldn't be swayed by a high salary offer. Eventually, all the reasons that you don't want to work there will surface, and you'll find yourself back in the job market. So move on to salary considerations only after you've first evaluated the rest of the offer.

It's All About the Money

Ah, the joy of salary negotiations. Many a job-seeker has been totally thrown by this part of the job hunt. Far too many candidates feel pressured to accept offers that are, simply put, not worthy of them, because they don't understand the rules of the game.

Know Your Worth

The first step to successful salary negotiations is to have an accurate picture of what you're worth. Some of the best resources on the Web are Dice.com, MCPMag.com, and Certmag.com. These sites sponsor annual salary surveys that can help you identify what you're worth based on job title and where you live.

But don't stop there.

Whether you're a desktop support engineer or a VB.NET developer, there are industry-specific magazines you can look to for more targeted information. Most of these magazines publish an annual salary survey. Check your library or online archives to find the most recent one. It's important to check multiple resources to make sure that the range presented is accurate.

Take your location into account. If you live and work in midtown Manhattan, you should expect a higher salary than if you live and work in, say, Point Pleasant, West Virginia.

SALARY NEGOTIATION MYTHS

Strong myths exist about salary negotiations. They are being kept alive by job candidates who are unsure of themselves and by unscrupulous interviewers who want to take advantage of candidates. Don't get caught up in these myths:

Myth #1: Everything the interviewer says is true.

It's the interviewer's job to bargain with you! That means not laying out all his cards. The less they pay you, the more money they have for other things. Don't let yourself fall into the trap of believing things that may be untrue.

Myth #2: Exceptions do not exist.

Situation by situation, organizations can always break the rules and make exceptions on salary amounts. If they really need you, they will find tangible means to convince you to join them.

Myth #3: The first figure is often a good one.

One of the most common errors is to believe that you have to accept the first offer made to you during the negotiation because you fear that it will be the only offer. Wrong! The first offer is just the starting point. Remember, if they want to hire you, they will negotiate.

Myth #4: Salaries are never negotiable.

Salaries are always negotiable. If an organization needs and wants you, they will negotiate.

Once you've established the basic range for your position and location, you know the range you should be asking for in your initial interviews. Ask for the higher end of the range if you have a lot of specific experience or something special to offer a company. If you're less experienced, you'll probably have to settle for the lower end of the range.

Strategies for Successful Negotiations

It's crucial to understand that salary negotiations are an expected part of the job search process. If you accept a company's first offer, you start off at a disadvantage. Likewise, if you start off by telling the company, "The absolute lowest amount I can accept is $X," guess what you'll get? You may not want to play this part of the game, but you don't really have a choice. Accept it, and play to win.

Rules of the Game

If your interview is arranged by a recruiter, you may be specifically told not to talk money. This is good and bad. You put the recruiter in the position of the bad guy who asks about money and negotiates a deal for you. You will probably get more money this way, but it may, in some cases, cost you the job. If the recruiter refuses to budge, you may never even hear about an offer he deemed too low, or the company may decide you're too expensive and choose not to pursue you.

Always be up front with your recruiter. If you're using a good recruiter, he'll be someone who companies trust, and he'll be poised to negotiate the best possible deal for you.

It goes without saying that if you've signed an agreement with the recruiter not to talk salary with the employer, you are bound by that agreement. Don't be swayed by an employee who promises not to tell. Such strategies always backfire. You'll lose everyone's trust.

Pass the Ball

When you are at liberty to negotiate your own salary, always try to delay. You should have some indication of a range being offered for the position, but avoid talking specifics until there is an actual job offer on the table. If the interviewer asks early in your initial interview—or at any point before a formal offer is on the table—what kind of salary you expect, your first counter should be:

"I'd prefer not to talk about salary unless you're offering me a job."

Say it pleasantly, and with a smile. Of course the interviewer will smile back and say, just as pleasantly:

"I understand, but I'd really like to get a sense of what you're expecting."

You can try again to turn it around. If there was an advertised range for the position, you can say, "I'm comfortable with the advertised range." If the interviewer still presses with something like, "But what's the lowest amount you would accept?" or some such drivel, you can probably quiet him with this:

> "I'm uncomfortable being pinned down to a number, especially since we're talking hypothetically. If you're ready to make me an offer, I'll be happy to talk specifics. I've given you the range with which I'm comfortable. What I'd really like to talk about now is if there's anything that's preventing you from making me an offer."

If the interviewer absolutely refuses to move on without a number, you should seriously consider whether you want to work for that company. Under no circumstances should you ever reveal the actual lowest number you've come up with. Always add something onto that number, otherwise you've eliminated all your wiggle room right off the bat.

STAND OUT!

Mentioning salary surveys can be helpful to you and the employer. Mention them to create a win/win scenario.

Crunch Time

At some point, though, you will have to do the actual salary negotiations. If you've done your research and you know your worth, you have nothing to worry about. Let's say the range you're looking for is $65,000 to $72,500 annually. The offer you're handed is for $65,500. Great! That's right in your range! Accept, smile happily, and be on your way.

Or not.

What you do right now sets the tone for the rest of your working relationship with this company. If you take their first offer, you indicate that:

- You're willing to accept anything they offer you.
- They don't have to offer you very much—in fact, they probably could have offered you less.
- You're not very savvy.

Granted, they won't rescind the offer if you accept immediately, but they'll probably be left thinking they might have just purchased a lemon. Think of it this way: You head on over to the used car lot to pick yourself out a nice set of wheels. You see something that catches your fancy. The sticker price listed is $5,000. "How about $4,500?" you say, and the salesman enthusiastically says, "Sure! No problem!" Hmmm... he sure seems in a hurry to unload the car, doesn't he?

If, instead, he shakes his head and says, "Sorry. Can't do it. This is a great car, and I can't let her go for less than $4,900," the very same car now seems more valuable. You want it even more, and you're going to have to work for it. Now, don't you think you're worth more than a used car?

So when that offer for $65,500 comes, instead of rushing to accept it, try this:

"$65,500. That seems a little bit low."

Look pensive. Don't speak. Do whatever you have to do to keep from speaking. Just sit there. And wait.

Silence makes people uncomfortable. You can repeat that in your head if you want. Just don't move your lips. Keep waiting. The silence will stretch out, and just when you think you are going to die, the employer will say, "Well, I guess we could come up to... $67,000." Just like that, you can upgrade to expanded cable. For ten seconds of discomfort, you've earned $1,500 more a year. Not bad!

Why It Works

Many candidates mistakenly believe that if they ask for more money, the company will rescind the offer of employment. It's not going to happen. Here's why.

If the company has gone to the trouble of making you an offer, they want you to work there. Although $1,500 is a lot of money to you, it's really not much to a big business, and it's only a little stretch for even the smallest businesses.

Remember, too, that companies hire people all the time. They've learned a thing or two about negotiating over the years. So if you truly believe them when they say, "Look, we're really not into all those salary negotiation games. We've come up with a number, and this is really it. This is what we can afford," you're deluding yourself. No true businessman will make his first offer with his final number.

And guess what? If the employer really, truly can't afford to go any higher and says so, at least he'll know that you believe you're worth more. He'll treat you better and have more respect for you. In addition, there are other ways he can boost the value of the overall offer—I'll cover those in a moment.

STAND OUT!

Benefits can mean much more than health insurance.

ADVANCED NEGOTIATION TECHNIQUES

Sometimes the negotiations can get a little more complicated. Here are some additional negotiation tips that will come in handy:

- If you're a naturally confident person, or if you've spent enough time rehearsing that you can fake it, try this: when you state your desired salary range, take the top figure of the employer's stated salary range, and extend it 5 to 15 percent above their range. The employer will see that you're in the general ballpark, but clearly think you're worth a little more than the average candidate. It won't turn them off—in fact, they'll work harder to get you, because they'll perceive you as being more valuable.
- If you're asked to share your present salary and it's lower than what you should be making, consider demonstrating the percentage increases you've enjoyed over your last few raises or job changes. You might still have to offer a final figure, but giving the percentage information may satisfy the interviewer.
- If you're pressed to share your current salary and it is significantly lower than market value, state your awareness of this fact: "The opportunity to work in the semiconductor industry was exciting to me as a new grad, so I was willing to accept a starting salary of $55,000. But the experience I've gained over the last two years means that I should be making closer to $72,000 now, and that's really what I'm looking for."
- If the company indicates at your first interview that their "budget" will only allow for a salary that is lower than what you want, remember that their budget is, in fact, an arbitrary number that has nothing to do with you. Ask if part of your compensation can be counted against next year's budget, or if money could come from a different part of the budget to pay you what you're worth. Always be pleasant and professional, but let the company know that you're not going to be bullied into accepting less than you deserve.

Additional Negotiations

It's important to look at the total compensation package. One job might offer a base salary that's higher than you expected, but if the company doesn't offer health insurance—or offers an HMO that doesn't provide the coverage of a PPO—you'll wind up with a lot of out-of-pocket expenses.

If an employer can't quite meet the salary you're hoping for, you can often negotiate increased benefits to make up the difference. Things to consider:

Vacation Can you get additional vacation time? If you have religious holidays that will cut into your time off, can you exchange days like Christmas and New Year's for those holidays without penalty?

Retirement Plan If the company doesn't currently offer a retirement plan, will they make your IRA contributions each year? Do they intend to start a 401(k) or other retirement plan? Have you seen something in writing to this effect?

Insurance Does the employer pay 100 percent of your premium? Are your spouse and children covered as well? Will the employer pay other insurance premiums, such as life, disability, or even homeowner's? If they can't offer health insurance from your first day on the job, will they pay your COBRA (or other insurance) premiums until you're covered by their policy?

Tuition Assistance Will the company pay for courses that will keep you current in your field? Can you get a master's degree or MCSD on the company's dime?

Childcare Will the employer contribute to your child's day care costs?

Flextime/Telecommuting Can you set your own hours or work from home on a regular basis?

Obviously, you shouldn't expect an employer to offer all of these benefits at the highest possible rate, but choose the ones that are most important to you and ask for them. Remember, always start off by asking for more than you want—within reason. You need room to negotiate, but you don't want to come across as greedy and obnoxious.

WHAT TO DO WHEN YOU'RE BLINDSIDED BY A LOWBALL OFFER

It happens. You did everything right—researched the market, came up with your range, presented it to the employer, and sat back in your chair. When the offer came in, it was for about $20,000 less than you anticipated. What do you do?

First of all, you can show the employer your honest reaction—laugh out loud. Don't be afraid, they're the ones who should be embarrassed. Now, explain why you're laughing. Be polite and succinct, and show them precisely why there's no way you can accept their offer:

> "I'm sorry. I don't mean to be rude, but you caught me off guard. When I presented you with the range I'm looking for, I didn't just pick a number out of thin air. I spent several weeks studying salary reports. I checked several Websites, read the annual salary reports published in *Certification Magazine*, *.NET Developer*, and several other industry publications, and I reviewed the ranges offered for other similar positions in the area. No one indicates that I should take less than $70,000 a year. You're offering $50,000. Unless you're prepared to revise your offer significantly, I'm afraid I'll have to decline."

The company may truly be clueless. You might provide them with a wake-up call, and their next offer could surprise you. Or they might shrug their shoulders and say, "Well, this is all we're prepared to offer you."

Thank them for their time and leave. You will find another company that is prepared to pay you what you're worth. When you stick to your guns, you show that you truly believe in your own worth. The company may ultimately make you a proper offer.

Remember, too, that your starting salary is just that—your *starting* salary. Especially if it's low (but even if it's at the high end of the range), you should have regular performance reviews. Most companies do so annually. Ask the employer what you can expect to be earning one, two, or five years from now. If you're forced to take a lower starting salary than you wanted, ask for an early salary review. Have them put in your contract that after three or six months (or whatever you agree on with the employer), you will have a salary review and that if you have met or exceeded expectations by then, your salary will be increased by at least X percent without any impact to your next annual review.

Get It in Writing

Always, always get everything in writing. If the employer promises a salary review at three months, get it in writing. If they say, "Sure, we'll make IRA contributions for you and your wife, and we'll set up that 401(k) for the company by next January," get it in writing. Words, sadly, mean nothing, and leave you with no recourse. You may also want to consider having any employment agreements reviewed by an attorney.

Checklist

If you play your cards right, salary negotiation and evaluating offers can be a lot of fun. And—stay with me now, because you've probably never heard this before—preparation is the key. If you've invested time in your research and know your market, your worth, and what other companies are paying, you're golden. You have the information you need to convince potential employers why they should pay you properly.

Ready to talk your way to the top?

- ☐ Did you put off salary negotiations until you had a concrete offer?
- ☐ Did you evaluate the company and how you feel about the job before you considered money?
- ☐ Did you do your salary research and prepare your case carefully?
- ☐ Do you feel confident that you deserve the salary you're asking for?

So what are you waiting for? Get out there and get that offer signed, sealed, and delivered!

Part V

Interview Encyclopedia

In This Part

Chapter 12

Getting Past the Technical Interview

The final chapter in this book is dedicated to helping you prepare specifically for your technical interview. In this chapter, you will find the following IT job profiles:

- Architect
- Business systems analyst
- Database administrator
- Desktop support technician (includes network support technician)
- Helpdesk manager
- Helpdesk specialist
- Independent consultant
- IT management (director of IT or IT manager)
- Network administrator
- Network engineer
- Developer/programmer/software engineer
- Team lead
- Project manager
- Quality assurance specialist
- Security specialist

These job profiles represent the top jobs in IT today and will most likely include your current job or the job you aspire to. Since many IT jobs overlap, you may also want to check out other similar jobs. We make it simple by providing references to other positions of interest.

Each of these job profiles includes the following sections:

Keywords Alternate names for the job or search strings that can be used in Internet job search engines to find jobs pertaining to this specialty

Job Description A short description of the position

Education and Certification Requirements Educational or certification requirements are listed; some are essential to qualifying for a position and some are highly recommended

Technical Skills Required Minimum technical skill requirements to be eligible for this position

Other Skills Required Other skills required, such as logic, interpersonal skills, and managerial skills that are essential to be successful at this position

Skills Check Skills checklist to help you assess your level of experience for each position using a simple grading system for self-assessment

Standing Out What it takes to stand out and be noticed when applying for this position

Interview Questions to Expect A set of 30–100 interview questions to practice with

There are several ways you can use these profiles. Start off by making sure you understand the key skills that interviewers seek for the job you aspire to. Cross-reference these against your résumé to ensure you meet the minimum requirements for the jobs you're applying for. We make it easy by providing standard skills descriptions (both technical and interpersonal skills) and lists of technology with which you should be familiar. You can incorporate these skills lists into the "Summary of Qualifications" section on your résumé and be prepared with matching asset statements to discuss with your interviewer.

Next, check the "Standing Out" section for tips on how to differentiate yourself on your résumé and during your interview. This section describes traits that will impress the interviewer and help you demonstrate the knowledge and skill behind the résumé. In most cases, you should have at least one asset statement that addresses the traits identified in the "Standing Out" section.

Finally, invest the time to rehearse your own answers to the interview questions presented. These questions have been developed from real-life interviewing situations. Each question pertains specifically to the job at hand and includes what the interviewer is assessing about you and your skills. In addition, each answer includes advice on how to respond in order to meet the interviewer's expectations. There are questions on your previous experience, your knowledge of how to do the job, your knowledge of the technology, and your problem-solving abilities. Wherever appropriate, a technical answer is also provided as an example of what is expected.

In reviewing these questions, you should note where you will need to have your personal examples to share with the interviewer. You should prepare your answers so that you can respond confidently and won't have to fish for an example or story to relate. But be careful. Don't memorize your answers so that they come across as too rehearsed. The idea is to be comfortable with the interviewing process. Always let your interviewer complete the question before responding. This chapter includes more than 1,000 questions that the interviewer *might* ask you. We can't guarantee that you will be asked these questions.

Another way of getting the most from this chapter is to review the job profiles for jobs other than the one you are interviewing for. This will provide you with a more rounded perspective, and who knows, you may learn a thing or two in technology areas you don't have a lot of experience in.

With this in mind, it's time now to start preparing for your IT job!

Architect

Keywords

IT architect, enterprise architect, information architect, business architect, software architect

Job Description

The IT architect position is one of the most in-demand positions in IT and will be for the foreseeable future. It's so important because of how quickly everything is changing in the IT industry. It requires the ability to pick up new skills quickly and to be a bridge across the different silos in IT. Enterprise architects aren't just technology experts. They are leaders with broad IT knowledge, the savvy to apply it to business problems, and the communication skills necessary to coordinate the people who will put their plans into action.

Education and Certification Requirements

An undergraduate degree in computer science, information science, or management information systems is generally required with an MBA highly preferred. The key certifications in this area are Open Group's IT Architect certification and Microsoft's Certified Architect programs (Infrastructure, Solutions, Messaging, and Database).

Technical Skills Required

IT architects require practical skills and experience with many application and infrastructure products, technologies, and services. While often relying on professionals with specialized skills for the construction, implementation, and operational aspects of solution delivery in many of these areas, the IT Architect must have enough skills and experience across them to be able to successfully architect appropriate solutions of heterogeneous components.

Other Skills Required

It's not enough to be a technical jack of all trades. The effective IT Architect is a leader, providing knowledge, business, technical, and team leadership skills in their work, to their clients, and for their teams. They have to be good communicators as well as consultants and client relationship managers. They spend their time problem-solving business and technical issues so they need to be capable of effectively identifying and framing problems, gathering information about the problem, and synthesizing this information so that the team can make effective decisions.

Architecture Skills Check

Use the following scale to rate your skills. You can later use these descriptors to help describe your skill level on your résumé.

1 (Beginning) Use the skill/product occasionally (basic functions; not primary job responsibility)

2 (Entry level) Use the skill/product on a daily basis

3 (Proficient) Can provide frontline support

4 (Expert) Can train others on this skill/product

5 (Escalation support) The person others turn to when they can't figure it out

Skills	Skill Level
Apply communications skills	
Lead individuals and teams	
Perform conflict resolution	
Manage architectural elements of an IT project plan	
Understand business drivers	
Develop IT architecture	
Use modeling techniques	
Perform technical solution assessments	
Apply, build, and teach IT standards	
Establish technical vision	
Define solution to functional and non-functional requirements	
Manage stakeholder requirements	
Establish architectural decisions	
Validate conformance to the solution of the architecture	
Perform as technology advisor	
Understand frameworks, e.g., Zachman, TOGAF	

Standing Out

This role is where business strategy meets technology strategy. It is therefore critical not just to develop technical competencies but business and leadership competencies as well. It is critical for architects to be savvy enough to understand business strategy and be capable of translating that into a compelling technical strategy.

Interview Questions to Expect

Q. What would you consider some of the critical success factors in your role as an architect?

A. As an architect it's not just about the technology. The interviewer wants to ensure that you see the broader picture. Working with people, gathering their input, and leading them informally are key parts of this job when combined with the architect's knowledge of design, experiences as a programmer, and interpretation of the business needs.

Q. Tell me about the most complicated architectural design you've done.

A. Architectures are supposed to be as simple as possible to meet requirements, future known and unknown growth, focus on areas of likely change. Describe how you met goals and eliminated unneeded complexity, while maintaining key areas that had to be thoroughly engineered.

Q. What are some of the most important architectural principles that you subscribe to in your designs?

A. Identifying key modules, rollout of features, separation of layers, security, and allowing for growth and reuse are important factors. Designing to the resources of the organization and planning for evolution may also be key parts of the architect's approach.

Q. Would you talk about what makes a successful architectural design?

A. A strong understanding of the business needs and the drivers are the key to ensuring that the architectural design addresses the right problems. The design needs to meet architectural principals, and then be reviewed with other key IT team members to determine what else needs to be included or modified. The design should include artifacts that can be presented to the business, including PowerPoint presentations or Visio diagrams, and additional technical details will be necessary to share the design in IT. Designs should be captured in common templates to facilitate presenting them to other team members. UML should be used to capture the technical details of the design, but should be used sparingly with the business.

Q. Describe a situation where you've had to rely on your non-technical skills to create support for your design.

A. The interviewer understands that it takes more than technical skills for being a successful architect. He is looking for examples where you've used your leadership skills for creating and communicating an architectural vision and your political savvy for understanding the organization. This helps you manage stakeholder hot-buttons, and influence and include others' ideas.

Q. Describe how you've worked with development teams to implement a design and ensure adoption of the architecture.

A. Implementing an architectural design is not as simple as just building and sending out a technology roadmap to the engineering community. It requires working in a collaborative manner with the engineers to help them understand the architecture and the rationale behind it and work through the details of how to implement it. Engineers have excellent ideas and capturing their experience by having strong relationships is key to engaging them in the design process.

Q. Describe examples of technology roadmaps that you've developed.

A. As a part of your answer, lay out the key objectives of the roadmap, as well as the business drivers, resources, and timelines. Explore the key areas that you feel were most important as the roadmap was formed, as it was initially delivered, and later after it had been in use for some time.

Q. How do you ensure that architecture is being consistently implemented after you've designed it?

A. IT departments have some level of governance that enforces and facilitates the architecture process; the rest of adoption of the design comes from relationships with the team members. Being approachable, knowing when to be flexible and when to be passionate about sticking with plans are key.

Q. What are some of the life cycle considerations for architecture?

A. Nearly all architectural efforts have constraints of time, money, and resources, as well as dependencies on third parties. They may also have to incorporate known or emerging security, regulatory, and industry requirements. Strong business participation is very helpful in the formation of the strategy and the revalidation of rollout timeframes of additional features. Implementation timeframes and architecture stages should map to typical timeframes acceptable in current or future business interactions.

Q. How do you continuously develop your skills?

A. There is a tremendous amount of change happening in information technology. It is important to keep core skills and industry interests up to date, as well as have good methods for learning new areas or emerging technologies. In addition, working through leadership, communication, and business knowledge development is also a must. Expressing the priorities you place on this activity and the methods you use is important. You're being hired to lead and implement the next generations of technology.

Q. Discuss some of the architectural tradeoffs that you architects make?

A. Many tradeoffs come from resource constraints. Other tradeoffs come from choosing one approach over another to achieve business objectives while staying within IT guidelines. Discuss how the style of the project and the depth of the business requirements affect what architecture decisions can be made.

Q. Describe some of your techniques for communicating the architectural vision.

A. Often architects rely on delivering information in a visual format. While this is an important format, in a business forum providing information in a textual format is also critical. When doing so it is important to eliminate all acronyms that don't come from the business. Confirmation questions should be used to ensure that the business understands the priority order, the systems capabilities, and limitations.

Q. Describe some of your techniques for gathering architectural vision inputs.

A. Discussions with the business, industry analysts, information technology employees, and partners help insure that important information is being considered. The roadmaps should be a guideline for technology decisions and be updated in accordance with evolving best practices and competitors actions. Confirming the drivers behind requirements is important. A lot of software has been built to solve the stated requirement and not the business driver. Using techniques like asking the five whys can confirm the validity of the business input and ensure that the correct problem and its source are being addressed.

Q. What programming languages should be used for which problems and why?

A. Good architects have a broad and deep understanding of different technologies. They have their favorite environments and programming languages and they can adapt their designs to whatever technologies are used by an organization. A good answer would demonstrate knowledge beyond trendy languages like C++, Java, or C#, as well as when to use other programming tools.

Q. What does your design process typically look like?

A. The interviewer is looking for you to describe a process that includes generating at least three alternate designs, assesses the advantages and risks of each of the designs, involves other project members and peers in reviewing the design review, as well as other business leaders in fully assessing the consequences. Designing for existing architectures may require fewer rigors; express when multiple alternate designs add value and how you as an architect make and communicate that choice.

Business Systems Analyst

Keywords

Business analyst, business systems analyst, systems analyst, computer analyst

Job Description

Business analysts are responsible for identifying the business needs of their clients and mapping solutions to business problems. This includes requirements development and requirements management. The business analyst is a like a translator within an organization, acting as a bridge between the client, stakeholders, and the solution team.

Education and Certification Requirements

An undergraduate degree in computer science, information science, or management information systems is generally required with an MBA highly preferred. The key certification in this area is the Certified Business Analysis Profession from the IIBA.

Technical Skills Required

Companies increasingly look for professionals with a broad background and range of skills, including not only technical knowledge, but also communication and other interpersonal skills. This position is 20 percent technical and 80 percent other. The 20 percent technical skills include knowledge of software development life cycle methodologies and modeling tools.

Other Skills Required

The "other" consists of analyzing, facilitating, negotiating, architecting, planning, communicating, strategizing, and managing change. This position also involves a solid foundation in business knowledge, business case development, and business process reengineering.

Business Systems Analyst Skills Check

Use the following scale to rate your skills. You can later use these descriptors to help describe your skill level on your résumé.

1 (Beginning) Use the skill/product occasionally (basic functions; not primary job responsibility)

2 (Entry level) Use the skill/product on a daily basis

3 (Proficient) Can provide frontline support

4 (Expert) Can train others on this skill/product

5 (Escalation support) The person others turn to when they can't figure it out

Skills	Skill Level
Requirements management	
Eliciting client requirements	
Facilitating client requirements	

Skills	Skill Level
Data gathering techniques	
Problem solving	
Decision making	
Systems thinking	
Information security	
Data modeling	
User centered design	
Writing use cases	
Organizational change management	
Negotiation skills	
Customer relationship management	
Systems engineering concepts and principles	
Communication of technical concepts to non-technical audiences	
Testing, verification, and validation	
Rapid prototyping	
Technical domain knowledge	
Ability to conceptualize and think creatively	
Requirements risk assessment and management	
Cost/benefit analysis	
Administrative, analytical, and reporting skills	
Time management and personal organization	
Business process improvement and reengineering	
Strategic and business planning	
Communication of business concepts to technical audiences	
Business outcome thinking	
Business writing	
Business case development	
Business domain knowledge	

Skills	Skill Level
Fundamentals of project management	
Capacity to articulate vision	
Team management	
SDLC Methodologies	
Rational Unified Process	
Agile	
Waterfall	
MFC	
Extreme Programming (XP)	
Tools	
Requisite Pro	
Rational Rose	
Rational ClearQuest	
MS Project	
MS Visio	
Test Director	

Standing Out

This role is the ultimate problem solver in IT. To wear the many hats of a BSA including analyst, facilitator, negotiator, architect, planner, communicator, diplomat, and strategist, you need to have broad experience including financial analysis, project management, quality assurance, organizational development, testing, training and documentation development. The more diversity of project experience the better to help you adapt to any new challenge.

Interview Questions to Expect

Q. What's the difference between a business systems analyst and a project manager?

A. In many organizations these roles are one—either the project manager is asked to do business analysis or the business analyst is asked to pick up project management responsibilities. The interviewer is trying to assess whether you can articulate the key focus of each job and perhaps how comfortable you are with working with a project manager. For the project manager this means ensuring that the project is delivered on time and budget by managing project resources. For the business analyst accountability lies in ensuring that the project is built according to requirements and is built correctly. Together, these roles ensure that the product meets the customer's expectations. They must work together on tasks like identifying project resources, identifying project milestones, identifying risks, estimating work, determining project milestones, determining project metrics, and communicating with stakeholders.

Q. What are the problems solved by business analysts?

A. This question is your opportunity to tie business analysis to business results—a very important consideration for all the work that you do. As a part of your answer, discuss how documenting the right business requirements will ultimately save time and money on projects by reducing rework and the development of unwanted features. This ultimately reduces the potential work for developers and testers.

Q. What are the tasks that you've been responsible for as a business analyst?

A. As a business analyst you are responsible for a broad range of tasks. The interviewer needs to get a sense of the responsibilities that you've held, the scope and size of the projects that you've worked on, and your business domain knowledge either in a specific industry or with a functional group (i.e., sales, finance, HR). Start your description of responsibilities with an overview of the industries and functional departments you've worked in. Include the number of years of experience you have in each of these areas. Then describe in general the categories of the responsibilities you've had. It is important to start with the big picture rather than just diving right into individual tasks. This demonstrates your ability to communicate effectively and not be narrowly focused on just the details—a very important skill set for the business analyst. In describing your responsibilities ensure that you cover all the bases: requirements planning and management, requirements elicitation, requirements analysis and documentation, requirements communications, and solution assessment and validation.

Q. What types of projects have you been involved in?

A. Perhaps all of your experience is with in-house custom-developed software projects. Be aware that there are other project types out there and you should be familiar with these as well. These include outsourced development, software maintenance, software package selection, process improvement, and organizational change. These different types of projects will have different requirements planning and management activities. Provide a comparison of the differences and similarities from your own perspective.

Q. What are your strengths and challenges when it comes to eliciting requirements?

A. The interviewer is looking for a self-assessment of the important skills as a business analyst. You'll want to comment on the following skills: eliciting and assessing information, interviewing, facilitating collaborative sessions, conflict resolution, thinking abstractly, and communicating with business users.

Q. How do you determine who should be involved in requirements elicitation?

A. At first glance, this may be a simple question, right? Of course you need to include the business stakeholders, but is that all? The interviewer may be trying to assess your business and organizational savvy in gaining early buy-in for the project by including other folks such as the finance department, and business and technical groups who may need to support the application. You should also describe how you've identified a complete list of stakeholders. These can include consulting reference materials, circulating questionnaires, and interviewing known stakeholders. Don't forget to mention how you've used a RACI matrix to then document roles and responsibilities.

Q. What are your responsibilities associated with managing scope?

A. Managing scope is one of the trickiest parts of any project. It's important how you respond to this question because it demonstrates your maturity as a business analyst. Your role is to establish and maintain a requirements baseline, tracing requirements and identifying impacts to external systems and/or other areas of the project, to identify scope changes resulting from requirements change, and maintain scope approval. Easier said than done so be sure to provide plenty of examples of how you've successfully managed scope on previous projects.

Q. What are your preferred requirements elicitation techniques?

A. There are plenty of elicitation techniques you can mention here but undoubtedly you have your favorites. Be sure to mention your most commonly used techniques and why. Then provide examples of how some of these are more appropriate than others depending on the project. For example, requirements workshops may be used in 95 percent of your projects. Surveys are good for when stakeholders are dispersed. System demonstrations may work best for COTS projects. A prototype may work well in iterative software development approaches. As memory joggers, the most common techniques are brainstorming, interviews, observation, storyboarding, focus groups, storyboarding, requirements workshops, JAD sessions, reverse engineering, and surveys.

Q. How have you used prototyping as a requirements elicitation technique and in what situations does it work the best?

A. Perhaps prototyping is one of the preferred elicitation techniques used by the hiring company. If you'll be involved in developing a lot of end-user applications, prototyping is a great way of getting the user interface right. It works well because you can get direct user feedback and they'll be more effective in articulating their needs using graphics or pictures.

Q. How often do you run requirements workshops and what challenges do you come across?

A. Requirements workshops are a staple of the business analyst role. You can't be a business analyst without the skills to facilitate a well-run requirements workshop. They are one of the most effective ways to deliver high-quality requirements quickly because they create trust amongst the project team, develop mutual understanding, and establish strong communications. The challenges that you may want to elaborate on include the difficulty of getting everyone into a room together and your own comfort with facilitating such a large group interaction, particularly if there are high-profile business stakeholders in the group.

Q. What are examples of documentation and project documents that you've been responsible for as a business analyst?

A. The types of documents that you describe will provide tangible examples of the complexity of the projects you've worked on and the depth of your experience. At a minimum you should feel comfortable discussing business architecture documents, feasibility study reports, business case documents, executive presentations, and risk assessments.

Q. What analysis and modeling techniques do you use to translate business objectives into system requirements?

A. This is a basic question to test your knowledge and use of common business analyst techniques. Your answer should include a broad overview of the analysis techniques you use (setting scope, identifying business-drive external events, establishing functional baselines, identifying critical development risks) and the modeling techniques like context diagramming, UML, and use cases.

Q. How do you manage risk on a project?

A. Managing risk is critical if your responsibilities include project management. With this question the interviewer is assessing how structured you are in your processes. Having a formal workflow process is the key for ensuring that projects meet the expectations of the business owners. If none exists, the number one priority is to create one with the help of your sponsor and IT managers. This process ensures effective customer service, communication, prioritization, validation, teamwork, quality, and productivity. You should also discuss whether you use risk management plans and how that integrates with the everyday tasks of managing project risks. For instance, you can provide examples of how you use weekly risks checks in your status meetings, and develop contingency plans as risks arise. Another example that you should discuss is the role of conducting lessons learned sessions or post-mortems as a part of closing out projects.

Q. What is Object Oriented Analysis and how have you used it?

A. This modeling technique is another staple of the business analyst role. Be sure to describe how you've used this technique and the methodologies that you've used, including UML. Describe the use of use cases, activity diagrams, and sequence diagrams.

Q. What types of modeling are you familiar with and when is the use of modeling beneficial?

A. Modeling is a critical part of the requirements gathering process. Be sure to include relevant examples of how you've used business rules, data dictionaries, class models, CRUD matrix, data transformation, entity relationship diagrams, activity diagrams, data flow diagrams, event identification, sequence diagrams, and workflow models. Discuss the benefits of these modeling techniques including how they help simplify the business environment and allow business analysts to focus on what is important and how the use of multiple models together helps to ensure a holistic view of the problem being addressed, which ultimately leads to a better solution.

Q. What are some examples of non-functional requirements?

A. A business analyst is not just concerned with the functionality of a business application. It's important to identify non-functional requirements impacting a project. The better you're able to describe these, the more experience and value you demonstrate to the interviewer. Be sure to provide examples of environmental requirements like regulatory constraints, audit and legal requirements, interface requirements for interacting with other systems, operational requirements such as how many users may use the system concurrently, performance requirements such as how much information the system must be capable of processing at a time, and quality requirements such as usability and maintainability.

Q. What documentation do you normally produce?

A. This question will provide the interviewer with insight into how structured your processes are. The basic response should include a mention of creation of a business requirements document (BRD) and the software requirements specification (SRS). A more advanced answer should include a mention of a vision document, a business process definition, and a request for proposal/request for quotation (RFP/RFQ).

Q. How would you handle a scenario where requirements change midway in the project?

A. Which project doesn't have its requirements change midway through? This is a common scenario. The interviewer is looking for how you reason through this situation. Do you evaluate how big the change is? Was it mis-scoped from the beginning because business requirements were not clearly defined or understood? Is it a new "nice to have" feature? Ultimately, this situation requires the BA/BSA to evaluate the impact on the timeline, cost, risks, and possible alternatives—push out the timeline, add more resources, or other creative alternatives such as other approaches to solving the business need and phasing of project deliverables. They then must bring this information to the project owner and allow them to determine which makes the most business sense.

Q. What are some of the problems business analysts run into when they are gathering requirements?

A. Requirements gathering is an art and a science. From a practical perspective, the biggest challenge that business analysts run into is the availability of the subject matter experts including end-users and managers. You may want to describe some of the ways that you structure your requirements gathering sessions to minimize the impact on their time. Other challenges include coming up with a way to gather requirements in a way that will make it easy for the end-user to understand and identify errors in the requirements. End-users will not know UML so do you use prototyping, screen diagrams, a written document, use cases, and so on? This question gets at your experience and your flexibility. Make sure you provide relevant examples of how you've identified these challenges and worked with the business to ensure that requirements gathering led to an end product that the customer was satisfied with.

Q. What's the difference between business process improvement and business process reengineering?

A. If you're asked this question, distinguish between the two (systemic approach to changing how an organization does business versus a management approach for increasing effectiveness and efficiency in how it does business) and provide examples of projects you've been involved in. Identify any personal contributions you've made to these initiatives and their business result.

Q. How important is software knowledge for a business analyst and why?

A. Fungibility—the ability to apply your skills in a new and different environment—is critical as a business analyst. After all, most folks don't have the luxury (or the desire) to work with the same client group or application for their entire career. You should focus your response on examples of how you've been able to apply your business analysis skills to different environments, applications, and client groups. Provide examples of what you've done to come up to speed quickly and the knowledge and skills you've been able to transfer.

Q. How do you go about learning domain knowledge in a new industry or organizational function?

A. The interviewer has several goals with this question: how structured are you about learning, your initiative, and resourcefulness. Unless you only apply for positions within the same industry or organizational function, it's important to quickly pick up new domain knowledge. There are several ways to do this.

1. Start off with a broad overview of the industry in order to better understand their business cycle of service—essentially how products are developed and sold, and customers supported. The Internet can be a resource prior to joining the organization. New employee orientation programs typically can also provide this information once you've joined the organization. If no orientation program is available then you can start searching for any PowerPoint presentations that the department may already have with this information.

2. Next, people or function organization charts can provide further breakdown of how people and work are organized to support the business.

3. Sitting down with a subject matter expert (either on the IT side or on the business side) is probably the next step so that you can ask the important questions like: "What are the most critical processes?" and "Where's the greatest volume of work?" and "What do I need to know about how work gets done?"

4. With this context, you can then sit down with business process diagrams and further study these if necessary.
5. Documentation can also be a good source of further detail about the function and application.
6. All front-end applications would also include a demonstration of the system.

Q. What is the difference between Agile and Unified Process methodologies?

A. Business analysts must be proficient in a broad set of SDLC methodologies because the SDLC methodology will impact requirements planning. The actual question that you may get can be a comparison of any of the methodologies that you list on your resume. In answering a question like this, you'll want to address: the pros and cons of each methodology, the similarities and differences in requirements gathering, development, project management, interaction with the business subject matter experts, the review processes, and the QA testing. You'll also want to provide examples of projects (their size, technology, and application) when one methodology is most appropriate over the other.

Q. How do you determine your communication strategy?

A. A business analyst must not just be good at analyzing situations but also good at communicating what they find in a way that matches the needs of the audience they are communicating with, be it developers (typically through SRS), the end-users (in validating requirements), or business sponsors. For example, to communicate to senior level management stakeholders, a presentation focusing on the high-level highlights of the project may be best.

Database Administrator

Keywords

Database engineer, database architect, relational database, SQL, Oracle, database programmer, data warehousing

Job Description

A DBA position is one of the most coveted positions within IT. For many, it represents much more than just responsibility for the company's treasured databases; it is the highest technical position on the team. A DBA does indeed maintain, archive, monitor, and tune the company databases. But he also works closely with business analysts and applications developers to determine the best database design based on systems specifications, and they create the underlying databases for applications. They work hand in hand with the development team to ensure that the architecture provides the greatest reliability, performance, and safety.

Education and Certification Requirements

A college degree is usually required as well as formal training in a leading relational database. The key certification for the two leading relations databases are the Oracle Certified Professional (OCP) DBA certification and the Microsoft Certified Database Administrator (MCDBA) for DBAs who have been working with SQL Server for at least one year. With database jobs ranking amongst the most difficult to fill in IT, certification is rarely required. Additional certifications include Cognos BI Architect and SAS Warehouse Architect.

Technical Skills Required

A solid foundation in relational database theory is required, as well as direct experience with a leading database. You should also possess in-depth experience in at least one major operating system. Along with database theory you should be familiar with various database utilities and performance tools that you will use as a daily part of your job, including report generators, online analytical processing (OLAP) tools, and data-mining software.

Other Skills Required

DBAs are the heart of the development department. Troubleshooting and problem-solving skills are a must, as is a detail-oriented work ethic. Highly developed oral and written communication skills for dealing with different members of the IT organization and creating documentation are also required. A DBA must work well with others as well as alone.

Database Administrator Skills Check

Use the following scale to rate your skills. You can later use these descriptors to help describe your skill level on your résumé.

1 (Beginning) Use the skill/product occasionally (basic functions; not primary job responsibility)

2 (Entry level) Use the skill/product on a daily basis

3 (Proficient) Can provide frontline support

4 (Expert) Can train others on this skill/product

5 (Escalation support) The person others turn to when they can't figure it out

Skills	Skill Level
Installation and configuration	
Security	
Data management	

Skills	Skill Level
Backup and restore	
Managing replication	
Automating administrative tasks	
Using linked servers	
Monitoring and optimization	
Troubleshooting	
Using indexes, clusters, and links	
Job queues and auditing	
Web publishing	
Tables and tablespaces	
Administering accounts, logs, and file management	
Reports and forms	
Database tuning	
Logical and physical database planning	
Managing a data warehousing project	
Design and development methodology	
Warehouse maintenance	
Use of OLAP tools	
Mining and analysis	
Database Management Systems	
Microsoft Access	
Microsoft SQL Server	
Oracle	
Reporting Tools	
Crystal Reports	
Impromptu	
Oracle Reports	

Skills	Skill Level
Online Analytical Processing Tools	
Microsoft SQL Server OLAP services	
Data Warehouse and Data Mining Tools	
Cognos Scenario	
Cognos Visualizer	
Oracle Darwin	
Operating Systems	
Unix	
Windows	
Web Development	
VB	
ASP	
HTML	
XML	

Standing Out

A DBA with programming skills will differentiate himself from other candidates. Programming skills allow a DBA to communicate more effectively with the programming team and increase the overall productivity of the team.

Interview Questions to Expect

General Questions

Q. What is the most challenging part of your job?

A. This question provides a clue about your mindset as a DBA. Be careful how you answer because it will determine whether you are the right fit for the position. First of all, whatever challenge you bring up should not be technical! You may want to bring up the challenges associated with getting the developers fast answers and accurate information—due, of course, to the incredible number of projects that you're working on.

Q. Describe your role as a DBA as it relates to the rest of the development staff.

A. The answer to this question is critical when evaluating a DBA candidate. Many DBAs, by virtue of their high pay and product-specific knowledge, tend to think of developers as underlings. In some cases, DBAs view developers with outright contempt, believing their queries to be naive. On the other hand, DBAs with the proper attitude will respond to this question by talking about the developers as clients to whom they provide data services essential to the application. In some shops, the DBAs may be responsible for code, or reviewing SQL queries or SQL statements written by developers, so a good relationship is vital.

Q. Why is it important to have separate test and production systems?

A. The answer to this question will often provide insight into your priorities. In many shops, the DBA doesn't perceive the test databases as being as important as the production database. The right DBA candidate will note that the data integrity of the test databases is crucial to the development staff because it is their "production" environment in many cases.

Q. Tell me about your experience in new system analysis.

A. The answer to this question will reveal a great deal about the breadth of your background. Although technical proficiency is an absolute requirement for the DBA, you must remember that DBAs need to have some tangential knowledge about the functional areas within the business they are supporting—for example, networking, Java syntax, or business-side concerns, like finance or accounting. DBAs with a strong business background will often be very useful to the initial design and implementation of new business functionality within their organization.

Q. Tell me about a situation when a project was falling behind schedule.

A. It's hard to find a project that doesn't fall behind schedule. It happens to the best of projects. How you handle the situation is a different answer. This question addresses several things: 1) how comfortable you are with sharing bad news with your manager, 2) your ability to assess pending risk to a project, and 3) your flexibility in handling the situation. There's only one right answer here—once the risk is identified, inform your management who will most likely bring in the project management team. While you're at it, you might want to throw in that this situation doesn't happen as often as it might have earlier on in your career since you've now learned to better estimate projects and have a solid relationship with your project management colleagues.

Q. What database environment do you prefer to work in?

A. This can be the easiest question during your interview or it can be the quickest way to be shown the door. Sometimes it happens—you respond to an ad for a great company that you've always wanted to work for but you find out that their development environment is Oracle but you only know MS SQL Server. What should you do? Be honest! Either you've got the skills for the job or you're a fast learner. Either way, you've got to clearly state your position. If you're looking to pick up experience in Oracle then let the hiring manager know that at the same time you mention that you're willing to invest your own time in getting there. You may also want to focus on your extensive experience in database architecture and design as a plus that you bring to the table. Honesty will probably get you further than faking it will on the first day.

Q. Describe the typical make-up of your development teams and how did you fit in?

A. Unless you know the exact requirements for the position, you want to stay as flexible on this answer as possible. Talk about the smallest team you've played on. Talk about the largest team. Describe several different types of projects that you've been involved in. And if possible find out if they are looking for team leadership experience. That should help you determine whether you should play up or play down your experience for this position.

Q. Describe your background in database design.

A. The hiring manager is interested in hearing the thought process that went into the planning of the database, particularly how you gather the data requirements for data fields and datatypes.

Q. Please describe the database design of one of your most recent projects.

A. Simply describe the steps that you and/or your team stepped through in designing your database. Include how you laid out the schema and identified which fields and datatypes were needed. Explain your reasons for using or not using a relational database. Give the interviewer the confidence that you know what you are talking about by supporting your statements with as much detail as possible.

Q. What was the worst disaster you were responsible for and how did you recover from it?

A. You must be careful how you answer this question because if your worst mistake resulted in your getting fired, you may not get this job either. Hopefully, your story will have a happy ending. I recommend giving a small-to-medium-size disaster that wasn't extremely critical to any systems. Make sure it doesn't reflect your not following directions or procedures.

Q. What are the major differences between <Database 1> and <Database 2>?

A. This is a question that tests your development loyalties. It's more of a cultural question than a technical question. Be honest but not too fanatical. You may also want to include how you were introduced to your favorite environment. If you're not familiar with Oracle, say that you have not had the opportunity to work with the product but would like to one day experience the differences yourself. This way you cover your bases regardless of the current and future environments. You never know what's in store and what the company's plans are going forward.

Q. Have you written or used stored procedures?

A. If you're interviewing for a DBA position, you'd better have. Go into details of how you've used stored procedures including how many sprocs you have written, how complicated they were, how many joins were in it, did it have parameters and how you optimized it, and the most complicated one you have written and what it did.

Q. What are the advantages of using stored procedures?

A. The interviewer not only wants to see whether you know how to write stored procedures, but he also wants to know whether you know when it's appropriate to use stored procedures. You should also know the advantages of using a stored procedure. For instance, you may want to state that the two main advantages of using stored procedures are for performance and maintainability. By using a stored procedure, the execution plan is cached, and everyone calling the stored procedure gains the benefit of not having to use the expensive query process every time the sproc is called. When explaining how stored procedures make it easier to maintain code, you may want to use the example of a change in a business rule, for instance, or a change in tax calculations. Using a stored procedure, you need only to make the change in one place, and all the code that relies on this stored procedure will take advantage of it, eliminating the need to update all applications and then recompile them.

Q. When would you not use a stored procedure?

A. Here is the corollary to the previous question. You should also be familiar with when not to use stored procedures. You should mention that it may not be an efficient use of resources when you're dealing with small amounts of data. In this case, a simple query may do the job faster.

Q. What is a trigger? What is the most complex trigger you have written?

A. Another common database element is a trigger. You should be prepared to discuss what a trigger is and give some examples of how you've used triggers in the past to implement business rules, audit, or extend referential integrity checks. Be specific and talk about the restrictions imposed by triggers, for instance, the fact that in SQL Server 6.5 you could define only three triggers per table and that in SQL Server 7.0 you may now create multiple triggers per action.

Q. What is a view? How do you use views?

A. This and other questions on specific features of SQL Server are the interviewer's test of your level of expertise with the database management system. You should answer these questions confidently, providing the pros and cons of using various techniques. For example, in responding to this question you could describe how a view is a subset of one or more tables created by a SQL statement, which provides a performance benefit by reducing the time for complex searches.

Q. What is a nested transaction and when would you use one?

A. The interviewer is assessing the level of complexity of your projects. The use of nested transactions represents relatively complex business rules. A nested transaction is a complicated concept. A great way to show that you understand the concept of a nested transaction is to simply explain what it does. For example, you might explain that a nested transaction is when you have one transaction happening inside another. Whatever happens to the outside transaction (committed or rolled back) will also happen within the inner transaction.

Q. What is an index?

A. The interviewer is testing you on your ability to optimize a database environment. Indexes are a key component of the optimization process. Some pointers on indexing that you should mention: 1) you don't want to have too many indexes because even though queries will run faster, data entry will slow down; 2) too many indexes will also gobble up disk space; 3) indexes on small tables makes performance suffer because a simple scan will prove faster than transversing the index. Indexes should only be used on tables with a large number of records.

Q. What is normalization?

A. This question is a great database question. Normalization is the process that separates data into distinct, unique sets. Some pointers on the use of normalization and denormalizations are: 1) normalization reduces the amount of repetition and complexity of the structure of the previous level; 2) denormalization is used to control the redundancy of the database design to help improve the query performance; 3) as normalization increases, so do the complexities of joins in order to retrieve data.

Q. Which OLAP tools have you used?

A. The interviewer is interested in your knowledge of automated analytical tools that enable data to be viewed from various dimensions. In organizations with heavy querying needs, OLAP's multi-dimensional capabilities enable more complex, sophisticated queries, making it easier to visualize data like cubes.

Q. How would you transfer data from Access to SQL Server?

A. As a database administrator, one of your common tasks is importing data from other databases or sources. There are many ways to transfer data from Access to SQL Server. The interviewer is assessing your basic database management skills.

Q. What benefit comes from using an outer join as opposed to an inner join?

A. This question tests your basic knowledge of joins. An outer join will return a complete list of data that is stored in one of the joined tables in addition to the information that matches the join condition. An inner join only returns data that matches the join condition.

Q. How is referential integrity enforced in a SQL Server database?

A. The interviewer is getting a feel for your knowledge of database design, including your understanding of the different types of referential integrity. Setting up and enforcing foreign key constraints is one way to enforce referential integrity. This is called *declarative referential integrity* because it is part of the table definition. You can also use other features as triggers to accomplish referential integrity. This is known as *procedural integrity*.

Q. How might you quantitatively measure an improvement made to a query?

A. Database optimization is a key task for a DBA. Knowing how to improve performance will differentiate you from amateurs. The best way to perform this task is to run the query in query analyzer and check the time it took to return the results. Alternatively, you can use the profiler to check the time, reads, and many other attributes of a query.

Q. How do you implement one-to-one, one-to-many, and many-to-many relationships while designing tables?

A. The interviewer is trying to figure out your level of experience in database design. One-to-one relationships can be implemented as a single table and rarely as two tables with primary and foreign key relationships. One-to-many relationships are implemented by splitting the data into two tables with primary key and foreign key relationships. Many-to-many relationships are implemented using a junction table with the keys from both tables forming the composite primary key of the junction table.

Q. What's the difference between a primary key and a unique key?

A. This question tests your basic knowledge of database design. Both primary and unique keys enforce uniqueness of the column on which they are defined. By default, the primary key creates a clustered index on the column, while a unique key creates a nonclustered index by default. Another major difference is that primary keys don't allow NULLs, but unique keys allow one NULL only.

Q. What is bit datatype, and what's the information that can be stored inside a bit column?

A. The interviewer is testing to see whether you understand datatypes. Beside this bit datatype example, it's a good idea to know them all because an interviewer may ask about a numeric or a varchar next time.

Q. Define candidate key, alternate key, and composite key.

A. The interviewer is testing whether you understand the database design and structure. A candidate key is one that can uniquely identify each row of a table. Generally, a candidate key becomes the primary key of the table. If the table has more than one candidate key, one of them will become the primary key, and the rest are called alternate keys. A key formed by combining at least two or more columns is called a composite key.

Q. What is a transaction, and what are ACID properties?

A. The interviewer is testing to see whether you understand how transactions work. A transaction is a logical unit of work in which all or none of the steps must be performed. ACID stands for atomicity, consistency, isolation, durability. These are the properties of a transaction.

Q. Explain active/active and active/passive cluster configurations.

A. The interviewer is testing your understanding and experience with clustering. Hopefully, you have some experience setting up clustered servers. If you don't have experience, at least be familiar with the way clustering works and the two clustering configurations.

Q. What are the new features introduced in the latest version of SQL Server? What changed between the previous version and the current version?

A. This question is generally asked to see how current your knowledge is. If you are not familiar with different versions of SQL Server, you can find quick summaries of changes by looking in the "What's New" sections of the latest books on SQL as well as in sections titled "Backwards Compatibility" (or similar chapter titles).

Q. What are the steps you will take to improve performance of a poor-performing query?

A. This is a very open-ended question—there could be a lot of reasons behind the poor performance of a query. The interviewer is more interested in whether you understand the causes of common performance issues. Some of the general issues that you could talk about would be the lack of indexes, table scans, missing or out-of-date statistics, blocking, excess recompilations of stored procedures, procedures and triggers without SET NOCOUNT ON, poorly written query with unnecessarily complicated joins, too much normalization, and excess usage of cursors and temporary tables.

You may also want to talk about some of the tools/ways that help you troubleshoot performance problems.

Q. What are the steps you will take if you are tasked with securing a SQL Server?

A. This is another open-ended question that tests your general understanding of SQL Server security. Some of the many things you can talk about in response to this question include: preferring Windows Server authentication; using server, database, and application roles to control access to the data; securing the physical database files using NTFS permissions; restricting physical access to the SQL Server; renaming the Administrator account on the SQL Server computer; disabling the Guest account; enabling auditing; using multiprotocol encryption; setting up SSL; setting up firewalls; or isolating SQL Server from the Web server.

Q. What is the difference between a deadlock and a livelock? How do they get resolved?

A. Obviously, the interviewer is checking your understanding of locks, when they occur and how they get resolved. If you're not familiar with locks, then you might want to do some research. The important point to remember for this question is that SQL attempts to resolve these locks automatically.

Q. What is blocking and how would you troubleshoot it?

A. Again, the interviewer is testing your understanding of common issues and how to resolve them. Blocking happens when one connection from an application holds a lock and a second connection requires a conflicting lock type. This forces the second connection to wait because it was blocked on the first.

Q. What is database replication? What are the different types of replication you can set up in SQL Server?

A. Replication is an important concept in database design. You should be familiar with different forms of replication that SQL Server supports and examples of when it would be appropriate to use each of these, including:

- Snapshot replication
- Transactional replication
- Merge replication

Desktop Support Technician

Keywords

Desktop support analyst, desktop engineer, desktop support coordinator, desktop support services, network specialist, technology support, LAN/WAN technician, network support specialist

Job Description

Desktop support is one of the positions that offers a step up from the helpdesk. Desktop support technicians spend one-on-one time with end-users solving desktop PC issues that the helpdesk wasn't able to resolve. You also set up and configure PCs for new users, handle upgrades, and install new applications. You'll need a wide range of knowledge and the ability to troubleshoot and solve a variety of computer-related issues. Some of these issues may also include troubleshooting network connectivity.

Education and Certification Requirements

These positions do not require a college degree, but certification is recommended. Microsoft Desktop Support Technician (MCDST) and CompTIA's A+, Server+, and Network+ certifications will provide you with a great background in network support. In addition, you may want to consider Red Hat Certified Technician or Cisco CCNA and CCENT. ITIL Certification is also a plus, since so many organizations are adopting ITIL best practices.

Technical Skills Required

Desktop support technicians have to be a jack-of-all-trades because they never know where the problem is going to be. That means that they require in-depth experience in PC hardware, operating systems and applications, peripherals, e-mail applications, Web browsers, internal corporate applications, and networking skills.

Other Skills Required

As a desktop support technician, you are a detective trying to solve the users' problems. Often they will not be able to articulate the cause of their problems or what steps they were carrying out when they encountered the difficulty. Through communication skills that allow you to explain computer concepts in plain English, you should be able to guide users through their issues and help resolve their computing woes. Patience is a virtue in this position as is knowing how to prioritize user requests, especially when they are from the CEO. A customer service attitude will earn you merits.

Desktop Support Technician Skills Check

Use the following scale to rate your skills. You can later use these descriptors to help describe your skill level on your résumé.

1 **(Beginning)** Use the skill/product occasionally (basic functions; not primary job responsibility)

2 **(Entry level)** Use the skill/product on a daily basis

3 **(Proficient)** Can provide frontline support

4 **(Expert)** Can train others on this skill/product

5 **(Escalation support)** The person others turn to when they can't figure it out

Skills	Skill Level
Hardware troubleshooting (motherboard, hard disk, power supplies, memory boards, video cards, sound cards, I/O basics)	
Desktop operating systems installation and troubleshooting	
Building and repairing a PC	
Hardware troubleshooting and maintenance	
Software installation and configuration	
Laptop configuration	
Peripheral installation (modems, printers)	
Network cards, cables, hubs, and network card drivers	
Internet Access	
Internet connectivity troubleshooting	
Web browsers	
TCP/IP configuration	
Disk management	

Skills	Skill Level
Security Management	
Virus protection software installation	
Password management	
Backup and recovery	
Response to virus infections	
Operating Systems	
Windows	
Linux	
Unix	
Macintosh	
Networking Basics	
Networking clients	
Network logins	
Login scripts	
Drive mappings/shares	
User profiles and policies	
Managing access control	
Group membership	
Network printing/printer shares	
Configuring printer drivers	
Troubleshooting printing problems	

Standing Out

Standing out as a desktop support technician is easy: get the job done quickly, accurately, and always with a smile on your face. People are extremely touchy when their systems are down. As long as you get them up and running again quickly, they will be indebted. While they're in this state of mind, ask them to shoot off an e-mail to your boss. Collect these e-mails as proof of your customer service skills. You can always refer to them in your résumé or on your next performance review.

Interview Questions to Expect

Q. What are you most proud of: your customer service skills or your technical skills?

A. Most interviewers like to start with big picture questions and then work their way into more technical areas. IT is a service organization and customer service is at its core. In particular, customer service skills are just as important as technical skills, particularly in panic situations when systems are down or the user has just deleted their board presentation that's due in 30 minutes. We've all had these situations. You should be prepared to talk about a specific situation where you've excelled and received accolades from an end-user. If the end-user put it in writing, mention that as well.

Q. What desktop operating systems are you familiar with?

A. Before you answer this question, you should have some background information on what operating systems are used within the organization you are interviewing with. Undoubtedly, you will be asked to elaborate on your skill set with each of these operating systems so it's best to tailor your elaboration to the operating systems that are relevant to the hiring manager. This being said, don't leave out mentioning experience in other operating systems. You never know whether the company may be evaluating the migration to a different OS.

Q. What desktop automation tools are you familiar with and which functionality were you directly responsible for?

A. Automation tools are an important part of your job as a desktop support technician. Hiring managers want to assess your in-depth knowledge and experience with using these tools. They certainly don't expect you to be an expert in the design and deployment of these tools but they will want to know whether you had a hand at building software packages for distribution or whether you simply pushed these out to your clients.

Q. What are the pitfalls of using desktop automation software?

A. This question is meant to assess how well you know these products, how sophisticated the environment was, and how you worked around the limitations of the tools.

Q. What do you like most about desktop support?

A. Hiring managers are looking for what motivates you. Hopefully your answer will match the characteristics of the job: being busy, working with different people, and the challenges of learning new operating systems and configurations.

Q. What do you like least about desktop support?

A. The hiring manager is testing whether you will fit in with the existing team. An appropriate answer here would be not being able to resolve a problem in a timely manner for reasons outside your control, such as hardware failure. Stick to things outside of your control for the best response.

Q. When solving a desktop problem, do you prefer to work with the end-user, your peers, or on your own?

A. This is another question to determine your fit within the organization. Hiring managers understand that to be successful as a support technician you will have to work in a team environment. This means working with other employees, vendors, and end-users on a constant basis.

Q. Describe a situation where you have had to deal with a difficult person. How did you handle it?

A. Desktop support can be very demanding some days. End-users only see their own priority needs and often are not interested in other demands on your time. This question explores how you deal with difficult end-users by understanding their problem, assessing priorities, and communicating a timeframe for resolution. Often, good communication can help both sides come to an agreement. Make sure you have an example with a successful outcome.

Q. Provide me with an example of a stressful situation and how you handled it.

A. Hiring managers are looking to see what coping techniques you can draw on to deal with stress. Sometimes from the answer, they can also determine whether you are prone to stress. When responding, some techniques for handling stress that you may want to talk about include continually evaluating what's on your plate and prioritizing, communicating with your manager on what your priorities are, and making sure that you take a break to reenergize, particularly at lunch time.

Q. What do you see yourself doing in three years?

A. Hiring managers want you to stick around. They realize that you will not be in this position forever, and they want to make sure there's a desire to move up within the organization as well as the right fit. They ask this question to see whether there's a growth path for you possible within the organization. As a desktop technician, natural growth paths are team leads, quality assurance, engineering positions, and entry-level development. Be honest about where you want to be in three years, and ask the interviewer whether they see your career path as a possibility.

Q. How do you learn new technologies?

A. Learning is an inherent part of the job. Hiring managers are looking for someone who enjoys learning technology on their own and who has the foresight to look for training opportunities. Besides the traditional books and manuals, don't forget to include user groups, eLearning subscriptions, and IT professional sites like TechRepublic.

Q. How do you prioritize tasks and manage your time?

A. What hiring managers want to know is whether you *have* time-management skills. Everyone manages their time differently, but think about how you handle e-mail, when you check voice mail, how you respond to pages, when you research and document, and how you pick up new trouble tickets.

Q. How would you handle the following situation: you receive three simultaneous calls from three executives needing assistance. Who would you help first?

A. Obviously, this is a trick question. What the hiring manager is trying to assess is how you set expectations with each of the individuals, knowing very well that you won't be able to assist all of them at the same time. They are also looking for how you will prioritize each of these incidents, including seeking assistance from peers and supervisors in order to meet user expectations. Don't allow the "tyranny of the urgent" to divert you from management-established support priorities.

Q. How would you work with a user who continuously misdiagnoses their technology issues?

A. By asking this question, the hiring manager is assessing your customer service skills. In this situation, you may want to discuss that the key is to not offend the user and turn them off to your support services. In handling this situation, you would pay particular attention to ways you can build trust with the user and lead them to the right resolution to their problem. These components may include:

- Acknowledging the user's diagnosis
- Asking the user to reproduce the problem
- Finding a solution that works

Q. What procedures have you used in the past for setting up new employees in an organization?

A. This type of question helps the hiring manager assess the types of organizations you've worked for in the past and how structured their processes were. Your role as a desktop technician is to make the first day on the job as seamless and painless as possible, so if you've got a few tricks up your sleeve don't hesitate to share them.

Q. How would you prioritize support issues?

A. It is unlikely that as a desktop support technician you will receive problem calls one at a time. Typically, when you receive one call, you already have three people waiting for service. For this reason, you must learn to prioritize. Your answer to this question will provide the interviewer with insight into how effectively you prioritize. It's not a trick question, though sometimes it can feel that way. You probably have a process that you use instinctually. Talk about it. It probably includes many of the following components:

- Total network failure (affects everyone)
- Partial network failure (affects small groups of users)

- Small network failure (affects a small, single group of users)
- Total workstation failure (single user can't work at all)
- Partial workstation failure (single user can't do most tasks)
- Minor issue (single user has problems that crop up now and again)

Q. What questions would you ask to help isolate a user's problem?

A. This question is used by the hiring manager to assess your problem-solving abilities. The following represent some of the common questions that you would ask the end-user to help diagnose a situation:

- When did the problem first start?
- Has the system ever worked properly?
- What was the last thing done to the system prior to the failure?
- Is the issue intermittent or ongoing/constant?
- Are there any error messages? If so, what are the specific error messages?
- Has any new hardware been added to the system?
- Has any new software been added to the system, including downloads from the Internet?
- Has anything changed with the system (for example, has it been moved) since the issue presented itself?
- Has anyone else had access to the system?
- Are there any environmental factors that could be causing the issue?
- Have you done any troubleshooting on the system on your own?
- Have you checked all the cables/connections for a tight fit?

Q. What are the main differences between the following operating systems?

A. Unfortunately, most companies have not been able to standardize the operating systems used by users. It's always critical that you know more than just the current version because there will always be a user who has a problem with an older version. By asking this question, the hiring manager is actually testing your knowledge of different operating systems that you may need to support.

Q. What are some of the ways to prevent virus attacks?

A. This is virus protection 101 just to ensure that you understand the basics of protecting against viruses. Possible virus sources include e-mail attachments, Internet downloads, and infected external media. To prevent virus infections:

- Use anti-virus software.
- Perform regular updates to the virus software definition files and scan engines. Verify updates have succeeded.
- Perform regularly scheduled virus checks.
- Configure software to check all files, not just program files.
- Educate users on virus attacks, their consequences, and how to prevent them.
- Know where all software came from.
- Do regular backups.
- Develop reporting mechanisms to inform server administrators of observed desktop infections and how these could impact the server environment (such as deletions or corruption of files on public shares, hidden payload files that might have been uploaded to servers, and so on).

Q. What are some of the guidelines you would recommend for implementing security at the user level?

A. Security is a major part of the desktop technician's day-to-day responsibilities. As the closest point of contact to the end-users, technicians need to be savvy on the different methods for enforcing security. Offer up some techniques around the use of anti-virus software, password security, and desktop security.

Q. Users are reporting that their e-mails to recipients outside the company are bouncing back. How would you troubleshoot this problem?

A. The interviewer will run you through a series of questions like this one to see how you would use your troubleshooting skills in a common, real-life situation. He not only gets to see how your mind works, but also begins to get an insight into your technical capabilities. In your answer, be methodical in your approach, identifying the most likely possibility and testing it. Be sure to let the interviewer know that if your first attempt doesn't work, you know how to move on to the next possibility.

Q. When a user opens up his browser he receives a "The page cannot be displayed" error message. What is the most likely cause of this problem?

A. This question starts the behavioral interviewing questions based on real-life situations that assess your problem-solving skills and your technical skills. They will range from the general (like this question) to very specific technical questions that determine your knowledge level and skill set. Don't worry if you don't have all the answers. The interviewer is mostly interested in how you would resolve the situation and what resources you would use to do so.

Q. A user is receiving the following message when they try to print: "This document failed to print." What do you think is causing it?

A. This question tests your troubleshooting skills. In this situation you may want to talk about which tests you would perform in order to resolve the issue. The range of solutions will vary from the printer being online to the user installed a new driver. The important thing when responding is to start with the obvious and then move on to the unlikely answers.

Q. What are the first things you check when a user is experiencing problems accessing the network?

A. This question assesses your basic network troubleshooting skills. You can't miss this one! You should be able to answer it in your sleep. You can liven up the interview by providing a funny story about user errors that you've encountered.

Q. A user cannot access the local intranet. What would you try first in helping to determine how to narrow the problem down to the intranet?

A. Don't make this question harder than it really is. Sometimes the interviewer will try to trip you up to test your common sense. Go for the obvious, rather than complicating the situation. In this case, simply trying to access the intranet from another workstation would help isolate the problem to the machine.

Q. Several users can't log in to the server. What would you do to narrow the problem down to the workstations, network, or server?

A. The situation gets a little more interesting. Again, keep it simple, such as checking the server console for user connections to see if other users are able to log into the server. If they can, the problem is most likely related to those users' workstations. If they can't, the problem is either the server or network connection.

Q. Which TCP/IP utility is most often used to test whether an IP host is up and functional?

A. TCP/IP is at the core of just about every network today. You must be familiar with the most often used commands for managing this network environment. This includes Ping, ipconfig, FTP, and tracert. You should also be ready to apply these commands and utilities to various situations, as the next question demonstrates.

Helpdesk Manager

Keywords

IT manager, helpdesk supervisor, helpdesk team lead, data operations manager, PC helpdesk manager, director of support

Job Description

How do you get anything done when your entire team's responsibility is to react to customer calls all day long? As the manager of the company's IT 911 system, you've got to make sure your managerial and project management skills are continuously sharp. The helpdesk manager is responsible for not only supporting the company and all their technical questions, but also for doing it economically.

Education and Certification Requirements

A college degree is recommended for this position, with specialized training in project management and helpdesk management a plus. Most helpdesk managers learn their roles on the job. Helpdesk management certifications are available and recommended from Helpdesk Institute (HDI).

Technical Skills Required

No one expects a helpdesk manager to get on the phone with a user and resolve their technical incident. Helpdesk managers are expected to be able to collect all the trouble ticket information that will allow the call to be properly logged, routed, and troubleshot by the appropriate technician. It is also expected that you'll be familiar with all the research tools available to look up a possible solution—after all, it was your responsibility to put the necessary tools in place, including knowledge bases, reference books, and training courses to aid technicians in resolving issues more quickly. You should have a general understanding of networking and applications and make it a priority to be familiar with custom applications specific to the company.

Other Skills Required

The primary responsibility of the helpdesk manager is to run the helpdesk as a business. That means understanding and emulating the principles of effective leadership, outstanding managerial and team building skills, and having an eye on the bottom line. As a helpdesk manager, your product is the customer service that your team provides. It's extremely important to have a highly motivated, customer-focused team running at all times, even when the circumstances are less than ideal. Dealing day to day with end-users can be frustrating for skilled support staff. The helpdesk manager must provide an atmosphere of motivation and encouragement for the team. This includes managing at the support team level as well as managing up—continually demonstrating the strategic value of the services your team provides.

Helpdesk Manager Skills Check

Use the following scale to rate your skills. You can later use these descriptors to help describe your skill level on your résumé.

1 (Beginning) Use the skill/product occasionally (basic functions; not primary job responsibility)

2 (Entry level) Use the skill/product on a daily basis

3 (Proficient) Can provide frontline support

4 (Expert) Can train others on this skill/product

5 (Escalation support) The person others turn to when they can't figure it out

Skills	Skill Level
Manage technology support services as a business	
Employee recruitment, training, and retention	
Professional development of self and team members	
Managerial skills for handling employee issues: motivation, skills, knowledge, and career development	
Define operational processes for running the call center	
Understand the technologies, processes, and key factors to consider in order to optimize helpdesk performance	
Manage service levels with customers and secondary support personnel	
Perform staff scheduling and workforce planning	
Determine appropriate use of technology for managing customer service, tracking helpdesk incidents, and analyzing performance data	
Design a new support center or analyze an existing center	
Consult on performance enhancements	
Re-engineer a support center for success	
Helpdesk Software	
HEAT	
Network Associates Magic Service Desk	
Remedy	
Asset Insight	

Standing Out

An effective helpdesk manager has two distinguishing characteristics: low turnover and high performance metrics. They do a great job in keeping the team motivated, productive, and efficient. You'll be a stand-out helpdesk manager if you realize the value of your people and the need to run support services as a business.

Interview Questions to Expect

Q. What do you see as the business of the helpdesk?

A. As the manager of such a critical part of the organization, the hiring manager wants to ensure that you understand that there's more to running a helpdesk than scheduling people to answer the phones. The helpdesk provides strategic support services for the people and companies that buy the company's products and services that lead to increased customer satisfaction and increased loyalty to products and services.

Q. What do you consider to be the key elements to running a successful helpdesk?

A. Here is your opportunity to demonstrate that you are more than just a supervisor of people. The key elements are strong leadership, effective policies and strategies, efficient people management, appropriate resources, systematic processes, employee satisfaction, customer satisfaction, and performance results to back up customer satisfaction. The hiring manager wants to know that he can count on you to not just run an efficient operation, but also to be a strategic part of the organization.

Q. As a helpdesk manager, describe how you would monitor and manage the bottom line performance of your department.

A. By asking this question, the hiring manager is assessing your experience with managing a budget. Managing the bottom line is done by establishing and living by a departmental budget, keeping costs in line, keeping turnover low, and continually looking for ways to streamline processes.

Q. What are some of the ways you can anticipate problems and develop contingency plans to prevent project delays?

A. Delays are inevitable in IT projects, and hiring managers know that. Some of the different ways you can work around these include segmenting projects into manageable phases, analyzing each phase of a project to determine areas of risk, and determining success/failure criteria for each phase. Breaking these down allows you to work with more manageable projects.

Q. What is your philosophy for recruiting and retaining people?

A. The recruitment process is probably the most important part of retaining people. The hiring manager wants to ensure that you have the right skills for hiring and retaining the right people. One of the key points you want to mention about the recruitment process is how making the right fit includes looking beyond the technical qualifications of individuals to determine whether their personalities will fit in well with the established team. One of the ways to do this is to have the candidate meet with existing team members. This also offers an opportunity to assess more technical skills specific to the job.

In providing insight into your retention strategies, you may want to include examples of how you actively work to develop your employees, such as regular performance reviews, skills gap analyses, and finding different opportunities or ways for them to diversify their skills.

Q. How do you use recognition and rewards to motivate your employees?

A. Recognition and rewards is a critical part of motivating high-performance teams. It is important to recognize all successes, not just strategic projects. The hiring manager is assessing your effectiveness as a motivator of your team. Be sure to include examples of how to reward employees for major and smaller accomplishments, such as passing certification exams.

Q. What are some of the ways you stay current with industry developments?

A. It's tough to stay current not just on your managerial skills, but also on the technology. Though hiring managers don't expect you to be wizards at the technical stuff, it is important to maintain your skills. Some of the common ways that helpdesk managers stay current include taking additional classes on project management, time management, and general leadership topics, attending conferences, subscribing to industry magazines, visiting leading Websites for IT managers, reading industry electronic newsletters, and joining newsgroups. You should also consider joining industry-related helpdesk organizations.

Q. What are some of the ways that you assess organizational development needs?

A. Helpdesks are typically comprised of entry-level individuals. In order to maintain productivity on the helpdesk, some of the tools you can use to assess training and development include a skills gap analysis, a position profile, and individual assessments using companies like Brainbench.

Q. What are some of your preferred methods for professional staff development?

A. Training not just on technology but also on the company's products, services, and operations is required to maintain a productive helpdesk. Examples of ways to train a staff include on-the-job training, computer-based training or e-learning, instructor-led classroom training, use of reference resources and knowledge bases, and subscriptions to industry publications.

Q. From your perspective, what do you see as the value of a service-level agreement? What SLAs have you implemented in your previous posts?

A. An SLA is an important tool for measuring performance. An SLA is used to set expectations regarding the types of services to be provided and the level at which those services are to be provided. You may want to mention whether you've used SLAs in the past and how you performed against them.

Q. Explain the following metrics: ABA, ASA, OCR.

A. With these questions, the hiring manager is evaluating your basic understanding of how helpdesks are measured. It is important to explain the relevance of these metrics.

Abandonment Rate (ABA) ABA is the percentage of customers who exited the call queue before the call could be answered (they gave up on getting an answer).

Average Speed of Answer (ASA) ASA is the average amount of time that a call is in the queue before it is answered.

One Call Resolution OCR means the problem was fixed on the initial call.

Q. How do ABA, ASA, and OCR measurements on the helpdesk impact customers?

A. You had better understand the impact of these metrics on your customers! If any of these metrics are out of line, the customer's perception of service may be negatively impacted. Extensive hold times and disconnects equal low customer satisfaction levels. Answered calls and problem resolution equal high satisfaction levels.

Q. What are some of the ways you monitor quality?

A. The quality of a helpdesk can be monitored in a number of different ways, including call monitoring, ticket monitoring, customer surveys, round tables, and focus groups. Quality is synonymous with service, and the hiring manager is hiring you for your delivery of quality service.

Q. How do you perceive call monitoring?

A. On the helpdesk, call monitoring is expected. It provides a coaching opportunity, ensures the highest quality, ensures consistency in call etiquette, and is an effective technique for training. Provide an example of how you've used call monitoring to coach an employee to higher performance. You may also include a humorous story that resulted from call monitoring. Most helpdesk managers have plenty of them.

Q. How does the rollout of new products and services impact the helpdesk?

A. The helpdesk is a reactive critical resource for users during new product rollouts. Some of the impacts to the helpdesk include driving call volume increases as rollout progresses and early feedback on problems to spot improvement opportunities. Change has an impact on organizational productivity, lowering it at first and then improving it.

Q. What are the benefits of outsourcing and what has been your experience with it?

A. For some organizations, outsourcing can be an effective solution. Outsourcing can provide a reduced overall cost for supporting end-users as well as increased productivity and quality of deliverables. It may allow you to reduce capital outlay and/or resources. Outsourcing can provide a reduced overall cost for supporting end-users. It can also reduce the complexity of your organization as well as freeing up staff to focus on new initiatives. If you've been part of an outsourced helpdesk solution, you should include mention of how you effectively worked with your customers to ensure that they were taken care of.

For more detailed technical questions, see the Desktop Support Technician, Network Administrator, and Network Engineer job profiles.

Helpdesk Specialist

Keywords

Helpdesk analyst, helpdesk technician, customer support representative, helpdesk engineer, technical support, desktop support

Job Description

A company's helpdesk is like the 911 system. It's where you first call when you can't log in or print or access the Internet. It's a stressful job that deals with IT problems all day long, and it's also the most common entry-level position into an IT department.

Education and Certification Requirements

A college degree is not generally required for this position. Certification is a plus. The most common certifications for this position are CompTIA's A+, Linux +, and Network+, and HDI's Computer Support Specialist.

Technical Skills Required

Helpdesk specialists have a tough job—you must be a generalist and know a little bit about a whole lot. That means you must know where to get the information on areas you aren't familiar with (see other skills required below). You must know popular applications packages such as e-mail packages, word processors, and presentation packages as well as all the different operating systems in the company. You'll need a good grasp of hardware and networking in order to troubleshoot connectivity. You must also be familiar with custom applications specific to the company.

Other Skills Required

In addition to the technical skills listed above, you must also think logically, be an excellent problem solver and great communicator, and provide exceptional customer service. Helpdesk specialists are like detectives trying to solve a user's problem by asking one probing question at a time. You must also be familiar with resources to help you do your job well, such as product manuals, knowledge bases, and customer support Websites. You must have a genuine interest in solving the user's problem even under the worst circumstances.

Helpdesk Specialist Skills Check

Use the following scale to rate your skills. You can later use these descriptors to help describe your skill level on your résumé.

1 (Beginning) Use the skill/product occasionally (basic functions; not primary job responsibility)

2 (Entry level) Use the skill/product on a daily basis

3 (Proficient) Can provide frontline support

4 (Expert) Can train others on this skill/product

5 (Escalation support) The person others turn to when they can't figure it out

Skills	Skill Level
Hardware troubleshooting (motherboard, hard disk, power supplies, memory boards, video cards, sound cards, I/O basics)	
Desktop operating systems installation and troubleshooting	
Building and repairing a PC	
Hardware troubleshooting and maintenance	
Software installation and configuration	
Laptop configuration	
Peripheral installation (modems, printers)	
Network cards, cables, hubs, and network card drivers	
Network printing	
Multi-function devices	
Internet access	
Internet connectivity troubleshooting	
Web browsers	
TCP/IP configuration	
Disk management	
Security management	
Virus protection software installation	
Password management	
Backup and recovery	
Response to virus infections	
Operating Systems	
Windows	
Linux	
Unix	
Macintosh	

Skills	Skill Level
Networking Basics	
Networking clients	
Network logins	
Login scripts	
Drive mappings/shares	
User profiles and policies	
Managing access control	
Group membership	
Network Printing	
Configuring printer drivers	
Troubleshooting printing problems	
Network Protocols and Clients	
IPX/SPX	
NetBEUI	
TCP/IP	
Applications	
E-mail	
Word processing	
Spreadsheet	
Database	
People Skills	
Managing customer expectations	
Handling challenging customers	
Adapting to customer knowledge levels	
Information gathering for problem resolution	
Understanding the escalation process	
Understanding the requirements for excellent customer service	

Skills	Skill Level
Helpdesk Software	
HEAT	
Network Associates Magic Service Desk	
Remedy	
Asset Insight	
GoToAssist	
Track-IT	
Dameware Utilities	

Standing Out

The way to stand out on the helpdesk is to be fast and service oriented. Your ability to diagnose and remedy a situation will determine how quickly you move out of the helpdesk position to a more senior position—QA, network support, or desktop support. How you treat your customers is how you will get noticed by peers, customers, and management. A combination of great customer service and quick resolution will have you moving out of the helpdesk in no time.

Interview Questions to Expect

The following are questions specific to the role of a helpdesk specialist. Additional applicable technology-specific questions are found in the job profiles for Desktop Support Technician, Network Administrator, and Network Engineer.

Q. What do you see as the primary responsibilities of a helpdesk technician?

A. The interviewer uses questions like this one to assess whether you understand the job at hand. The foremost responsibility of someone in this position is to consistently deliver outstanding customer support. This is accomplished by ensuring response time and resolution time objectives are met, providing technical phone support to resolve IT-related service requests, maintaining technical product knowledge by learning new products as required, and enhancing customer relationships with the helpdesk and organization.

Q. What are the steps to logging a call?

A. This is another basic question that identifies your knowledge of how to do the job. The steps include:

1. Identify name of caller.
2. Verify eligibility/entitlement of service.
3. Identify priority/severity of the call.

4. Document caller's request.
5. Identify any special requirements.
6. Confirm facts/details with the caller.
7. Set caller's expectations for next contact.
8. Provide call reference (tracking) number.

Q. What information should be logged for calls?

A. Here is another question that tests your basic knowledge of how to do the job. The important information that should be logged on every call is

- Name of caller
- Contact information
- Phone number
- E-mail address
- Priority/severity of the call
- Caller's description of the request/problem
- Platform specifics
- Hardware, operating system, applications, and network
- All information pertaining to attempted and successful resolutions
- Conversation with the customer as it pertains to the problem
- Steps taken during the call, steps that will be taken after the call
- Next contact date
- Commitments made to the customer

Q. Have you used any helpdesk software to log calls?

A. The interviewer uses this question to assess whether you can hit the ground running or whether some retraining will be necessary on the basic tools to do the job. You should include the name of the application you've used and the feature set that provided the most efficiency in getting your job done. If you've worked on a helpdesk for more than a year, you probably have experience in customizing the software for your company's environment. Be sure to provide specific examples of your experience.

Q. Describe how you can use open and closed questions to gather necessary data from the user.

A. Your questioning techniques are synonymous with your experience and proficiency as a helpdesk technician. At the core are the types of questions that you ask in order to gather the necessary information from the user. Provide examples of open-ended questions that can be used to draw information from a user. For example, "Can you tell me what you were attempting to do when the application crashed?" Closed questions can be used to focus the user and get more specific information to help identify the true nature of the problem—for example, "What version of Microsoft Word are you using?"

Q. When should you escalate a call?

A. By asking this question, the interviewer is assessing your ability to understand the gravity of a situation in order to resolve customer issues quickly. Some of the instances when a call should be escalated include when the customer requests to speak to a manager, when an outage occurs that affects revenue, when you have a senior level/executive support personnel issue, and when you do not have an existing workaround.

Q. Why is it important to keep the customer informed of the current status of the problem and the next steps that will be taken?

A. The interviewer is assessing basic customer service skills. Obviously, keeping a customer informed improves customer satisfaction levels, sets customer expectations as to when a problem may be resolved, and increases employee productivity. If you can, provide an example that resulted in positive feedback from the customer.

Q. You work on an international helpdesk. Explain the impact of language barriers when interacting with others.

A. Many organizations provide international support, so you never know who will be on the other end of the line. Language barriers produce unique situations and require special attention. The language barrier may lead to a misunderstanding of the issue, misunderstanding of the instructions to resolve the issue, and general frustration on both ends of the phone. If you have experience working on an international helpdesk, you most likely have a few examples of how you've had to go out of your way to provide exceptional customer service. Provide these to increase your credibility.

Q. Sometimes customers build affinities with a particular technician. How do you encourage the customer to be open to using other helpdesk resources?

A. This question is part customer service, part a test of your ego. As a team player, you want to ensure that customers receive the same level of customer service regardless of who answers the phone. The interviewer is interested in hearing specific techniques that you would use to encourage the acceptance of other technicians. These may include helping the customer understand the long-term importance of great customer service by using all of the resources available.

Q. Why is it so important to document and properly fill out a call ticket?

A. A helpdesk thrives on processes and procedures that are consistently performed. Filling out a call ticket is a critical procedure for the immediate resolution of the problem and long-term customer service. The interviewer wants to know whether he can count on you to fill these out consistently and contribute to the success of the helpdesk and increased knowledge among the team members.

Q. The customer calls in with a question regarding a product you don't support. How would you respond?

A. This is a common question on any helpdesk. The interviewer wants to determine how you will be accommodating and at the same time not get carried away supporting a product that does not generate revenue for the company. Provide an example of a situation where you've redirected the customer to the proper support vehicles without impacting your customer service level or creating a negative experience for the customer.

Q. What are some of the ways you can build a better relationship within other parts of the IT department?

A. The hiring manager wants to ensure that you are a team player and will work effectively with other departments as you resolve customer issues. Some of the cardinal rules of being a team player include not blaming other departments when a bug/issue/mistake is discovered, treating others as you'd like to be treated, and whenever possible, assisting other departments with accomplishing their objectives.

Q. Describe some ways to empathize with the customer.

A. Empathy means putting yourself in the customer's place and is a common way of winning the customer over whenever they've encountered a particularly difficult problem. When answering this question in an interview, some of the phrases you might use to express empathy are: "I understand how scary that can be," "Oh, this is critical for you...," and "I'm sorry for the inconvenience."

Q. Describe an example of when you provided service beyond the call of duty.

A. This is an opportunity to stand out from the crowd with a real-life testimonial of your performance. Be sure you're prepared before the interview so you don't have to think of a situation on the spot.

Q. How would you determine the severity of a problem?

A. The interviewer is assessing your knowledge of protocol and processes. Incident severity policies should be a part of the helpdesk operating procedures or the service-level agreement with the customer. If there are no clear definitions, the following guidelines should be used to determine the severity of the problem: determine the number of personnel affected, determine the impact to the organization, assess the workload at the helpdesk, and determine the ability to provide a workaround.

Q. How do you properly close a call?

A. This is a test of your customer service skills. As a guideline, mention the following points:

1. Using the customer's name, recap the call to ensure all relevant data has been collected.
2. Verify that the customer data is correct and complete.
3. Provide a call reference (tracking) number.
4. Summarize problem resolution and/or steps to be taken, if any.
5. Set expectations for follow-up.
6. Ask if the customer has any other questions.
7. Thank the customer for calling.

Q. What's your method for problem solving?

A. The interviewer is assessing your skills in properly resolving problems to ensure that they fit in with how the rest of the department works. The steps to problem solving include several major components: problem identification, identifying possible causes of the problem, developing a plan, implementing the plan, observing and evaluating the results of the plan, repeating the process until the problem is resolved, and documenting the solution. It's a good idea to walk the interviewer through a problem that you had to solve recently.

Q. What are some of the resources you turn to for help in researching a problem?

A. Experienced technicians have a complete list of resources available to them that they depend on. Some of the resources that may be included are the vendor knowledge bases, user groups, product online help, and search engines like Google and Ask.com. Interviewers want to ensure that you won't be dependent on simply asking the guy next to you for all the answers.

Q. What are some of the metrics that you've been measured against in the past?

A. The typical metrics used to evaluate helpdesk employees include:

ASA Average speed of answer, or how long someone has to wait before they speak to a technician

ABA Abandonment rate, or how many customers gave up on waiting to speak with a technician

Talk Time The amount of time each caller talks

OCR One call resolution, or the ability to resolve the problem on the first call

Customer Satisfaction Measured via surveys
You should be aware of your own performance in these areas, particularly OCR.

Q. How many days did you miss in the last six months?

A. Your attendance record is extremely important as a helpdesk technician. An unscheduled absence can wreak havoc on your teammates. Obviously, the hiring manager will not have access to your attendance records, but they can certainly check with your references if they happen to be associated with your previous employers.

For more detailed technical questions, see the Desktop Support Technician, Network Administrator, and Network Engineer job profiles.

Independent Consultant

Keywords

Contractor, independent contractor, IT consultant

Job Description

The rule with IT consultants is the more specialized the position, the greater the need for them. For example, highly specialized database administrators who can performance-tune a SQL box can demand a very nice hourly wage. Independent network administrators, on the other hand, may have a hard time finding work. Contractors are typically brought in to work on specific projects.

Education and Certification Requirements

See the appropriate job profile.

Technical Skills Required

See the appropriate job profile.

Other Skills Required

In addition to any technical skills that are required for the position, consultants must also be skilled in other areas. Marketing skills will help you stay employed. Project management skills will help you complete projects successfully. Communication skills will help you keep the project going, set expectations, and ensure that everyone is in alignment with the project's progress. In addition, there is a set of hidden skills that will make an independent consultant successful. These include being able to prioritize with minimal information, the ability to quickly read system specifications and identify errors in logic or processes, skill in solving complex business problems, the ability to understand common business practices, and the ability to weed through voluminous information to draw conclusions.

Independent Consultant Skills Check

Please see the Skills Check for the position you are consulting for.

Standing Out

To stand out as a consultant, you must be prepared to provide references and testimonials of your past work. Testimonials go a long way. Preferably these references will be in the same industry as the company with whom you are interviewing.

Interview Questions to Expect

Q. Tell me about your past experience on this type of project.

A. This is generally an opening question that the interviewer will use to dig deeper into your experience. The goal is for the interviewer to be able to picture you completing the project at hand. Find out as much as you can about the open project so that you may tailor your experience to what will be needed to get the job done.

Q. What is the most challenging project you've worked on?

A. Here is an opportunity for you to take control of the interview by telling a story. Make sure that the story has a successful conclusion and that you include the challenge, the circumstances, how you approached it, the outcome, and what you learned.

Q. What type of contracting agreement do you typically negotiate?

A. You should have a standard contracting agreement that you use on every engagement. The company may also have their own version. If they insist on using their own agreement, make sure that you have your legal counsel review it before signing.

Q. How do you propose to hit the ground running?

A. Consultants are retained to deliver. Getting up to speed is costly and, in itself, provides no value to the organization. Generally, the smaller the burden to the organization in time and effort, the better. This means asking up front for what you need to do your job quickly and well, such as project definition documents, network documentation, security policies, and database schemas. It also means sitting down with the right people (project managers, development leads, project stakeholders, and even end-users sometimes) to fill in the details and get the big picture.

Q. How do you ensure that your projects meet deadlines and requirements?

A. The interviewer is checking out your project management skills. Do you strive in a structured environment, and how do you create structure for yourself when the organization doesn't naturally provide it?

Q. Describe a situation when you've been called upon to reengineer a process. What challenges did you encounter?

A. Consultants are change agents. Luckily, they typically don't have to stick around for long after the changes have been made. Change creates fear, uncertainty, and doubt in an organization, so you must be prepared to handle these emotions. Many assignments are for the purpose of restructuring the way something is done, reengineering a process, or acting as an advisor. Such situations require creative thinking and a willingness to challenge the status quo. You should address some of the ways in which you have handled similar situations in the past, including how you used communication to ease some of the high emotions.

Q. Describe a project that was headed for trouble when you were brought in to work on it.

A. It's unlikely any experienced person has not been involved in a project or assignment that has gotten into trouble. How you respond to these situations tells a great deal about your capabilities. Explain how you reestablished roles and responsibilities, assessed what went wrong, reset priorities, and adjusted the project plan as necessary.

Q. Describe a situation when you've exceeded customers' expectations.

A. One of the values a consultant brings is a wealth of experience that allows them to look beyond the status quo and identify opportunities for improvement in efficiency or more effective alternatives for achieving departmental or organizational goals and objectives. Provide an example of when it made sense to extend a contract, bring in other consultants, or provide additional management advice.

Q. What interests you about this position, and why are you confident you can successfully meet the requirements of the role?

A. You should point out how this project fits into an area in which you already have experience. You should then explain how your years of experience as a contractor have provided you with the ability to handle whatever might come up (provide an example). Whenever possible, project enthusiasm for the work, and stress your ability to foresee problems and head them off at the pass.

IT Management (Director of IT or IT Manager)

Keywords

IT operations manager, manager of business systems, engineering manager, technical services manager, telecommunications manager, systems manager, quality control manager, development manager

Job Description

A career in IT management is not for everyone. Your first IT management position may be one of the toughest transitions you will have to make. After years as a techie, you are willingly shifting what drives you. You're changing what you're willing to give up and what you're willing to take on. When you join the ranks of IT management, there is a fundamental shift from managing systems to managing people who manage systems. With the change to management, you no longer need to keep your technical skills up to date, including your certifications that took you so long to earn, because you no longer need to fix all the problems yourself. You now have a staff of people who are responsible and to whom you will have to delegate problem resolution. What you take on is planning, people management, running a business, and interfacing with other managers and executives, either within the IT department or outside your department. This typically means more meetings, more reports, and more presentations.

Education and Certification Requirements

A four-year degree in computer science or management information systems is a requirement as you move up the management ranks. Along the way, technical certification will set you apart by demonstrating your initiative. An M.B.A. degree as well as leadership and professional development seminars are additional pluses.

Technical Skills Required

IT managers should get a solid grounding in technical skills early in their careers. As you rise in the ranks of IT management, maintaining your technical skills can be done by reading IT periodicals, attending industry conferences, and through day-to-day management of the IT department and vendors.

Other Skills Required

In addition to technical expertise, you will also need managerial skills, which include people skills, recruiting, motivating, getting consensus, and team building. Emotional stability and tolerance to stress are also important, and project management is a major plus. Above all else, you must have a strong desire for leadership in order to willingly forego keeping your technical skills up to date.

IT Management Skills Check

Use the following scale to rate your skills. You can later use these descriptors to help describe your skill level on your résumé.

1 (Beginning) Use the skill/product occasionally (basic functions; not primary job responsibility)

2 (Entry level) Use the skill/product on a daily basis

3 (Proficient) Can provide frontline support

4 (Expert) Can train others on this skill/product

5 (Escalation support) The person others turn to when they can't figure it out

Skills	Skill Level
Functional experience in one area of IT	
Budgeting	
Conducting ROI analysis	
Staffing and HR issues	
Performance management	

Skills	Skill Level
Managing vendor negotiations and relationships	
Project management	
Maintaining IT corporate standards	
Technologies	
Web technologies	
E-business	
Helpdesk management	
Security	
Outsourcing	
Networking/WANs	
Storage solutions	
Software engineering	
ERP	
CRM	
Systems integration	

Standing Out

If you're just getting into IT management, your project management skills will provide you with an efficient framework for your upcoming management responsibilities. Having a project management certification will provide instant credibility. You may want to consider this certification as a way of making the next step from manager to director.

Interview Questions to Expect

Q. Describe your current IT management position.

A. The interviewer is looking for you to address the following: the size of your present IT organization, the functional groups within it, specifics on which groups you manage, how long you've been in that position, your strategic responsibilities and your day-to-day responsibilities. You should also include what's different about the organization since you took the job, paying particular attention to the improvements you have contributed to. Your asset statements should encompass your accomplishments.

Q. What were your three most impressive tangible contributions to your company?

A. Go back to your "So what?" statements. How did you save the company money? Implement a process? Increase revenue? What awards did you receive?

Q. What are some of the common threats that IT departments face and how do you reduce the risks?

A. The interviewer wants to see the depth of your experience. One way of assessing this is by asking you to identify the biggest challenges that you'll face as an IT manager. Some of these include viruses, natural disasters, sabotage by disgruntled employees, theft of confidential information, and damage or loss of key operating information. You must also be able to offer insight in how to rein in these challenges. For example, to prevent virus and hacking threats and minimize their impact, you must be a master at risk management. You can elaborate on answers such as these by talking about the measures that you would put in place to deal with these challenges, such as creating and regularly updating disaster plans, ensuring that security and virus detection are key focuses, enforcing physical security of valuable equipment, and protecting the company legally in all contract negotiations.

Q. What are some of the different ways that you've ensured cooperation and success in managing projects that affect other departments?

A. The interviewer is looking for examples of how well you handle building cross-departmental buy-in for projects that involve other parts of the organization. The key here is to talk about the importance of communication in ensuring that everyone understands their roles and responsibilities. In well-run IT organizations, this can be done through a formal project management department within IT whose purpose is to bring all respective stakeholders together to build the project scope and provide key business expertise. As an IT manager, you should be able to talk about your specific experience in project management.

Q. What kinds of problems do you feel you are uniquely qualified to solve? Give an example of how you have demonstrated this.

A. Your résumé should easily identify what your strengths are. To ensure that you answer this question appropriately, you should have already identified what unique challenges the organization faces. That way you'll be able to customize your answer to their needs. IT directors are always looking for managers they can rely on to bring projects in on time and under budget, so managing a well-run group is important. They look for managers who can align their priorities with the business priorities. Other situations that provide challenges include ensuring that the IT department is seen as an effective service organization—systems are reliable and resources are managed so that projects can be completed on time.

Q. What ideas have you sold to your management? Why? What happened?

A. The interviewer is looking for your resourcefulness, your creativity, and your business acumen. As an IT manager, you should always be looking for ways to improve the bottom line by improving business processes, reducing the staff that it takes to accomplish business goals, and creating efficiencies in the resources required. Some of the ways that you can accomplish these goals might include the creation of standards for desktop operating systems and computer platforms supported. Also, implementation of a knowledge base and adoption of a project management process are excellent ways to demonstrate that you are not happy with the status quo.

Q. Give an example of a project you were responsible for starting. What did you do? How did it work out?

A. This is an opportunity to discuss your project management style. As an IT manager, you should be ready to discuss a very specific *successful* project that you were responsible for, like a new product rollout or an upgrade to an environment. The larger the scale, the better. By being as specific as possible in your example, you will help the interviewer see you performing those same functions within their organization.

Q. What is the biggest error in judgment you have made in a previous job? Why did you make it? How did you recover?

A. This is a tough question, but it's often asked. You can't guarantee how the interviewer will take it. Some safe bets on what to mention: selecting an ISP or a vendor that went out of business. These are safe bets because everyone has been burned by an IT vendor at one point or another. Through these experiences you have the opportunity to learn what to watch out for in your next selection. Be ready to talk about one specific experience and what you learned from it.

Q. How do you keep up with the changes in technology (terminology, information) in your field?

A. As an IT manager, you are not expected to sit down and code an application fix, but you are expected to make the right decisions when it comes to selecting the right vendors, understanding the strengths and weaknesses of the technologies that can get the job done, and being able to lead the group in solving a problem like the WAN being down. In order to do this, you have to maintain your skills. There are a number of ways to do this, ranging from what you read on a regular basis to the professional groups you are a part of, the conferences that you attend, and the type of knowledge sharing that happens regularly at your organization. Most importantly, you need to pay attention to how problems get resolved by holding a debriefing after the problem is fixed so that your entire team can learn from the situation. Some excellent free resources include *ComputerWorld* magazine, TechRepublic.com, and the CIO.com Website. You should talk about which resources are particularly helpful to you in maintaining your skills. Don't forget—IT management isn't just about managing technology, so mentioning additional resources that provide insight into management is an excellent idea.

Q. What methods do you use to make decisions? Please give an example of your approach.

A. As an IT manager, you will have to make hundreds of decisions on a daily basis. The interviewer is looking for consistency and thoroughness in your decision-making process. You should talk about how you go about defining the problem, collecting information on resources needed, identifying alternative solutions, choosing one of the solutions, acting on the solution, and evaluating the results. Be prepared to discuss a specific situation to illustrate your effective decision-making skills.

Q. When, in a past job, did you find it important to disagree with your boss? How did you approach him or her, and what was the result?

A. Talking about disagreements with bosses is rough because the interviewer will immediately put himself or herself in the position of the previous boss. It doesn't really matter what the topic was that you disagreed about. What is important is how you approached your boss. In all situations, you should never disagree in public; you should always give the benefit of the doubt that they know what they are doing, and you should be prepared to truly see the situation from their perspective. You might ask for a private meeting to discuss this, and if you are still of the same opinion, ask for permission to present your case further in the form of a report or presentation with the research to back it.

Q. What do you typically do when you hear of a problem in your area? Give a current example.

A. The interviewer is testing your resistance to jumping to conclusions. Communication is the only way to resolve issues, and as a manager you are going to run into many problems on a daily basis. The first thing you should do is meet with the manager or supervisor of the suspected source of the problem to see whether in fact there is a problem. If there is a problem, and it is not mission critical, you could then allow the supervisor to make it right before further action, holding them accountable to future follow-ups. If the problem is with a direct employee, you would proceed with them.

Q. How have you planned for performance improvements in employees who report to you?

A. Managers know that handling performance problems is one of the most dreaded responsibilities of being a manager. How you handle these situations will determine your fiber as a manager. What the interviewer is looking for is to determine your discipline in handling these situations. The first part is the assessment of the performance problem: skill deficiency or motivation. The second is the recommended course of action: training to fill the gaps or training for more advanced skills. The last component is the follow-up: continued termination, further training, or dismissal of the employee.

If you have experience with handling performance improvements, talk about an example that illustrates how you handled the situation professionally yet humanely. If you don't have personal experience, refer to the ideal scenario above.

Q. What responsibility do you have for budgeting?

A. Managing the IT budget is an important responsibility, especially since IT is generally seen as a cost to the organization. The interviewer wants to know how big the budget was, whether you built the budget, how close you came to the budget, and—especially—that you didn't go over the budget. Be ready with numbers and percentages in this area.

Q. Describe any cost savings programs that you have implemented within your department.

A. A major issue with IT is overspending. It's important to always keep an eye on cost savings programs. These may include monitoring license usage, consolidating telecommunications and negotiating better rates, centralized purchasing, bringing outsourced functions in-house, outsourcing, and improving on existing processes. Provide specific examples on cost-saving programs that you have implemented for previous employers.

Q. How would you monitor/manage consultants?

A. Managing consultants takes managing to a whole new level. Most IT managers will have had experiences (good or bad) with consultants. The key points to mention (along with providing specific examples on projects where you've had to manage consultants) include being clear on objectives, reporting procedures for work assignments, and project milestones. A technique that's often used is to insist on weekly status reports correlating the billing hours and the work accomplished.

Q. How would you work with an employee who seems to be consistently late on deliverables?

A. Questions like these allow the interviewer to test your skill in managing difficult situations. Disciplining employees is tough for every manager. In this particular situation, the key is to isolate the cause of the problem. There are many possible solutions here, but honest communication with the employee is best. It may turn out that the employee may not have the proper training for the job and it may be beyond what the person is capable of performing. The employee may also have too much on their plate, with everything being a top priority, or there may be a lack of understanding of how to prioritize tasks.

Q. Your team is primarily junior level and you are behind schedule with a drop-dead deliverable date. What would you do?

A. Here is yet another question that assesses how you would manage a difficult situation. This particular situation is very common, as new teams often get assigned projects beyond their capabilities. One way to handle this situation is to start off with a skills gap analysis to help define whether training will fix the problem. An additional option would be to hire qualified consultants to act as mentors and coaches. If you've been in this situation before, you should discuss how you solved the problem.

Q. Describe what expertise you have relative to network security or disaster recovery planning.

A. This is an intentionally very broad question to assess your knowledge on the various aspects associated with security. Hiring managers are looking for your knowledge on firewalls, virus protection, keeping software up to date with the latest patches, perimeter defense systems, single sign-on, and authentication techniques. Be prepared to talk about previous policies that you may have implemented within other organizations.

Disaster recovery is also an important area to focus on. Be descriptive of how your company implemented redundant systems, managed backup of critical information, and provided succession planning in case of emergencies.

Q. What groups of people in the organization or company must an IT manager develop good, sound relationships with?

A. IT managers must develop relationships above and below them. Above them includes upper management (department director, VP, CEO, board, director). Below them may include clients, other departments, and IT staff.

Q. What is your role in managing up?

A. An IT manager/director's role in managing up the organization includes keeping executives informed and involved at the right level on initiatives they have sponsored, gaining approval for major new initiatives, recognizing changes that are needed regarding projects, getting executive support for changes affecting the rest of the organization, and explaining overall IT costs versus volumes and unit costs.

Q. As an IT manager/director, what are the key areas that you focus on?

A. Questions of this nature assess your strategic thinking ability. As a part of management, you will be expected to tactically manage your team and to also be part of a higher-level team that will have to define key focus areas that align themselves with the business objectives. If you're not new to IT management, you can address this question with specific examples of working on strategy meetings. You should also include your experience in interfacing with executive management, developing an IT strategy to meet business goals, budgeting, resource planning, negotiating contracts with vendors, ensuring that key policies are in place (security, e-mail usage, and so on), and ensuring that projects are delivered according to plan.

Network Administrator

Keywords

Systems administrator, maintenance, troubleshooting, support, upgrades, NetWare, Windows Server/Vista, Linux admin, sysadmin

Job Description

To become a network administrator—that's every Microsoft Certified Systems Engineer's dream. Network administrators are responsible for the administration of a company's local area network. An organization may have more than one admin to handle all their networking requirements. The job entails installing servers, managing and upgrading network operating systems, and overall network maintenance including installing and configuring applications, creating users, and security. Networks inevitably have issues and much of a network administrator's job may be to work with the helpdesk to troubleshoot any network issues. Since the network is the core of the IT department, network administrators are key members of the IT department.

Education and Certification Requirements

A college degree in computer science or management information systems is usually required, though equivalent on-the-job experience may be appropriate. Certification will definitely give you a leg up in this position.

Technical Skills Required

You should have network operating expertise in the latest and most popular operating systems, including Windows Server, Solaris and Linux. In addition, you should understand and be proficient in Internet connectivity, basic security skills, and network hardware infrastructure, including hubs, switches, routers, and firewalls. Network administrators must also be familiar with network topologies and wide area networking.

Other Skills Required

As with other network-related positions, troubleshooting and problem-solving skills are required. Great communication skills are a plus for helping users figure out their problems.

Network Administrator Skills Check

Use the following scale to rate your skills. You can later use these descriptors to help describe your skill level on your résumé.

1 (Beginning) Use the skill/product occasionally (basic functions; not primary job responsibility)

2 (Entry level) Use the skill/product on a daily basis

3 (Proficient) Can provide frontline support

4 (Expert) Can train others on this skill/product

5 (Escalation support) The person others turn to when they can't figure it out

Skills	Skill Level
Server installation and configuration	
Configuration of advanced file systems and name services	
Security and user administration	
Developing disaster recovery plans and managing daily backup and recovery	

Skills	Skill Level
Server administration	
Installation of print services	
Active Directory administration and configuration	
Network performance monitoring and planning	
Troubleshooting and end-user support	
Evaluating new hardware and software and making purchasing recommendations	
Anticipating network issues and putting preventive measures in place	
Timely notification of network maintenance outages	
Creating documentation for the systems	
Hardware	
Hubs	
Switches	
Routers	
Bridges	
Networked storage devices	
Modems	
Network Protocols and Technologies	
TCP/IP configuration	
VPNs	
WAP	
Active Directory	
DNS	
Ethernet	
SNMP	
NFS	
AppleTalk	

Skills	Skill Level
Network Software	
Microsoft Exchange Server	
Novell NetWare	
Unix	
Solaris	
Linux	
Windows Server	
Lotus Notes	
Microsoft Internet Information Server (IIS)	

Standing Out

You can stand out as a network administrator by having in-depth experience with the latest technology. This includes Windows Active Directory and security.

Interview Questions to Expect

General Questions

The following questions provide you with an opportunity to demonstrate the application of your networking skills, including planning, installation, configuration, and troubleshooting. Using these general questions, the interviewer will assess your overall network administration skills. Additional operating system–specific questions will enable the interviewer to determine your experience level with these systems. The interviewer may also ask you to take an assessment exam to further rate your knowledge level in particular technologies.

Q. Please describe the technical environment of your current (or most recent) position.

A. When describing the technical environment that you currently support, be sure to include the number of users you support, the number of IT staff, the technical infrastructure including servers, types of connections, desktop operating systems, your job duties, and your work schedule.

You should be prepared to talk about each of the positions you have listed on your résumé in this way. Also be prepared with a follow-up statement of your most significant accomplishment.

Q. How do you keep your technical knowledge and skills current?

A. Keeping your skills current demonstrates initiative and a desire to perform at high standards. Be prepared with a list of resources including professional groups.

Q. What has been the greatest challenge in your career and how did you work through it?

A. Ah, an opportunity for a story. Great examples to draw on: how you taught yourself a new operating system, the installation of a complex system, integration of multiple systems, building of an e-commerce Website.

Q. What are some of the tools you use to make your job easier?

A. All network administrators have a bag of tricks. You should share some of your trade secrets as a way of demonstrating that you can be efficient in your job as a network administrator.

Q. What's the minimum documentation you should have for your network?

A. One of the toughest parts of network administration is keeping track of an always changing environment. You must have basic documentation for user administration, file system planning, and address planning. Share your documentation with your interviewer.

Q. What are some of the things you need to take into consideration when planning an upgrade from one network operating system to another?

A. This is the mother of all planning activities because it will affect so many resources. The key here is testing and backups and that's what the interviewer wants to hear. Other considerations include:

- Network documentation
- Ensuring that your hardware meets the minimum hardware requirements for the new operating system
- Creating a test network for testing the compatibility of applications, hardware, and drivers with the new operating system
- Gathering all updated drivers and patches/service packs required for upgrade compatibility
- Identifying workflow issues before converting
- Separating workstation conversions from server conversions
- Ensuring you have backups of data and the servers so that you can revert back
- Network addressing scheme

Q. Describe the backup/restore policy you use most.

A. First of all, the interviewer wants to ensure that you do backups! There are different methods, but the most common backup strategy used is to perform incremental backups Monday through Thursday and a normal backup on Friday. An alternative backup strategy is to perform differential backups Monday through Thursday and a normal backup on Friday.

Q. How would you ensure that your servers are secure?

A. Security always begins at the physical level—it makes little difference that you've provided all the security the operating system and software can provide if someone can walk away with the box or the portable hard drive. The next step is to ensure you have the latest service packs for the operating system and applications running on the server.

Installation

Server installation is a major part of your job as a network administrator. The following questions will provide the interviewer with insight into your skills in this area.

Q. What steps do you go through as part of your server installation process?

A. The interviewer wants to know whether your typical work habits are to just jump in or whether you do some planning. You obviously want to ensure that your hardware meets the minimum requirements, that you have all the right drivers for the new operating system, and whether you need a ROM upgrade for your hardware. Depending on how many installations you've done, you may have a process that you like to follow. If you do, describe it to the interviewer.

Q. What's the last thing you should do when you install a service pack or a software patch?

A. The interviewer wants to make sure that testing is an integral part of your routine whenever you install software or make updates to systems. You may also want to review the Event Viewer logs and look for any errors that have been registered. It's a good idea to also examine the administrative interfaces for SQL and the e-mail server to satisfy yourself that no anomalies have appeared there.

Q. What methods are available for configuring a WINS server for use by various Microsoft computers?

A. This question demonstrates to the interviewer that you are familiar with the various methods for configuring routing using WINS. You can either configure the WINS server manually or by way of a Dynamic Host Configuration Protocol Server.

Q. What are some of the ways you can automate the creation of users to save time?

A. By asking you to describe multiple ways of getting the job done, the interviewer can assess your experience level with the operating system. Some of the correct answers to this question include the following:

- You could copy an existing user's account to create a new account. However, the rights and permissions for the new, copied account will be based purely on its group memberships, not permissions granted strictly to the original account itself.

- Using Active Directory, you could use the CSVDE.exe program to create a new account with specific group memberships; however, this program is usually intended for bulk creation of accounts in your domain.
- You could create the new account from scratch, assigning group permissions or individual rights manually.

Q. What are some of the alternative ways for mapping a drive letter to a file server if you wish to connect to one of the server's shared folders?

A. This question tests your experience by asking for alternate methods of getting the job done. In addition to mapped drives, you can use a Universal Naming Convention path: \\servername\sharename. You can also browse the Network Neighborhood.

Q. You shared a printer from your Windows 2003 Server. What could you do to ensure that the printer is easily accessible to your Windows 98 clients?

A. You may have to support older clients on your network. This question tests your experience with older technology.

Q. A user contacts you and reports that their Windows workstation is having trouble connecting to the Web. You run the ipconfig command on the computer and you find that the computer is not referencing the correct primary DNS server. What must you do to remedy this?

A. Using this question, the interviewer can assess your routing troubleshooting skills, an essential part of network administration. Walk the interviewer through reconfiguring the client computer.

Q. A user is having trouble sharing a folder from their Windows workstation. What is a likely cause?

A. The interviewer is testing your basic knowledge of rights. In order to share a folder you must be logged on as an administrator, server operator (in a domain), or power user (in a workgroup).

Q. You've shared a folder and set the share permissions to "Everyone = Full Control." However, none of the users can save information in the folder. What's the likely cause?

A. This is another question that tests your knowledge of permissions. The likely cause is that someone has set the NTFS permissions in a more restrictive manner than the share permissions. Between those two categories of permissions, the more restrictive of the two always applies to users accessing the folder over the network.

Q. What is the most likely cause for the failure of a user to connect to a Windows remote access server?

A. Supporting remote users may be a big part of your job. It's important to understand the proper configuration and troubleshooting of RAS.

Q. A remote user calls in for help. You determine that you'll need to access some hidden files on the remote machine. The user is logged in using Terminal Server. Which tools do you use to solve the situation?

A. Remote troubleshooting is a key component to a network administrator's job. You should be familiar with different tools that allow you to do remote management of users' computers.

Active Directory

In order to manage an Active Directory Services environment, you must be comfortable with planning, security and permissions, authentication, and synchronization. The following questions may be asked by the interviewer to assess your experience with performing these functions. These questions will provide you with a baseline of technical knowledge for your interview.

- What is the Active Directory schema?
- What is the default protocol used in directory servers?
- What are the physical and logical components of Active Directory Services?
- What is the global catalog server?
- What is the file responsible for the Active Directory database?
- What rights must a user have in order to create a Windows forest?
- What rights must a user have in order to add a domain to an existing forest?
- What would you look for if you received an error message stating that the Domain Naming Master cannot be contacted?
- Why is Domain Name System so important to an Active Directory forest?
- What rights does a user need in order to create computer accounts in an Active Directory domain?
- What's the difference between local, global, and universal groups?
- Where are group policies storied?
- Which has highest priority—group policies or computer settings?
- How can you restrict running certain applications on a machine?
- An administrator accidentally deleted an entire organizational unit containing 200 users from the domain. How can you recover the organizational unit?

For more detailed technical questions, see the Helpdesk Specialist, Desktop/Network Support Technician, and Network Engineer job profiles.

Network Engineer

Keywords

Systems engineer, infrastructure engineer, network architect, technology architect, network design engineer

Job Description

Network engineer is the next step up from a network administrator. Whereas a network administrator is responsible for the local area network, a network engineer is primarily responsible for an organization's wide area network infrastructure. This means everything from deciding on the type and number of servers required to perform a group of functions to designing the infrastructure required to support the network. It also means troubleshooting the network. You work with third-party providers to build the network resources. You are also responsible for capacity planning, analysis, design, and testing of the WAN. You may also have the responsibility of setting up an automated network management system. Given the complexity of the position, you generally need two or more years of LAN administration experience to qualify.

Education and Certification Requirements

A college degree is usually required as well as formal training in network administration or engineering. The key certifications in this area are Microsoft, Linux, and Cisco engineering certifications. These include MCSE, RHCT, RHCE, RHCSS, RHA, CCNA, and CCIE.

Technical Skills Required

This is a highly technical position. Network engineers need to have extensive knowledge of the latest technologies for local area networks and wide area networks. Additional skills may be required in telecommunications.

Other Skills Required

Network engineers need very fine-tuned problem-solving skills because of the many disparate systems that make up today's networks. You must be systematic and methodical to handle problem isolation and remediation. You must also be good at documentation and ensuring that the documentation is kept up to date. You must work well in a team because you will work closely with other IT departments, including development and project management. The position of network engineer is the highest point of networking and systems escalation. The most important qualification is your desire to learn. At the rate of today's technology changes, you'll be learning a new technology a week.

Network Engineer Skills Check

Use the following scale to rate your skills. You can later use these descriptors to help describe your skill level on your résumé.

1 (Beginning) Use the skill/product occasionally (basic functions; not primary job responsibility)

2 (Entry level) Use the skill/product on a daily basis

3 (Proficient) Can provide frontline support

4 (Expert) Can train others on this skill/product

5 (Escalation support) The person others turn to when they can't figure it out

Skills	Skill Level
Analyze and resolve technical problems for established networks	
Plan, test, recommend, and implement network, file server, mainframe, and workstation hardware and software	
Provide network documentation, training, and guidance to computing system clients and programmers	
Serve as technical specialist in network problems and emergencies	
Troubleshoot and resolve network production problems	
Conduct technical research on network upgrades and components to determine feasibility, cost, time required, and compatibility with current system	
Recommend network solutions for short-, medium-, and long-range network projects	
Install, configure, and maintain network components	
Determine plan layout for new hardware or modifications to existing layout	
Install, upgrade, and configure network printing, directory structures, user access, security, software, and file services	
Establish user profiles, user environments, directories, and security for networks being installed	
Work as a team member with other technical staff, such as systems to ensure connectivity and compatibility between systems	
Work with vendors to resolve complex network problems	
Maintain confidentiality with regard to the information being processed, stored, or accessed by the network	
Document network problems and resolutions for future reference	

Skills	Skill Level
Technology	
Bridging	
Routing	
LAN switching	
Bandwidth management	
Intranets	
Extranets	
Certificate services	
Active Directory	
Routing Protocols	
TCP/IP addressing, subnet masks	
Default gateways, static and dynamic routing	
Distance-vector	
IGRP-EIGRP	
IPX/SPX, RIP and NLSP	
Link-state protocols	
OSPF, ABR, and ASBR	
RIP	
AppleTalk	
DNS	
NAT	
DHCP	
WINS	
WAN Types and Topologies	
RAS	
ATM	
ISDN	
Point to point	

Skills	Skill Level
Star, hub and spoke, mesh	
VPN	
X.25 and Frame Relay	
Analog and digital modems	
Cable modems	
DSL	
FDDI	
PSTN	
Satellite	
Wireless technologies	
SMDS	
Mask and default gateways	
Troubleshooting tools	
SNMP applications and agents	
Bluetooth	
WLAN (802.11)	
WiFi	
Traffic Management	
AAA (authentication, authorization, and accounting)	
Compression and queuing	
Extended access lists	
SAP traffic management	
SNMP	
SNTP and NTP	
Standard IP access lists	
Standard IPX access lists	
Vendors	
Cisco	

Skills	Skill Level
Citrix	
CheckPoint	
Linux	
Windows	
Nortel	

Standing Out

Extensive knowledge of security and wireless technologies will help you stand out in the crowd.

Interview Questions to Expect

Q. Describe the network environments of the organizations that you have supported in the past.

A. This general question provides you with an opportunity to start the conversation regarding the technologies that you have experience with. Be descriptive in your answer. Include the number of users, number of remote sites, types of systems, type of connectivity between sites, network configuration, ISP used, routers/switches used, and the size of the overall engineering team. Also include who you reported to and the management style of that manager.

Q. Describe TCP/IP and its protocols.

A. This is a great question in that it forces the candidate to display their knowledge of the protocol.

Q. What routing protocols have you configured?

A. Another application question. Be specific with your answer.

Q. What routing problems have you troubleshot?

A. It's not just about setting up the networks but how you handle the common problems. Obviously, there are the issues with not being able to connect to the outside world but go a little deeper into your answer—router not forwarding IP packets, routing loops caused by filtering redistribution, mismatched neighbor parameters in OSPF, etc.

Q. As a part of your interview, you can expect to be asked how you've used common networking commands and protocols. Some of the questions you can anticipate include:

- When do you use BGP, IGRP, OSPF, and static routes?
- What is UDP and TCP. How do they differ?

- Describe how SNMP works.
- Describe what a VPN is and how it works.
- Describe how VoIP (Voice Over IP) works.
- Describe methods of Quality of Service (QoS).
- How do you distinguish a DNS problem from a network problem?

Q. Describe how traceroute, ping, and tcpdump work and what they are used for? Describe a situation where you used these tools for troubleshooting a network problem.

A. It's easy to find the definition of these commands. The hard part is providing an example of when you would use one command over the other. Obviously, be sure that you know the difference and have plenty of examples to talk about how you've used these commands for troubleshooting.

Q. Describe the last major networking problem that you were able to troubleshoot and solve on your own?

A. This question gets at the heart of whether you can do the job. When describing the situation be sure to include: overview of the situation, the impact on users, how you diagnosed the cause of the problem, how you identified solutions, and which solution was the answer. Describe how long it took you from start to finish and what you did, if anything, to prevent this situation in the future.

Q. What network analyzers tools are you familiar with and provide an example of how you've used them to solve a network problem.

A. What's your bag of tricks? Provide a variety of examples which demonstrate your proficiency with the tools. Include the tools, whether you've received any formal training in its use, and the situations where you've applied the tools.

Q. Which name resolution system is implemented with TCP/IP by default?

A. Although WINS is a name resolution that is implemented by TCP/IP by default, it only works on Windows-based networks. The only true name resolution system that almost every TCP/IP network uses is DNS.

Q. Provide an example of how you've used the OSI model to troubleshoot a connectivity issue.

A. As an engineer, you must know the OSI model inside and out. TCP/IP is the standard protocol for the Internet, and it strictly follows the rules set forth in this reference model. As a quick refresher, here is the OSI model:

Application Layer Responsible for end-user–friendly protocols like HTTP, FTP, and telnet.

Presentation Layer Responsible for isolating different data formats from each other.

Session Layer Responsible for maintaining a registry of all current active connections.

Transport Layer Responsible for transparent flow of data between devices, without consideration to hardware details. This layer is concerned with the reliable transfer of data packets from point to point.

Network Layer Responsible for providing logical paths for data packets to pass through; provides switching and routing facilities.

Link Layer Responsible for encoding and subsequent decoding of data packets at various network points.

Electrical/Physical Responsible for defining various electrical standards such as cables and bitstream sizes for communicating between devices.

Q. How do you approach a technical problem? Give an example.

A. This question is a necessary evil to ask a network engineer and one that you are guaranteed to be asked. Everyone has a different system. What's important is that you have a system. Describe your method and also provide a recent example that demonstrates it in action from start to finish.

Q. What role does network planning play in successful project implementation?

A. This question shows the necessity of having a solid foundation for any project. Any infrastructure is only as good as the basic network that it's built on.

Q. Have you ever been in a situation where you found yourself without the specific technical knowledge to perform a task essential to your project? What did you do?

A. This question is one that every engineer should have an answer for. It should be relatively easy to answer—be truthful without showing a weakness in ability. This is when a good researching talent comes in handy. No one expects an engineer to have memorized all of the information necessary to perform his job, but you need to have the skills to find the correct information quickly.

Q. Describe what a password policy is and the reasons for having one. Give an example of a policy and its rule set.

A. This is one of the most important and overlooked details in a secure network. You'll get pushback from the users, but they will adjust. An engineer must be well versed in security and the policies required to implement and maintain it.

Q. What is offsite storage and why is it important to a disaster recovery plan?

A. This is a subject that no one ever pays much attention to until it's needed. It is also one of the biggest reasons engineers lose their jobs. Offsite data storage guarantees that no matter what happens to your data center or servers, you will always have a copy of your data elsewhere. This is just a small part of an overall plan, but one of the most critical.

Q. How (and how often) should you test your disaster recovery plan?

A. Again, disaster recovery plans are a critical part of a network engineer's job. A disaster recovery plan should be tested by doing an actual rebuild and restore of critical systems at least once every six months (or when major data or infrastructure changes occur).

Q. How often do you change the administrator passwords and accounts on local machines and domains?

A. Here is another area that doesn't seem to get the attention it deserves. These passwords should be changed as part of a global password policy, and immediately upon any change of personnel who have knowledge of or access to the accounts and/or passwords.

Q. How often should a server be accessed to have the logs and drive space checked?

A. Although there is no set rule for this, it is a good idea to physically access each server at least once a week to check its overall health. There are a variety of applications that will alert you to errors and error conditions, but nothing replaces actually being logged into the server itself to get a good look at its performance.

Q. How many servers were you responsible for monitoring, maintaining, upgrading, and handling disaster recovery?

A. For effective coverage, an engineer should be able to manage 20–25 servers. There are often times when this number is much higher. This is when a good knowledge of the third-party tools available is handy. Certain systems, such as SQL, require more attention more frequently.

Q. How do you balance customer service skills and technical skills?

A. IT is a service organization. As such, customer service skills are just as important as technical skills, particularly in panic situations when systems are down or the user has just deleted their board presentation that's due in 30 minutes. At these times, staying calm and being empathetic to the user are just as important as being able to quickly bring up the system or recover the file.

For more detailed technical questions, see the Helpdesk Specialist, Network Support Technician, and Security Specialist job profiles.

Developer/Programmer/Software Engineer

Keywords

Application developer, developer, software engineer, programmer, Java, C#, .NET

Job Description

Over the years, the term "software engineer" has become synonymous with "computer programmer," "developer," and "programmer." Generally speaking, a software engineer or programmer develops, optimizes, and otherwise improves computer software. Developers turn business requirements into applications that an organization can use to accomplish their work. It's the most creative of the IT positions though it's getting tougher as technology changes so quickly.

Education and Certification Requirements

Certifications from Microsoft (MCSD) or Sun Microsystems (Sun-certified Java developer) don't necessarily make a candidate more attractive. In fact, these certifications are next to meaningless. They teach very basic skills that don't prepare candidates for problems that can occur in the real world. What counts is real-world experience.

Technical Skills Required

Programmers have to have a broad range of technical skills, though you'll typically acquire these over the years, thanks to the different platforms you develop on. At the bare minimum, a solid understanding of the systems development life cycle is required. Next, you should be proficient in at least one of the core modern programming languages: .NET, C#, or Java. Additionally, basic networking skills are necessary, particularly in a client/server environment.

Other Skills Required

Developers are problem solvers who apply great attention to detail, reasoning, and logic. You are constantly producing new ideas for solving problems. You search for new and better programming techniques that can be applied to new and existing programs. You need the ability to concentrate in distracting conditions and interpret intricate system specifications, thinking critically and adjusting to change quickly. As a developer, you must persevere in solving problems and have the ability to attack problems from many angles. You must also have great people skills, including being open to suggestions, being able to relate to people, having patience, and showing tact when dealing with others.

Programmer Skills Check

Use the following scale to rate your skills. You can later use these descriptors to help describe your skill level on your résumé.

1 (Beginning) Use the skill/product occasionally (basic functions; not primary job responsibility)

2 (Entry level) Use the skill/product on a daily basis

3 (Proficient) Can provide frontline support

4 (Expert) Can train others on this skill/product

5 (Escalation support) The person others turn to when they can't figure it out

Skills	Skill Level
Understand business processes	
Analysis and design of systems according to specifications	
Maintenance of existing programs	
Creation of specifications	
Database design and management	
Prepare test data and test programs for error checking	
Create system documentation	
Troubleshooting systems	
Ability to create procedures from specifications	
Understand software configuration management	
Unified Data Modeling	
Networking fundamentals	
Platforms/Technologies	
VB.NET	
C#	
VBScript	
ASP.NET	
ISAPI	
API	
Java	
JavaScript	
HTML	
JDK	
CORBA	
C++	
Visual C++	
CGI/Perl	
Microsoft SQL Server	
J2EE	

Standing Out

Really great programmers stand out by meeting deadlines and writing clean code. This means getting through QA with minimal bugs to ensure that deadlines are met. If you're known for these characteristics, make sure you have an asset statement ready on this outstanding trait.

Interview Questions to Expect

Q. What has been your experience in developing applications?

A. This question provides the interviewer with insight into why you have chosen software development as your career. It's an opportunity to demonstrate your passion for programming. When describing your work experience, feel free to use phrases like "That's why I love programming" or "That was one of my most interesting projects."

Q. Tell us about a difficult or complex programming assignment you've had. What steps did you take and how successful were you?

A. The interviewer is testing your mettle. Though everyone will have a different answer based on their experiences, you must be prepared with specifics on the project. Without specifics, the interviewer will be able to see right through your lack of experience. Include a short description of the project, the technology you developed in, the user requirements, the components that made it challenging—was it the technology, the user requirements, project management, working as a team?

Q. What SDLC methodologies are you familiar with?

A. The interviewer is looking to see if you worked with different styles of software development—agile, waterfall, etc. Explaining how they might favor a particular style of project may be helpful to the interviewer. Confirming whether they have a preference for a style could be important, so that you do not unintentionally criticize a style they prefer.

Q. What is rapid application development?

A. Rapid application development is a process for fast-tracking the development process so that a system can be developed within 60 to 90 days. The interviewer may also ask you whether a project you've worked on has been implemented using RAD, in which case you should talk about how this process was used to build a system with integrity while meeting the project deadlines. Undoubtedly, there will have been some challenges, such as proper definition of system requirements, QA, and documentation. You should talk about methods that might have been used to ensure that all requirements were still met despite the challenges.

Q. What is "good code"?

A. Good code is code that works, is bug free, and is readable and maintainable. Some organizations have coding standards that all developers are supposed to adhere to, but everyone has different ideas about what's best, or what is too many or too few rules. There are also various theories and metrics. You may want to comment on how quickly your software passes QA testing and how reusable your code is based on the methods you've used.

Q. What techniques and tools can you use to ensure that a new application is as user friendly as possible?

A. First, talk about your own experiences with creating user-friendly software. If you've been in the field for a couple of years, you have probably developed some of your own. Some common techniques include working closely with the end-user to ensure that your perception of user-friendly matches with their use of the application. Another technique involves having the end-user participate in customer acceptance testing (CAT) to help identify areas that may seem tedious for the end-user.

Q. What actions can you take to ensure that user requirements are appropriately addressed in the implementation of a new application?

A. To ensure that user requirements are properly addressed, it is important to gather and properly document these up front. Having the end-user sign off on the requirements is the best way to ensure that you both agree on the direction of the project. This also allows the user to understand what the end result will be and will help minimize scope creep.

Q. What are your preferred platforms for development and why?

A. The only right answer here is to be honest no matter how much you want the job. Let the interviewer know what your strengths are. If they aren't the same platforms that their company develops on, then this may not be the job for you. If you're interested in diversifying your skill set, it's important to stress that you are a quick learner. Once you've mastered one development language, you can easily pick up another. You will need to provide examples of how you've done this in the past in order to get your point across.

Q. Why do you need a source code control system? Have you ever used any?

A. Source control is very important in protecting your code. It allows a developer to go back to previous versions not only to see what changes have been made between versions, but also to allow the developer to roll back code to a working version if something goes wrong. One of the most common source code control systems is Visual Source Safe.

Q. What is error logging? Why is it important in programming?

A. Error logging is the process of documenting errors within a log file. Error logs help debug problems within the application, data, or network. They are used for troubleshooting and provide insight to where an application may be failing. They are a critical component of development.

Q. How do you prioritize multiple projects?

A. Everyone has their own way of handling multiple tasks, so present your way. You should emphasize how you take completion dates into consideration, consider overall priorities to the organization based on their business needs, and take into account the role project management plays in setting priorities.

Q. If someone tells you that your program is not working, how are you going to approach this problem?

A. The first thing is not to take it personally. Then it is important to gather all the relevant information about the problem. Next, it's time to start working the problem from the beginning to the end using a structured approach. You should never jump into a problem without fully understanding it, otherwise you may simply be spinning your wheels.

Q. Which do you prefer, writing code or managing a project? Why?

A. Most developers prefer writing code. If you have been programming for more than four or five years, you may be interested in moving into a development manager position. This is the interviewer's way of assessing whether you want to be a programmer or a manager.

Q. What's more important, time spent testing a product or getting into the market first?

A. It truly is a trade-off that depends on the market situation. Typically, this type of decision is not made by developers, but by the management team overseeing the project. With that said, you can express your opinion.

Q. How would you go about learning a new programming language under high-pressure conditions?

A. This should be an easy question for any programmer or developer, especially with the constant changes in technology. One common technique is to study sample programs whose tasks are related to the tasks involved with the new project. After mastering simple tasks, you can then move on to larger tasks that bring everything together. This goes hand in hand with the philosophy that ideal programming should involve algorithmic design first, then pseudo-code, and then the actual syntax of the new language.

Q. Tell me about a product that you helped create from scratch.

A. This question is similar to the question on the software development life cycle. Be specific. Examples demonstrate that you have the experience. The interviewer should not have to pull this information out of you.

Q. Have you been involved in a project that missed a release date? Why did that happen?

A. Every programmer has missed a deadline, so don't even think of answering no. Be frank with the interviewer. Explain why the deadline was missed, making sure not to place blame on anyone. Remember, you're a team player and the project was a team effort.

Q. Do you prefer working on back-end or front-end programming?

A. This depends completely on you and where your expertise is. Be specific about your preference. Provide examples of projects of both types and explain what you enjoyed best about your preferred development area.

Q. What is n-tier development? Name the tiers.

A. N-tier is also known as three-tier development. The interviewer is simply confirming what you may have put down on your résumé. Don't get caught off-guard by simple questions like these.

Q. What is a stateless object?

A. A stateless object is one that does not hold or change values from its original or default value. The interviewer is simply assessing whether you know the difference between a stateless and a stateful object.

Q. What are design patterns? Can you explain the singleton pattern?

A. Design patterns are repeatable solutions for common problems faced in development. Patterns are similar to templates for architectural solutions for common issues. The singleton pattern is probably the most common and basic pattern. The singleton pattern is used to restrict the instantiation of an object. The singleton pattern checks to see if an instance already exists and if it does it simply returns that instance; otherwise, it creates a new instance that all subsequent calls will use.

Q. What is Service Oriented Architecture and what are its benefits and its drawbacks.

A. SOA is very popular today and you should be familiar with it. It is an architectural design where the application business logic is accessed through a data service via the Internet or local network. SOA is helpful in promoting reuse of code and consolidating business rules. Another benefit for SOA is that an organization can expose parts of its business layer to partners and vendors. Drawbacks include security concerns about placing an organization business layer on the Internet, which can possibly be hacked. Another drawback is performance. Since every message that is sent must be wrapped within an envelope, the data will suffer from bloating. Bloated data or simply large datasets will take much longer to send to the requester based on Internet speeds.

Q. What is abstraction?

A. Abstraction is the process of extracting key functionality into a single functional group and exposing only the necessary parts of an object. Abstraction is used to simply code, increase efficiency, improve code reuse.

Q. What is polymorphism?

A. Polymorphism is the ability for an object to take on the shape of another type. Polymorphism happens when a type takes on the shape of either its own type, its base type, or an interface that it has inherited from.

Q. What are generics?

A. Generics are used to allow developers to extract logic that can be used by different types. The types are passed into a generic method or class when the client code is executed.

This provides for type safety but also promotes code reuse because multiple objects of different types can be created from a generic class. Generic methods promote reuse because a single method can take different types as a parameter but provide the same functionality.

Q. What does an interface like ICar enforce?

A. Interfaces are contracts that can only be inherited from. All objects that are derived from the ICar interface must supply the implementation for the methods defined within the interface (drive, turn, gas, break, etc.).

Q. What is an abstract class?

A. An abstract class is a class that cannot be instantiated. The abstract classes can only be derived from. All classes that are derived from the abstract class are forced to override the abstract classes' methods.

Q. What is the difference between an interface and an abstract class?

A. An abstract class and an interface are both used as contracts. Interfaces, however, are not classes; they are entities that are defined by the Interface keyword. Derived classes can inherit from multiple interfaces but only one abstract class.

Q. Give two examples of how you have promoted code-reuse.

A. For this you can give an example of a time you used inheritance, abstraction, polymorphism, abstract classes, generics, or interfaces. You can also include any services that you have created.

Q. What is refactoring?

A. Refactoring is the process of revisiting code in an effort to improve implementation. Refactoring is used to improve performance and to clean up code for future readability.

Q. Please explain the basic concepts behind unit testing. Why is unit testing important?

A. Unit testing is a way for a developer to validate that a single unit of code operates as it should. Unit testing should only test one single unit of code, typically a method. Unit testing helps save costs by reducing the number for regression bugs that can be introduced into a system. Unit tests can also reduce costs by helping reduce the number of quality assurance resources needed for a project.

Q. What is test driven development?

A. Test driven development is the process of writing code by creating test cases that the code should pass. When using test driven development a developer should only write the minimum code necessary to pass the test case. Requirement must be written before any code is developed so that proper test cases can be created.

Project Manager

Keywords

Project coordinator, project controller

Job Description

With so many IT projects late and over budget, this position has risen in importance in the last five years. For many, it is the first rung on the IT management career ladder. It is a very important position because, as a project manager, you are responsible for the final project, whether it's an enhancement to a current system or a brand-new system. It takes more than a solid knowledge of networks and technical knowledge to be an IT project manager. Planning, budgeting, and interpersonal professionalism are perhaps more important—especially since, when it comes down to it, it's all about delivering a project to meet business objectives.

Education and Certification Requirements

A college degree is a must for this position, as it's typically the first real management position in IT. After that, a project management certification is a requirement in order to move up. Professional certifications include CompTIA's IT Project+, Project Management Institute Project Management Professional, American Management Association, APM from the Association of Project Management Professionals, the CPMP, or the IPMA Certificated Project Manager.

Technical Skills Required

The technical skills required of a project manager are varied. There are many successful project managers who have never programmed a line of code or rebooted a server in their entire careers. There are others who can jump right in and start coding with the rest of the development team. The key to successful project management is to have enough experience with the technology to be competent at scoping projects, understanding when problems might occur, and knowing when team members are putting up unnecessary road blocks. That means an understanding of networking, development, and databases. It also means understanding technology architecture, prototyping and design techniques, testing techniques, configuration management, and documentation.

Other Skills Required

This position is 20 percent technical and 80 percent "other." The "other" consists of scoping project requirements, identifying resources, scheduling these resources, tracking each team member's progress, managing changes and updates, and keeping everyone informed of the project progress. That's on a good day. On the other days, you have to overcome challenges in missed deadlines, get feuding departments to work together, and explain to management why the project will be delayed because the outside contractor went bankrupt. And all with a smile on your face.

Project Manager Skills Check

Use the following scale to rate your skills. You can later use these descriptors to help describe your skill level on your résumé.

1 (Beginning) Use the skill/product occasionally (basic functions; not primary job responsibility)

2 (Entry level) Use the skill/product on a daily basis

3 (Proficient) Can provide frontline support

4 (Expert) Can train others on this skill/product

5 (Escalation support) The person others turn to when they can't figure it out

Skills	Skill Level
Define the project management process to be applied to the project	
Select team members	
Prepare project plan and obtain management approval of the project plan	
Ensure that all team members understand their roles and accept their responsibilities	
Apply project resources according to the approved project plan	
Analyze risk and instigate avoidance activities	
Establish contingency plans and identify trigger events and responsibility for initiating corrective action	
Track and report on progress of plan	
Ability to analyze the actual performance against the plan and make adjustments consistent with plan objectives	
Proper communication to keep all stakeholders informed of progress and issues	
Involve functional expertise in design reviews and key decisions as well as risk strategies	
Ensure timely adaptive action is taken	
Manage change to preserve business plan commitments	
Negotiate the performance of activities with team members and their managers	

Skills	Skill Level
Coordinate management and technical decisions	
Arbitrate and resolve conflicts and interface problems within the project	
Provide input on the performance of project team members to their supervisors	
Tools	
Microsoft Project	
FastTrack	
PlanView PM Software	
Primavera Software	
Turbo Project	
Nexxiom	

Standing Out

Your track record is your most distinguishing quality as a project manager. This means the number of projects you have delivered on time and under budget. Obviously, to be this good you will also have to demonstrate how you are an effective leader: effective communication skills, excellent conflict resolver, good organizer, goal-oriented motivator, and an outstanding team player.

Interview Questions to Expect

Q. What formal training do you have in the area of project management, and are you certified?

A. Formal training and certification is an important way to build credibility as a project manager. If you don't have certification, at least point to other training that you have received that will increase your likelihood of getting hired.

Q. What project management methodology are you most familiar with?

A. There are different schools of project management methodologies and each organization that you work for will have their variation on the methodology that they use. The most popular are COCOMO, a software development cost estimation model, and PMI's PMBOK framework. If you have not been formally trained in these methodologies, be prepared to describe any company-specific methodology that you have been practicing.

Q. How do you define the key success factors for any project?

A. The success of the project is always measured against the requirements specified by the client at the beginning of the project. Provide examples of some of the projects you have worked on and be specific about how the project was measured.

Q. Why is a scope statement important?

A. A scope statement is important because it provides the basis for making future project decisions. It also identifies what the project will and will not do, which will help keep scope creep under control. The interviewer will be interested in how you managed to that scope. You will have the opportunity to discuss various projects.

Q. How would you go about building a project plan?

A. The interviewer wants to assess your ability to build the project plan. They will want to ensure that it includes phases with the necessary tasks under each phase. They are also looking for how resources are appropriately allocated to each step, including their dependencies, and how you determine the necessary time each task would take to complete, remembering to include enough time for requirements gathering, design, and testing. In addition, they will be looking for details on how you incorporate any known holidays, training requirements, vacations, or other resource downtime to ensure you have an accurate completion date. A final step would involve reviewing the draft plan with support groups, upper management, and business users for additional input and final approval.

Q. How do you establish detailed plans, requirements, and procedures for the project?

A. The interviewer wants to ensure that you have your act together as a project manager. By asking you questions on the development of standard project management processes, he will be able to assess your skill level. This is a pretty complex question to respond to, so you may want to pick a specific project and walk the interviewer through the processes you would use to establish the plans, requirements, and procedures. You should intersperse anecdotal information throughout your answer, including how use cases help identify missing requirements, how flow charts are critical for identifying required sign-offs, and how scope changes and customer acceptance must be agreed upon *before* the project begins.

Q. How much information do you need to get started on a new project or assignment?

A. Are you a go-getter, eager to start any new project, or do you stick with the same methodology on each project? The interviewer will be able to assess your work style by how much information you need in order to get started. Of course, you want to get started right away, but it is critical to stay focused on the key aspects of project management: a detailed list of business requirements, what is driving the need for the project, what operating systems or platforms are involved, what the expected business benefit is, and how the success of the project will be measured. It is also important to find out who the audience is, as well as all departments, customers, and vendors that may need to be involved and considered. You must also find out whether the project is time sensitive or has cost constraints.

Q. What type of methodology, tools, and techniques have you used to assist project management?

A. The interviewer is seeking insight into the tools that you use during project management and how you use these tools for efficiency. Having a structured methodology, such as the PMBOK methodology, helps to frame the project management process. Using a tool like Microsoft Project is also key to staying on top of tasks and due dates. Each project is different, but by analyzing what has worked in previous projects, best practices can be used to facilitate new projects.

Q. What would be the first thing you would do as a project manager?

A. We all know that you want to make a great first impression and hit the ground running, but in project management sometimes it's better to be more like the tortoise than the hare. The first step as a brand-new employee of an organization is to orient yourself with the organization. The best way to do this is to meet with various departmental managers to identify the priorities. Meeting with the users and staff and obtaining status reports and appraisals of all team members will also provide the foundation that's needed to later make informed decisions.

Q. How do you evaluate progress against the plan and make adjustments?

A. Established milestones are the measures used to evaluate whether a project is progressing against the plan. The goal is to always meet or exceed those milestones. However, if the quality or customer acceptance of the deliverable is in danger of being jeopardized to make a timeline, you must always adjust the project plan accordingly, either by extending milestones or bringing in additional resources. Err on the side of caution and you can't go wrong.

Q. A key objective of project management or program management is to minimize risk and ensure project coordination by providing a framework for project execution. How have you accomplished this at your present job?

A. Having a formal workflow process is the key for ensuring that projects meet the expectations of the business owners. If none exists, the number one priority is to create one with the help of managers within the IT department. This process ensures effective customer service, communication, prioritization, validation, teamwork, quality, and productivity.

Q. Have you ever been assigned several important projects at roughly the same time? How did you go about setting priorities for your time?

A. As a project manager, you are there to manage the projects. Determining the priorities of projects is a job left up to upper management. The interviewer wants to ensure that you clearly understand the boundaries of the project manager role.

Q. How do you get cooperation from other departments (vendors, suppliers, customers)? Give an example.

A. Project managers don't just manage internal resources; they may also be responsible for managing outside vendors. Getting vendors, departments, and customers to cooperate is an art that starts with communication. It also means clearly establishing roles and responsibilities, asking other parties to participate in key planning and decision review, and keeping them informed.

Q. At what point do you find it necessary to bring others into your decision-making process? Why?

A. Project stakeholders must be kept in the decision-making process to ensure that the business rules are clearly defined and that the project is in alignment with these rules. This means including all departments that may be involved to ensure that one wrong decision does not affect other departments that have dependencies on one another. Having business experts in the room or reviewing decisions before they are finalized usually helps identify anything outstanding or validates the correct decision has been made for all areas.

Q. How do you determine staffing requirements?

A. With this question, the interviewer is assessing your knowledge of IT project management to ensure that you don't leave out critical groups like quality assurance and the end-users. He is also checking on the method by which you build your project plan. You can use an example from a previous project to step the interviewer through your process for identifying roles, tasks, the resources that will be necessary, estimating the amount of time for each task, and incorporating additional considerations such as turnover, downtime, and training.

Q. Ideally, communication between the project manager and the project team members should take place how?

A. The interviewer is assessing your communication style. Though you may have a preference, the best answer to this question is that communication should always be both written and oral to ensure that the message has been received and understood.

Q. A project loses a contractor in the middle of a project. A new project team is formed to replace the role of the lost contractor and their team. As a project manager, what is the first topic that you would address to the team in the kickoff meeting?

A. In asking questions such as this, the interviewer is assessing how you will react in high-pressure situations. Successful project management is all about having clear roles and responsibilities and having a team that will live up to them. When taking over a project, as you will undoubtedly run across, the first step is certainly to identify team roles and responsibilities.

Q. What's the objective of fast-tracking a project?

A. The objective of fast-tracking is to reduce project duration. This is often used today when projects are mission critical. You should provide an example of a project where you've had to fast-track its development. You should include where you decided to cut time and resources and what the respective risks were in doing so.

Q. You are working on a project for your company to offer its product on the Internet. The company has no previous experience in this area, but it believes knowledge is needed rapidly. You are asked to start planning for this project. What is the first step to take as you begin planning?

A. This type of behavioral question allows the interviewer to see you in action under sticky situations—like ensuring that even fast-tracked projects adhere to a project plan. The correct answer here is to gather the stakeholders and plan the scope of the project.

Q. What are some of the elements of a changing project schedule?

A. The elements include obtaining the appropriate levels of approval, submitting the appropriate change requests, and evaluating the impact of a change to the schedule.

Q. How do you ensure that others are familiar with the project management methodology that you will be using for the project?

A. The devil is in the details, and training is often one of the details that is overlooked with project management. The interviewer will gain a deeper appreciation of your skill set when you talk about training—from the need to review the tools that will be used to business process-specific training that will ensure that everyone clearly understands the requirements of the project.

Q. How are you going to determine your stakeholders and link that to your communication plan?

A. The interviewer wants to make sure that you can properly identify all the stakeholders and rank them according to their "power and influence" on the project decision-making process. Those with the power and influence must be involved and informed throughout the project life cycle to get their support and backing. Stakeholders are identified through team meetings and interviews.

Q. What types of reviews are part of your project management methodology?

A. The interviewer wants to ensure that you are inclusive in your reviews with the right stakeholders. There are different types of reviews used throughout the development life cycle. Status reviews include core team meetings, milestone reviews, and post-project reviews. Technical reviews include software requirements gathering, architecture planning, design, code, test case building, and test case inspections. Executive reviews include steering committees and executive/board reviews.

Q. Do you plan to produce a risk management plan? And how often do you intend to update the plan?

A. A risk management plan is created early in the planning phase of the project so that contingencies are included in the project schedule and cost estimate. This is a sign of an experienced project manager. The risk management plan should be updated regularly as more information is gathered throughout the project life cycle.

Q. What is more important: the senior management and sponsor are satisfied with the product, but the project ran over budget due to change orders, or the project met cost and time goals, but did not meet all the client expectations?

A. As a project manager, your customer always comes first. You may want to provide a first-hand example of this type of situation and talk about the things that you did to ensure that management was kept apprised of the situation, such as ensuring that they signed off on any change orders.

Q. How would you handle a team member who is not performing?

A. This type of question is used by the interviewer to assess how you'll handle challenges throughout the project, such as handling team members who aren't performing. You may want to start off with a specific example from your past experiences and use it as the model for how to handle this situation. For example, the first step is to determine the reason they are not performing by speaking with them to ensure they are aware of expectations. Then you may want to mention documenting a recovery plan, which may include any necessary training. You may also include discussing solutions with their supervisor. The last resort that you may want to include is removing the individual from the project.

Quality Assurance Specialist

Keywords

Software tester, QA engineer, QA tester, QA

Job Description

A QA specialist tests the functionality of software, programs, and Websites or other technologies to ensure they work as defined by the system specs. As a QA specialist, you write and implement test plans, often relying on test automation tools to test the functionality of the system. You track quality assurance metrics such as defect counts. You must communicate these to the project management and often work hand in hand with the development team to identify problems and future vulnerabilities for failure. You also work with users to identify usability issues and suggest ways to improve the usability of the system being tested. A QA specialist wields incredible power—all systems must pass their scrutiny in order to be released.

Education and Certification Requirements

A college degree in computer science or management information systems is usually required. A certification in software quality testing is a plus, especially if you aspire to manage the quality assurance department. The Quality Assurance Institute offers three certifications: Certified Software Quality Analyst (CSQA), Software Test Engineer (CSTE), and SPICE Assessor (CSA).

Technical Skills Required

QA specialists need a wide range of skills in all the technologies you will be testing, including basic programming, database design and management, and networking skills and Web technologies. You also need an understanding of the company's IT infrastructure, hardware, and the operating systems the application will be deployed on.

Other Skills Required

QA specialists must be detail-oriented, persistent, analytical, and thick-skinned. You need excellent troubleshooting and problem-solving skills. But the most valued skill of all is your mastery of how to work within a team of users, other QA testers, developers, and project managers—especially when a project is behind schedule and they've just uncovered a high-priority bug that will put the project behind.

Quality Assurance Specialist Skills Check

Use the following scale to rate your skills. You can later use these descriptors to help describe your skill level on your résumé.

1 (Beginning) Use the skill/product occasionally (basic functions; not primary job responsibility)

2 (Entry level) Use the skill/product on a daily basis

3 (Proficient) Can provide frontline support

4 (Expert) Can train others on this skill/product

5 (Escalation support) The person others turn to when they can't figure it out

Skills	Skill Level
Configuration management process	
Error reporting methodology, including using available tools and bug report writing	
General testing knowledge, including prioritization of testing tasks, terminology, the testing process, and working effectively with the project management team	
Performance measurement, including test management and using a testing matrix	
Understanding the need and role of testing according to the software development process, including testing design specifications, functionality, components, configuration and compatibility, and integration	
Using automation tools to develop testing scripts	

Skills	Skill Level
Writing test plans to test use cases from the functional systems specification	
Programming languages (VB, Java, C, C++, SQL)	
Network operating systems (Windows NT, 2000, NetWare, Linux, Unix)	
Desktop operating systems (Windows 95/98/2000/XP/Vista, Linux, Unix, Macintosh)	
Browsers (IE, Netscape)	
Web technologies (ActiveX, ASP, applets)	
Test Tools	
JTest	
QARun	
Rational Robot	
SilkTest	
TestPartner	
Visual Test	
WinRunner	
e-Test	
LoadRunner	
QALoad	
Test Director	
QTP	

Standing Out

As a good QA specialist, you'll have one thing on your mind at all times: how can I break this application/Website/system? Your job is to break things. You must think like a user—looking for how a user would use the application and ensuring that everything works as expected. That can be tough, as this study can result in delays in project releases, which can put a strain on the relationship between developers and project managers. You must, therefore, possess tact, diplomacy, and an ability to communicate with both the technical and non-technical team members. Previous software development experience is an added plus, which gives you an appreciation for the developers' point of view, and reduces the learning curve in automated test tool programming.

Interview Questions to Expect

Q. What is software quality assurance and why is it important?

A. Interviewers like to start all interviews with general concepts. There's no better way to get your perspective on the roles and responsibilities of the job you are interviewing for. Some key points that you should include in your response: Software quality assurance is an integral part of the entire software development process and focuses on the prevention of system errors. It ensures that software is written according to specification and that problems are found and dealt with before the software is released. Quality software is reasonably bug-free, delivered on time and within budget, meets requirements and/or expectations, and is maintainable. By thoroughly testing software, you are helping to prevent system meltdowns that could cost a company a lot of money in downtime and in erroneous business data.

Q. Define "good code."

A. This question may seem open-ended, but you can actually define "good code." It's a way for the interviewer to assess your philosophy around what's important about quality programming. At the end of the day, "good code" is a program that works and is bug-free. In addition, it may be concise, requiring few lines of code to accomplish a task. It may also be maintainable, meaning that others can add to it or change its functionality easily. Finally, another way that you can describe good code is by how many times it had to go back to the programmer before it passed bug-free.

Q. What are some common sources of software bugs?

A. This question is a way for the interviewer to assess your experience and the complexity of the systems you've worked on. Bugs are not just a result of a mistyped command. Some of the common sources for bugs include:

- Poorly written specifications.
- Miscommunication about expectations of the functionality of an application or system.
- The complexity of current software applications, requiring integration with many varied systems.
- Simple programming errors.
- Changing requirements without understanding the impact of the changes, coupled with the interrelationship of shared resources for other projects and the reassignment of team members may also cause things to slip through the cracks.
- Time pressures lead to shortcuts being taken and mistakes being made.
- Poorly documented code.

Q. What is validation?

A. The interviewer wants to assess your systematic approach to QA. Validation is another name for the testing that actually takes place to ensure that code meets up with the expectations.

Q. Please describe some of the types of testing that you have personal experience with.

A. This is an opportunity to show your experience. The interviewer is testing your formal experience in QA. The more tests that you can rattle off, the better. The following are some common examples:

- Alpha and beta testing for major enterprise applications with high visibility
- Usability testing of Websites and end-user applications
- Load testing of database access and client server environments
- Functionality testing that matches requirements to actual components
- Security testing of commerce applications and those applications requiring authentication
- Compatibility testing of upgrades and Web applications
- Integration testing of disparate systems
- Acceptance testing for sponsor sign-off on functionality

Q. How do automated testing tools make testing easier?

A. When QA is your career, you figure out efficiencies in getting the job done. There are plenty of automated testing tools to facilitate testing on larger projects. For small projects, the time needed to learn and implement them may not be worth it. For larger projects or ongoing long-term projects they can be very valuable. Automated tools can include:

- Record/playback type
- Code analyzers
- Coverage analyzers
- Memory analyzers
- Load/performance test tools
- Web test tools

Q. What formal training have you had in any of these tools?

A. QA testing tools are not something that you pick up and play with in your spare time. The more proficient you are with these tools, the more valuable you will be to an employer. Be specific about any training you've undergone or any special mentoring you have received as a result of working with someone highly specialized in these tools and methodologies.

Q. Why is documentation important in QA?

A. Is QA a career or the step in between the helpdesk and the development department? All professional quality assurance specialists know that documentation is mandatory. A good answer here will let the interviewer know that you consider yourself a professional. The reason you must document QA practices is so you can repeat your tests as updates are made. In addition, you must also have documentation for specifications, business rules, configurations, test plans, test cases, and bug reports. Because of the incredible amount of paperwork, you should have an easy-to-manage change management process that will help identify which document contains what information.

Q. Why do you need test plans and what should they include?

A. The interviewer is assessing your ability to create necessary documentation. A test plan provides information on the overall objectives, scope of the project, and designated approach. It should be created prior to beginning the actual testing and should include a sign-off process to ensure that it aligns with the overall project definition. The individual components of a test plan will vary based on the breadth of the project, but the following provide a general idea of key components:

- Project name, owners, and version
- Business application overview
- Testing overview and objectives
- QA team roles and responsibilities
- Assumptions, dependencies, and limitations of the testing
- Overview of the testing environment, including software and hardware
- Setup requirements, including software and hardware configurations
- Special testing tools configuration
- Location of any test scripts to be used
- Testing process outline
- Process for tracking errors and bugs
- List of open issues

Q. Why do you create test cases?

A. The interviewer is assessing your basic understanding of QA processes. A test case is a document that describes how an application should work given the documented data or action. It should include the data that will be used for testing the application and the desired response. Without a test case, you wouldn't know what you're testing or what you expect to happen.

Q. What do you do when you find a bug and what should you report?

A. Bug reporting is a standard process within a QA department. The interviewer is checking on your consistency in reporting bugs and tracking them. Bugs should be entered immediately into a problem-tracking system so they can be reported and assigned to developers who can fix them.

Q. What do you do if software is so buggy it cannot be fully tested?

A. This type of question tests how you will react in a difficult situation. After all, you may have brought the whole project to a halt. Be careful how you answer. It's not your responsibility to fix this situation—the development process as a whole is probably faulty. The best thing to do is to try to isolate the most critical bugs and log them. Next, notify managers with the proper documentation to support your suspicions of larger issues. Do not try to handle this situation on your own.

Q. How do you know when to stop testing?

A. The interviewer is testing your persistence and perfectionism. Hopefully, the decision has already been made for you either through a deadline or through a test plan that identifies the number of tolerable bugs.

Q. What do you do if there isn't enough time for thorough testing?

A. Another test by the interviewer: It is not up to the quality assurance specialist to make this determination. If this happens, project management should raise the issue with executive management and decide whether to extend the deadline or risk a faulty product. In all cases, the decision should be made after a careful risk analysis is conducted.

Q. Should testing be the same regardless of the project?

A. It depends on your environment and company policy. You may want to ask the interviewer what their policy is and be ready to talk about your experiences with other companies you've worked with. In the end, it depends on their impact on the end-user and how mission-critical the application is.

Q. How would you deal with a situation where requirements weren't locked down?

A. This question addresses your adaptability to change. One of the hardest parts of your job will be juggling multiple projects and shifting priorities. Even though shooting the project manager may be your favorite option, there are other ways to address the situation:

- Speak with your management to devise a course of action. It's critical to keep them informed to ensure that you are meeting their expectations.
- Work with project management to come up with alternate plans.
- Build the necessary time for testing into the schedule.

- If you know you're going to be testing the same processes over and over, build test scripts to ease the pain.
- Start testing what's least likely to change.

Q. How do you introduce QA processes into the software development process without grinding it to a halt?

A. Admit it, this is a tough order. The interviewer is looking for personal examples on best practices. For example, if an organization is not familiar with QA processes, they should be introduced slowly and over time. Everyone on the project must buy in to these processes because they affect users, project management, development, and the QA team. You can go into further detail on helping team members understand that problem prevention will lessen the need for problem detection, there will be less panic-driven development and burn-out, and a lot less wasted effort. The key to introducing QA into an organization is minimizing the paperwork, keeping the overall process simple, and minimizing meeting time.

Q. What's the most important test in a client/server environment?

A. This question tests your familiarity with QAing in a client/server environment. That means you need to be familiar with specific use cases of stress testing the system to uncover system limitations and capabilities.

Q. What are the typical tests you would run a new Website through?

A. The same applies to this question. Website testing is some of the most common testing that QA professionals perform. You should be familiar with all these common testing requirements as well as with the typical environment the Website will be accessed from. As a part of this testing, you should include:

- Browser compatibility
- Different connectivity speeds
- Time between page loads
- Validating that internal and external links work
- Testing all applications on the Website, including CGI scripts, ActiveX components, and other client- and server-side applications
- Testing all security settings required
- Testing for access from an outside domain
- Usability for the major functionality and ease of use
- Accessibility testing for navigation without the use of the mouse

Q. Describe your experience with programming, database management, and networking.

A. Additional experience in the programming and development world will make you a more valuable QA specialist. It will certainly help in communication and resolving bugs.

Q. How would you resolve communication issues that arise with the development team, customers, and the project management team?

A. The interviewer will ask you this question to see whether you'll fit in with the team. You may want to express that you've had a very good relationship in the past with all of these different departments and that you work very hard to maintain that relationship. In the case when you may have had an issue, you've used open communication to resolve it and have always kept the project management team informed of anything that might affect the project timeline.

Security Specialist

Keywords

Security analyst, network security, security administrator, security architect, security engineer

Job Description

A security specialist saves the day on a regular basis from the moment you log in to well after you go home. With viruses, denial-of-service attacks, network break-ins, and other security incidents on the rise, the job of the security specialist never ends. This makes this one of the fastest growing positions in the IT job market. The daily tasks include assessing network vulnerabilities from all possible areas of attack—software, hardware, and physical attacks inside and outside the server room; configuring the security policy and deploying it; monitoring the network infrastructure; setting up security perimeters, and detecting and preventing intrusions; automating incident response and enforcement capabilities; and setting up reporting, auditing, and communication capabilities. And then you get to come back the next day and do it all over again.

Education and Certification Requirements

A college degree is usually required as well as formal training in network and systems security. There are a number of vendor certifications available from Cisco, Symantec, and CheckPoint. Beyond these, vendor-neutral certifications demonstrate a broader knowledge of security concepts and techniques. Vendor-neutral certifications are available from CompTIA, SANS, $(ICS)^2$, ICSA Labs, and Security Certified Program (SCP).

Technical Skills Required

The security specialist needs quite a diverse background in networking and system administration. Not only do you need to have the skill set to set up and administer these systems, you need to know the vulnerabilities for every single network component so you can properly protect valuable company resources.

Other Skills Required

A security specialist is a security guard and a detective in one—sleuthing to find system vulnerabilities and tracking down attackers. You must enjoy problem solving. You must be methodical and detail-oriented, and work well under pressure.

Security Specialist Skills Check

Use the following scale to rate your skills. You can later use these descriptors to help describe your skill level on your résumé.

1 (Beginning) Use the skill/product occasionally (basic functions; not primary job responsibility)

2 (Entry level) Use the skill/product on a daily basis

3 (Proficient) Can provide frontline support

4 (Expert) Can train others on this skill/product

5 (Escalation support) The person others turn to when they can't figure it out

Skills	Skill Level
Network security philosophy, hackers, and law enforcement	
Physical infrastructure security	
Hacker profiles, tools, and techniques	
Encryption	
Security holes in server operating systems	
How to properly harden servers	
Proper password practices	
Active Directory security	
Implementing IIS security	
Implementing DNS security	
Use of network scanners and packet sniffers	
Scripting for security	
SQL Server security	

Skills	Skill Level
E-commerce security	
SSL security	
Proper use of digital certificates	
Dial-up security	
Firewalls	
Packet Filters/IPFilt	
Packet Filters/Router ACLs	
Proxies/Proxy Servers	
Proxies/SOCKS	
Proxies/TIS Toolkit	
Topologies/Bastion Host	
Topologies/DMZ	
Topologies/Dual Homed Gateway	
Virtual Private Networking/IPSEC Virtual Private Networking/PPTP	
PKI	
Cryptography	
API	
Network design and implementation	
Anti-virus Tools	
Symantec	
Trend Micro	
Network Associates	
Computer Associates	
Central Command	

Standing Out

To stand out as a security specialist, you've got to have some time in the industry—typically four or more years with a very in-depth background in various operating systems. There are three things that make a great security specialist: a passion for learning, attention to detail, and a broad knowledge base. For added impact, add some programming experience to your operating system experience.

Interview Questions to Expect

Prevention

The following questions may be used by the interviewer to assess your general knowledge of the prevention of security breaches. Ensuring a secure infrastructure starts with prevention. The questions included in this section help the interviewer gain a deeper understanding of your experience with each of these best practices. These questions focus on planning and understanding basic security technology.

Q. What are some of the threats against security within an organization?

A. This is the typical first question. It allows the interviewer to assess your general knowledge of security threats and their impact on business systems. Your answer should focus on the typical points of vulnerability and the impact on users, access to proprietary information, interruption of service, obtaining trade secrets, and obtaining customer information. The affected devices may include desktop systems, network resources, server resources, and database and information services.

Q. What security standards are you familiar with?

A. The interviewer may then progress to your familiarity with security standards. The most often referred to security standards document is ISO 7498-2, *Security Architecture*, which defines security as minimizing the vulnerabilities of assets and resources. It also defines pervasive mechanisms including trusted functionality, event detection, audit trail, and security recovery as part of an overall security strategy.

Q. What is the Computer Emergency Response Team (CERT)?

A. This organization is the highest point of escalation in the security world and is "the" place everyone turns to when new attacks are discovered. The interviewer may ask you how you have relied on CERT in the past. CERT is based out of Carnegie Mellon University, and is devoted to dealing with computer-related security issues. It is a part of the Internet Society, which establishes the protocols that govern the Internet. It is the place to report any attacks and to keep up to date with possible security breaches.

Q. How would you go about creating an effective security policy?

A. A security policy provides the company's overall strategy for handling cyber and physical attacks. This question is used by the interviewer to determine your experience with developing an effective security policy. You will want to describe your involvement in the development of such policies and then share your best practices. Your answer may include the steps for creating an effective security policy, such as:

- Classifying systems according to their criticality to the business operations
- Assigning risk factors according to the likelihood that a hacker would attack a resource
- Defining acceptable and unacceptable activities, such as who has permission to modify files and directories
- Defining the appropriate security techniques for each resource in the network—for instance, packet filtering
- Defining education standards about the key security principles
- Identifying who is responsible for administering the security policies

Q. What must you balance with the implementation of an effective security policy?

A. This question may provide the interviewer with an overall impression of how stringent your security policies are. Keep in mind that there's a critical balance between ensuring secure resources and allowing employees to do their jobs as quickly as possible. You don't want to come across unreasonably overzealous about your security policies.

Q. What types of attacks are servers most vulnerable to?

A. This common question is used to determine just how much experience you have by your knowledge of these common attacks. For instance, the most common attacks on servers include unauthorized entry, service interruptions, and Trojans.

Q. What are some of the security threats against Internet transactions?

A. Some examples of vulnerabilities are spoofing (the creation of illegitimate sites that appear to be published by established organizations), unauthorized disclosure (when hackers intercept transmissions to obtain customers' sensitive information), and data alteration (when transactions are intercepted and altered en route). You should include any real-life experiences you may have with these vulnerabilities and how they can be secured using a certification authority like VeriSign.

Q. What is social engineering and how can you prevent it?

A. Interviewers understand that sometimes hackers don't really need technology to break into a network. Hackers can be very deceptive, as is the case with socially engineered attacks. The interviewer would like to know how you can prevent these hackers from conning your network users into giving out sensitive information. In answering this question, you should focus on the role of educating users as the best means to preventing these situations.

Q. What goes into a physical security plan?

A. Physical security is the practice of making sure that no one can steal the entire server or any of its constituent parts. You should discuss how you've put together physical security plans that ensured unauthorized users from walking up to a network server and unplugging it and other similar situations. Include security systems, intruder detection systems, and company policies about leaving PCs turned on as examples of components of your plan.

Q. How does a firewall work?

A. Even though this is a basic question, it's still an important one to demonstrate that you understand not just the basic functions but some of the more advanced features. Ask the interviewer which type of equipment his company uses and, if you are familiar with it, describe your experience in more depth. If you've worked on other equipment, include the name of the vendor and model of the equipment and describe your preference in equipment based on its features.

Q. What are some of the basic concepts in critical firewall design?

A. This is a test of your security planning knowledge. You should provide an overview of your security strategy and describe how the firewalls fit into the overall strategy.

Q. What steps are important when creating a contingency plan for your firewall system?

A. Your backup plan for your firewall system is extremely important in case the primary system goes down. As part of your answer, you should discuss simple steps like creating an identical copy of the software, configuring an identical system and keeping it in safe storage, and ensuring that all software necessary to install the firewall is accessible, including having rescue disks.

Securing Your Systems

These next questions provide the interviewer with insight into your general knowledge on securing systems against attacks. The interviewer uses these questions to ensure you have a solid foundation in the area of security.

Q. How does packet filtering provide network security?

A. This is a basic question to determine whether you understand the concept of packet filtering as an effective security measure. Packet filtering is the process of using a router to process and scan packets for acceptable and unacceptable activity at the network layer.

Q. How does SSL work?

A. SSL is a very basic concept when it comes to Internet security and one that you should be familiar with. The interviewer is interested in knowing whether you understand how SSL works to encrypt data between the Web server and the client machine.

Q. Why is it important to safeguard information like the contents of a DNS server, routing tables, user and account names, and banner information?

A. These resources are fundamental in ensuring a secure environment. The interviewer is making sure you understand how the contents of the resources can be used in an attack.

For example, with this information hackers can identify the type of operating system and Internet service that a host is running, which may facilitate their ease of penetration.

Q. Why should you protect open ports on your system?

A. This is another fundamental question used by the interviewer to determine whether you understand how hackers can use these resources to make it easier to attack systems. In this instance, open ports allow a hacker to infiltrate the inside network.

Q. How do you protect against root kit attacks?

A. The interviewer is testing your familiarity with applications that help protect your network resources. Applications like Tripwire or Windows File Protection utility will protect against illicit changes being made to system files. They will detect and reverse these changes.

Q. Describe the legitimate and malicious uses of ICMP.

A. Various utilities use ICMP as their protocol for troubleshooting connectivity. For example, the ping program can be used to test name resolution, as well as whether or not a system is up. The *tracert* and *traceroute* commands use ICMP to test router connections. The interviewer wants to see whether you understand how hackers can use ICMP to wage denial-of-service attacks against servers. Using relatively simple applications and equally modest band width, a hacker can quickly fill up a corporation's T3 line with ICMP packets.

Q. What's the biggest known risk to SMTP?

A. The interviewer wants to know whether you understand the vulnerabilities of all components of a system. In this case, SMTP is an e-mail protocol and the biggest vehicle for sending and receiving viruses and Trojan horses via e-mail attachments.

Q. What measures can you take to secure an e-mail server?

A. Like the previous question, this question is basic but is used to identify whether you understand the vulnerabilities of something as simple as an e-mail server. You may want to discuss reducing the size of e-mail attachments, forbidding attachments, scanning e-mail attachments, and/or imposing a limit on the number of messages a user can receive.

Q. In what way is Telnet vulnerable to security threats?

A. This is yet another question about the vulnerability of common applications or utilities. With this utility, the vulnerability lies in the fact that it sends all usernames and passwords in plain text.

Q. What are the implications of a hacker attacking a DNS server?

A. A DNS can provide a hacker with a lot of sensitive information that can be used to create further destruction on a network. The interviewer wants to see whether you understand the sensitivity of this information and how it can be used to penetrate the network.

For instance, using zone files, anyone can learn the IP addresses and computer names of all systems in that zone and target those systems.

Q. Why might it be unwise to allow write access to an anonymous FTP server?

A. The interviewer wants to ensure that you know the reason for requiring authenticated logins to an FTP server. Authenticated logins can be tracked and can be used to prevent a malicious user from filling the drive, which might lead to a denial-of-service attack.

Q. What measures can you take to secure an FTP server?

A. Securing an FTP server is basic protocol. The interviewer wants to ensure that you know the fundamental aspects of this task. In this case, by altering the FTP server's default settings.

Q. What measures can you take to harden an operating system?

A. Similarly, this question addresses the need to secure an operating system. The interviewer is looking for the basics because there are obviously various steps that are OS specific.

Q. What measures can you take to secure a wireless network?

A. Wireless networks are standard these days. This question tests your currency of knowledge. Be sure to include references to establishing a WLAN security policy, securing the WLAN (strong encryption, modifying the SSID, using VPNs, physically hiding access points to secure tampering, etc.), enabling wireless devices with security services, and enlisting employees in safeguarding the network through education.

Detection and Recovery

The next step in network security is detection, and the interviewer will want to assess your ability to troubleshoot, detect, and recover from an attack.

Q. What are some of the tools you can use to respond to an attack?

A. An important part of your job is ensuring that you have the right tools for the task. The types of tools that you use can tell a lot about your experience. The interviewer is also interested in how you would use these tools to respond to an attack. In general, it is usually unwise to respond aggressively to a hacker, though you can use various applications to log or end connections to prevent further damage.

Q. What tools does an administrator have for trapping a hacker or forcing him to leave behind evidence of tampering?

A. This question tests your knowledge of how to find out more information about the identify of a hacker. The interviewer wants to know whether you know how to use a tripwire technique.

Q. How do the system logs help in identifying security breaches?

A. This question assesses your depth of knowledge on system logs, which can be used to prove that the network has been infiltrated. You'll want to describe the types of information that you look for from system logs in order to gather the evidence that you seek.

Q. How can you prevent the destruction of evidence that a hacker may have left behind?

A. The interviewer wants to ensure that you know how to preserve evidence for later analysis to identify the hacker. What they are looking for from your answer is that it's imperative to stop all activity, even normal use, in order to prevent further damage to any of the systems.

Q. How would you repair an infected system that has been attacked by a root kit?

A. The interviewer must determine whether you can repair the damage hackers leave behind. This particular attack is very difficult to detect and cumbersome to repair. You would have to completely erase and reinstall the operating system. When reinstalling the operating system, you have to make sure that you do not reinstall from backups, as they can be affected by the Trojan. You would also have to replace the affected binaries.

Q. What is the purpose of denial-of-service attacks, and how can you recover from them?

A. This type of question provides the interviewer with insight into your overall knowledge of the various attacks that may affect your organization. You should have a clear understanding of the objective of common attacks such as denial-of-service. For instance, this attack has three purposes: to crash a server or make it unusable to everyone else, to assume the identity of the system that is crashing, and to install a Trojan or a root kit. You should also know how to recover from these attacks, as in this case, by simply rebooting your machine.

Q. What are the things that you should document when you've been attacked?

A. Documentation is key, especially in network security. The interviewer is interested in the type of documentation that you are accustomed to keeping whenever your network has been infiltrated. For a thorough answer you should include the time and date of the attack, the nature of the attack, the affected systems, the traffic type, the servers that were involved, the names of all company employees who were contacted during the response, and any applications used.

Q. How do you determine the scope of a breach?

A. This is the interviewer's way of assessing your investigative skills. Some of the things you should include as a part of your response are

- Determine which accounts have been affected
- Identify which files have been read, altered, or substituted
- Trace the hacker's activities in your system

- Consult audit logs
- Determine whether any permissions have been reset

Q. What should your response plan consist of?

A. A security policy is critical if you're a network security specialist. With this simple question, the interviewer will know whether you know the basics of network security. As a refresher, your security policy should include:

- Contacting affected individuals (users, management, ISP)
- Breaking the link or creating a "jail"
- Calling the police or other authorities (CERT)
- Contacting the hacker
- Tracing connections and conducting other checks to further map the hacker's activity
- Reconfiguring the firewall

Q. What should you do after a security incident has been resolved?

A. This is a perfect closing question that wraps up the topic of network security and your interview. Your answer should include analyzing your security policy, your security mechanisms, and your team's response. As a matter of habit, you should assess the strengths and weaknesses of your response and how you could improve on them.

Index

A

B

C

D

E

F

G

H

I

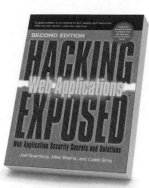

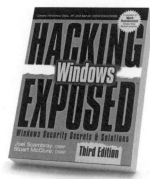

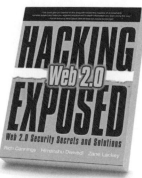

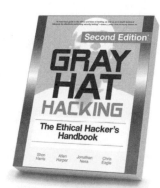

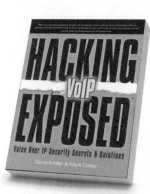

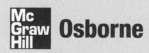